Network Intrusion Detection and Prevention

T0135078

Advances in Information Security

Sushil Jajodia

Consulting Editor
Center for Secure Information Systems
George Mason University
Fairfax, VA 22030-4444
email: jajodia@gmu.edu

The goals of the Springer International Series on ADVANCES IN INFORMATION SECURITY are, one, to establish the state of the art of, and set the course for future research in information security and, two, to serve as a central reference source for advanced and timely topics in information security research and development. The scope of this series includes all aspects of computer and network security and related areas such as fault tolerance and software assurance.

ADVANCES IN INFORMATION SECURITY aims to publish thorough and cohesive overviews of specific topics in information security, as well as works that are larger in scope or that contain more detailed background information than can be accommodated in shorter survey articles. The series also serves as a forum for topics that may not have reached a level of maturity to warrant a comprehensive textbook treatment.

Researchers, as well as developers, are encouraged to contact Professor Sushil Jajodia with ideas for books under this series.

For other titles published in this series, go to www.springer.com/series/5576

Ali A. Ghorbani • Wei Lu
Mahbod Tavallaee

Network Intrusion Detection and Prevention

Concepts and Techniques

 Springer

Ali A. Ghorbani
Faculty in Computer Science
University of New Brunswick
Fredericton NB E3B 5A3
Canada
ghorbani@unb.ca

Wei Lu
Faculty in Computer Science
University of New Brunswick
Fredericton NB E3B 5A3
Canada

Mahbod Tavallaee
Faculty in Computer Science
University of New Brunswick
Fredericton NB E3B 5A3
Canada

ISBN 978-1-4614-2474-1   e-ISBN 978-0-387-88771-5
DOI 10.1007/978-0-387-88771-5
Springer New York Dordrecht Heidelberg London

Printed on acid-free paper

Springer is part of Springer Science+Business Media (www.springer.com)

Dedicated to all those who are helping to make the world safer and more secure and to our families for their love and support.

Preface

Great changes are taking place is the area of information supply and demand due to the wide spread application of computers and the exponential increase of computer networks such as the Internet. The Internet has become a popular medium of commercial activities and this raised the stakes, both, for attackers and security personnel. Trillions of dollars of transactions occur daily at each major financial institution. For example, Visa processes 4,000 transactions per second, which means that if Visa's system goes down for one minute because of a distributed denial of service attack (DDoS), and assuming only $100 per transaction, over $24 million in transactions is lost in one minute.

Today the world of business computing is faced with the ever-increasing likelihood of unplanned downtime due to various attacks and security breaches. In this environment of uncertainty which is full of hackers and malicious threats, those companies around the globe which are the best at maintaining the continuity of their services (i.e., survive the system) and retaining their computing power, enjoy a significant competitive advantage.

Network downtime results in financial losses and more harms to the credibility of commercial enterprises especially ISPs. Minimizing or possibly eliminating the unplanned downtime of the system establishes the continuity of the computing services. Minimizing unexpected and unplanned downtime can be done by identifying, prioritizing and defending against misuse, attacks and vulnerabilities. The challenge is to reduce the likelihood of catastrophic incidents by: a) using appropriate machine and statistical learning techniques to assess the relative danger of individual threats and b) autonomously providing effective and appropriate response to the relevant threats.

Intrusion Detection System (IDS) is a rapidly growing field that deals with detecting and responding to malicious network traffic and computer misuse. Intrusion detection is the process of identifying and (possibly) responding to malicious activities targetd at computing and network resources. Any hardware or software automation that monitors, detects or responds to events occurring in a network or on a host computer is considered relevant to the intrusion detection approach. Different IDSs provide varying functionalities and benefits.

An attempt to break or misuse a system is called "intrusion". An intrusion normally exploits a specific vulnerability and must be detected as quickly as possible. An intrusion detection system is a system for detecting such intrusions. Intrusion detection systems are notable components in network security infrastructure. They examine system or network activity to find possible intrusions or attacks and trigger security alerts for the malicious activities. They are generally categorized as signature-based and anomaly-based detection system. Other categories are network-based and host-based intrusion detection systems.

Network-based IDSs are placed at a strategic point or points within the network to examine passing network traffic for signs of intrusion, whereas, host-based IDSs are run on individual hosts or devices on the network and look at user and process activity for signs of malicious behavior.

In most networks, signature-based IDSs, which are very effective against known attacks, are deployed. Signature-based systems (also know as misuse detection systems) detect attacks based on known cases of misuse. Advantages of misuse detection are high confidence in detection, low false positive rate and an unambiguous detailed identification of attack. They are also more well understood and widely applied. Disadvantages are inability to detect unknown attacks and the need for expert knowledge to create signatures.

For defense against unknown attacks, an anomaly detection scheme has to be used, which creates a model of normal bhaviour of the system and detects deviation from this model. Techniques used in detecting anomalies include data mining, clustering, and statistical signal processing. The main advantage of anomaly based systems is the ability to detect unknown attacks. The disadvantages are high false positive rate and difficulty in identification of attack type. Moreover, since what is considered normal could be different in different environments, a distinct model of normalcy need to be learned individually.

A more recent class of intrusion detectors is the *specification-based* detectors, which try to reach a common ground between misuse-based and anomaly-based systems. They are mainly based on specifications derived from protocols and detect deviations from these specifications. Although they combine the benefits of anomaly detection and misuse detection, they suffer from the disadvantage that complete specifications are hard to create especially with most protocols being constantly extended.

Due to the exponential growth in size, distribution, and complexity of communication networks, current IDS technologies are not very effective against new attacks and have severe limitations as far as performance, scalability, and flexibility are concerned. Moreover, the improvements to the IDSs are often too slow and too little to keep up with the innovations by the attackers.

The main drawbacks of the current IDSs are: 1) the large number of false positives; 2) the inability to detect unknown attacks; and, 3) an inability to properly assess the relative danger of the misuse and provide an appropriate response. There is a general consensus that the primary focus of the intrusion detection technologies must be: a) to reduce the rate of false positives; b) to develop non-signature-based intrusion detection methods; and, c) work on prevention instead of detection.

There is a critical need to be able to deliver systems that can automatically detect intrusion patterns and performance bottlenecks, and dynamically defend themselves. The main goal of an intrusion detection system is to survive the system and retain its essential services. Survivability is often defined by resistance, recognition and recovery. Resistance deals with hardening a system to prevent a break-in or other malicious acts. The goal of recognition is to detect intrusive behavior from normal behavior. Recovery deals with ways of surviving malicious acts.

Any solution to the survivability problem must handle three basic criteria, including: dynamically changing network traffic patterns, occurrence of unpredictable events (security breaches), and non-finite base of network traffic environment. One way to develop survivability tools capable of blending seamlessly into current dynamic network environments is to design them as an agent-based distributed system. The key element of such a system is an intelligent agent, which is capable of analyzing a situation, making decisions and communicating with other agents and users. Multiagent systems together with the fuzzy systems can be used to establish a community of intelligent agents with features such as autonomy, self

During the past number of years, machine learning and data mining techniques have received considerable attention among the intrusion detection researchers to address the weaknesses of knowledge-base detection techniques. This has led to the application of various supervised and unsupervised techniques for the purpose of intrusion detection. This book provides a comprehensive review on current trends in intrusion detection systems and the corresponding technologies. We present a set of experiments which are carried out to analyze the performance of unsupervised and supervised machine learning techniques considering their main design choices.

During the last decade, anomaly detection has attracted the attention of many researchers to overcome the weakness of signature-based IDSs in detecting novel attacks. However, having a relatively high false alarm rate, anomaly detection has not been wildly used in real networks. This book presents data driven approaches to automating network behavior modeling. One of the approaches is the technique we developed to create an ARX model of network signals and using it for detecting network anomalies caused by intrusions. Network signals are nonstationary, highly volatile and hard to model using traditional methods. Our modeling technique using a combination of system identification theory and wavelet approximation is very effective at addressing this issue.

Alert correlation is an important technique for managing large volume of intrusion alerts that are raised by heterogeneous IDSs. The recent trend of research in this area is towards extracting attack strategies from raw intrusion alerts. Knowing the real security situation of a network and the strategies used by the attackers enables network administrators to launch appropriate response to stop attacks and prevent them from escalating. In this book we present alert management and correlation technique that can help to automatically extract attack strategies from a large volume of intrusion alerts without specific prior knowledge about these alerts.

The intrusion detection books on the market are relatively unfocussed. They tend to leave out details of a variety of key techniques and models. Additionally, many books lack much detail on different types of attacks, theoretical foundation of attack detection approaches, implementation, data collection, evaluation, and intrusion response. In this book, our goal is to provide simple yet detailed and concise information on all these subjects. Additionally, we provide a detail overview of some of the commercially/publicly available intrusion detection and response systems. On the topic of intrusion detection system it is impossible to include everything there is to say on all subjects. However, we have tried to cover the most important and common ones.

This book is divided into 8 chapters and one appendix as follows:

Chapter 1 (Network Attacks):   In this chapter we first discuss different attack taxonomies and then present the details of a large number of known vulnerabilities and strategies to lunch attacks.

Chapter 2 (Detection Approaches):   Detection approach describes the attack analysis method used in an IDS. In this chapter different detection approaches that are currently available to detect intrusions and anomalous activities are given. Misuse, rule-based, model-based, anomaly and specification-based detection approaches are explained in detail.

Chapter 3 (Data Collection):   Intrusion detection systems collect their data from various sources. Such sources include log files, network packets, system calls, or a running code itself. In this chapter, we provide detail information as to how this very important step in the life of different intrusion detection systems (i.e. host-based, network-based and application-based) can be accomplished.

Chapter 4 (Theoretical Foundation of Detection):   Understanding the strengths and weaknesses of the machine learning and data mining approaches helps to choose the best approach to design and develop a detection system. Several approaches to the intrusion detection research area are introduced and analyzed in this chapter.

Chapter 5 (Architecture and Implementation):   Intrusion detection systems can be classified based on their architecture and implementation. This classification usually refers to the locus of the data collection and analysis. This chapter introduces the centralized, distributed and agent based intrusion detection systems.

Chapter 6 (Alert Management and Correlation):   Intrusion Detection Systems trigger too many alerts that usually contain false alerts. Decreasing false positives and improving the knowledge about attacks provides a more global view of what is happening in a network. Alert management and correlation addresses the issue of managing large number of alerts by providing a condensed, yet more useful view of the network from the intrusion standpoint. The correlation function can relate different alerts to build a big picture of the attack. The correlated alerts can also be used for cooperative intrusion detection and tracing an attack to its source.This chapter introduces different approaches to cluster, merge and correlate alerts.

Chapter 7 (Evaluation Criteria):   This chapter provides a number of approaches that can be used to evaluate the potential intrusion detection systems for accuracy, performance, completeness, timely response, cost and intrusion tolerance & attack resistance.

Chapter 8 (Intrusion Response):   The objective is to enable automated reasoning
    and decision-making to aid in human-mediated or automatic response. The cost-
    benefit analysis of response is the key for effective response. This chapter ex-
    pands on this and other approaches for providing effective and sensible re-
    sponses.
Appendix A (Examples of Commercial and Open Source IDSs):   A brief introduc-
    tion to some of the current commercial and open source IDSs are given in Ap-
    pendix A.

Audience: This book provides students and security professionals with the necessary technical background to understand, develop and apply intrusion detection
systems. Some background of machine learning and data mining is helpful to understand the approaches presented in this book. We also assume that the readers of
this book have a good command of data communication and networking. After reading this book, you should have a solid understanding of technical basics of intrusion
detection and response systems. In addition, you should know how to develop reliable and effective detection systems and be able to install and manage commercially
available IDSs.

Fredericton, Canada,   *Ali A. Ghorbani*
July 2009   *Wei Lu*
                                                                              Mahbod Tavallaee

Acknowledgements

We would like to recognize the contribution of a number of people to the book. This book is basically the result of the work of research associates, postdoctoral fellows and graduate students at the Faculty of Computer Science, University of New Brunswick, Canada, under the supervision of one of the authors (Ali A. Ghorbani). In particular, the authors would like to thank Drs. Peyman Kabiri, Mehdi Shajari, Mehran Nadjarbashi, Iosif-Viorel Onut and Mr. Bin Zhu for their effort and hard work. They contributed a great deal to some of the original wording and editing of what now became this book. Their work in putting together a comprehensive technical report on intrusion detection and response systems, from which this book is inspired, has been invaluable. The authors truly appreciate their efforts. The authors recognize that the contents of the following chapters inspired and in some cases are partially from this technical report.

- Chapter 1 (Network Attacks), Contributors: Dr. Mehdi Shajari, Dr. Peyman Kabiri and Dr. Iosif-Viorel Onut.
- Chapter 2 (Detection Approaches), Contributors: Dr. Mehran Nadjarbashi, Dr. Iosif-Viorel Onut, andDr. Peyman Kabiri.
- Chapter 3 (Data Collection), Contributors: Mr. Bin Zhu, Dr. Iosif-Viorel Onut, Dr. Mehdi Shajari, Dr. Peyman Kabiri.
- Chapter 4 (Theoretical Foundation of Detection) Contributors: Dr. Peyman Kabiri, Dr. Mehdi Shajari, Dr. Mehran Nadjarbashi, and Mr. Bin Zhu.
- Chapter 5 (Architecture and Implementation), Contributors: Dr. Mehdi Shajari, Dr. Peyman Kabiri, and Dr. Iosif-Viorel Onut.
- Chapter 6 (Alert Management and Correlation), Contributors: Mr. Bin Zhu, Dr. Mehdi Shajari, Dr. Peyman Kabiri.
- Chapter 7 (Evaluation Criteria), Contributors: Mr. Bin Zhu, Dr. Mehdi Shajari, Dr. Iosif-Viorel Onut, Dr. Peyman Kabiri.
- Chapter 8 (Intrusion Response), Contributors: Dr. Mehran Nadjarbashi, Dr. Iosif-Viorel Onut, Dr. Peyman Kabiri, and Dr. Mehdi Shajari.
- Appendix A (Examples of Commercial and Open Source IDSs), Contributors: Dr. Mehdi Shajari, Dr. Iosif-Viorel Onut, and Mr. Bin Zhu.

We gratefully recognize the opportunity the Springer gave us to write this book. The authors would like to also recognize the financial support from Atlantic Canada Opportunities Agency (ACOA) under the Atlantic Innovation Fund.

Contents

Chapter 1
Network Attacks

Network attacks are defined as a set of malicious activities to disrupt, deny, degrade or destroy information and service resident in computer networks . A network attack is executed through the data stream on networks and aims to compromise the Integrity , Confidentiality or Availability of computer network systems. Network attacks can vary from annoying email directed at an individual to intrusion attacks on sensitive data, computer information systems and critical network infrastructure. Examples of computer attacks include viruses attached to emails, probing of a system to collect information, Internet worms , unauthorized usage of a system, denial-of-service by abusing a feature of a system, or exploiting a bug in software to modify system data. Some general approaches that attackers can use to gain access to a system or limit the availability of that system include Social Engineering, Masquerading, Implementation Vulnerability, and Abuse of Functionality. In particular, the social engineering is an attack method for misleading a victim by aggressive persuasion or using other interpersonal skills to obtain authentication information or access to a system, e.g. email Phishing and email Trojan horses; a masquerading is a type of attack where the attacker pretends to be an authorized user of a system in order to gain access to it or to gain greater privileges than they are authorized for, e.g. bypassing the authentication mechanism through the use of stolen logon IDs and passwords; the implementation vulnerability is a software bug in trusted programs that an attacker can exploit to gain unauthorized access to a system, e.g. buffer overflows, race conditions, and mishandled of temporary files; the abuse of functionality stands for a malicious activity that an attacker perform to push a system to failure by overdoing a legitimate action, such as filling up a system process table through opening hundreds of telnet connections to other computers. We discussed in this chapter all these network attacks in detail.

A.A. Ghorbani et al., *Network Intrusion Detection and Prevention: Concepts and Techniques*,
Advances in Information Security 47, DOI 10.1007/978-0-387-88771-5_1,
© Springer Science + Business Media, LLC 2010

1.1 Attack Taxonomies

Although classification is simply the separation or ordering of the objects into classes, a taxonomy is the theoretical study of the classification, including its bases, principles, procedures and rules [44]. The purpose of attack taxonomies is to provide a theoretical and consistent means of classifying computer and network attacks, thus improving the efficiency in information exchange when describing attacks. In this section, we reviewed three typical taxonomies for computer and network attacks from the perspective of general usage, specific usage and the attacker, respectively.

The taxonomy called VERDICT (Validation Exposure Randomness Deallocation Improper Conditions Taxonomy) presented in [47] shows that all computer attacks can be classified using four improper conditions, namely validation, exposure, randomness and deallocation.

During an improper validation, an insufficient or incorrect validation will lead an unauthorized access to critical information or a protected system. The errors caused by an improper validation constitute a broad category. In a typical operating system, a protection error will happen for the whole system if its critical components and operators receive unconstrained or invalid data. In order to avoid the improper validation, the parameters that are passed between two system components or between a system component and an external entity must be validated according to a set of conditions, namely presence or absence, data types and formats, number and order, value ranges, access rights to associated storage locations, consistency among parameters [42].

The improper exposure always happens if the specific exposure conditions are satisfied. For instance, an inferior process might obtain the access to privileged information located in the storage or privileged information is transferred to an inferior process indirectly through the acknowledgment or timing. In this situation, the critical information system will be improperly exposed to the attack.

The improper randomness can result in an exposure to attack. A crucial aspect in cryptography is to generate random numbers. However, due to the lack of true random sources, pseudo-random numbers are used in current computer systems instead, which makes the development of unbreakable ciphering units extremely difficult.

The improper deallocation means the information stored in the system is not properly deleted after use, and thus it will lead a system vulnerability to the attack. A typical example of improper deallocation is the deletion of a file from a disk. In practice, most of the operating systems do not actually erase the file data from the disk, instead they just simply deallocate the occupied sectors from the allocation tables. A deletion is not completed until the location of that file on the disk is overwritten entirely with certain patterns.

Although the VERDICT is successfully applied to classify the existing attacks and find numerous new vulnerabilities on a wireless network, there are still a few shortcomings to this taxonomy. In terms of a security organization like CERT (Computer Emergency Response Team), the VERDICT cannot be used to identify and classify the day-to-day new attacks. It is general and abstract and does not give a description of attacks in terms of viruses, worms, Trojans and malwares, which is how the attacks are usually described in reality.

Next, we review another typical taxonomy work proposed by Hansman [32] in terms of specific attack classes. Compared to VERDICT, Hansman's taxonomy is more complete and practical, which includes four dimensions:

- 1st dimension covering the main behavior of the attack.
- 2nd dimension allowing for classification of the attack targets.
- 3rd dimension classifying vulnerabilities and exploits the attackers use.
- 4th dimension taking into account the payloads for an attack to have an effect beyond itself.

In the first dimension, the attacks have been classified into ten 10 categories that are listed below:

- **Virus:** self-replicating program that attach itself to an existing program and infects a system without permission or knowledge of the user.
- **Worm:** self-replicating program that propagates through network services on computers without any intervention of users.
- **Trojan:** a piece of program made to perform a certain benign action, but in fact perform different code for malicious purpose.
- **Buffer overflow:** a process that gains control or crashes another process by overwriting the boundary of a fixed length buffer.
- **Denial of service:** an attack which prevents intended legitimate users from accessing or using a computer or network resource.
- **Network attack:** an attack that crash the users on the network or the network itself through manipulating network protocols, ranging from the data-link layer to the application layer.
- **Physical attack:** an attack that attempts to damage physical components of a network or computer.
- **Password attack:** an attack that aims to gain a password and is usually indicated by a series of failed logins within a short period of time.
- **Information gathering attack:** an attack that gathers information or finds known vulnerabilities by scanning or probing existing computer networks.

In the second dimension, attacker's targets can be very specific target, such as IIS 4.0 or can cover a class of targets such as MacOS systems, Unix systems, etc. Targets can be hardware or software . Hardware targets are usually composed by computer, network equipment and peripheral devices. Computer targets are all computer related components, such as CPUs and hard disks. Network equipment can be devices like routers , switches or hubs. Peripheral devices are devices that are not essential to a computer's operation, for example mouse, keyboard, etc. Software targets include three main classes: operating system, applications and network. Operating system targets stand for the different OS families, such as Linux, Unix, Windows, etc. Application targets are targets that are running on top of the operating system, consisting of server application (e.g. database server, web server) and user application (e.g. email client, word editor). The network target focuses on the network itself or its protocol, such as transport-layer protocol.

In the third dimension, vulnerabilities and exploits used by the attack are covered, which are usually classified as Common Vulnerabilities and Exposures (CVE) entries. The CVE project is designed to produce common definitions of vulnerabilities [1], which is originally proposed by Mann and Christey in [50]. Since vulnerabilities are wide and varied, they usually apply to specific versions of a piece of software or operating systems. Once vulnerabilities that an attack exploits are known, the relevant CVE entries can be found.

Attacks with payload are dealt in the fourth dimension since different payloads may have different effects beyond that attack itself. For example, a worm attack may have a Trojan payload. As a result, the taxonomy allows for attacks classified in first dimension to launch other attacks defined in the fourth dimension. The payloads are classified into five categories in the fourth dimension, namely:

- First dimension attack payload.
- Corruption of information.
- Disclosure of information.
- Theft of service.
- Subversion.

The first dimension attack payload is defined according to the attack class in the first dimension. The corruption of information payload alters or destroys some information. The disclosure of information payload discloses information without the authorization of the victim. The theft of service payload access services of systems without any authorization and without any impact on the services of legitimate users as well. The subversion occurs when the payload can gain control over part of the target and then use it for its own purpose.

1.2 Probes

Network probes are usually attacks scanning computer networks to gather information or find known vulnerabilities, which are exploited for further or future attacks. The goal of this information gathering is to find out about computer and services that are present in a network as well as to detect the possibility of attack based on known vulnerabilities [29]. In this section we introduce several publicly available scanning tools that are used for network probing.

1.2.1 IPSweep and PortSweep

The IPSweep attack determines which hosts are listening on networks through a surveillance sweep. The Portsweep is used to scan which ports of a specified computer are opened in a network (or subnet). The IPSweep and PortSweep attack determine the running host and its service types, and then the collected information can be used by attackers in staging attacks and searching for vulnerable computers. Detecting an ongoing IPSweep or PortSweep attack is rather easy, especially if it is performed in a linear single-source fashion. It is harder to detect if multiple hosts or spoofed source IPs or non-time-linear are used during the sweeping.

1.2.2 NMap

NMap is a free and open source utility that mainly performs IP scans, port scans, firewall scans and OS fingerprinting using raw IP packets directed at victim computers. The inter packet timing is adjustable and ports can be scanned sequentially or randomly. Detecting scans conducted by NMap is difficult due to the distribution of multiple sources and slowing timing schedule of the attack that make the probing stealthy over a long time period.

1.2.3 MScan

MScan uses DNS zone transfers and brute force scanning over the whole domains and complete ranges of IP addresses to discover active computers and probe them for well known vulnerabilities in various network services such as statd, NFS, cgi-bin programs, open X servers, pop3, imap and finger. There exist different signatures for MScan attack detection are various, depending on which flaws and how many target computers are being probed.

1.2.4 SAINT

SAINT is the acronym for Security Administrator's Integrated Network Tool. It gathers a large amount of information from networking services, such as finger, ftp, telnet, tftp, NIS, NFS, rexd, statd, and some other services. SAINT is not an attack tool in its very basic form. It, however, gathers information that can be exploited for attackers to start further intrusions. The information mainly contains misconfiguration of network services, well-known vulnerabilities in operating systems or network utilities, and weak policy decisions. SAINT provides three optional modes of operation, namely light mode, normal model and heavy model. In light mode,

SAINT scans the target computer for discovering RPC and DNS vulnerabilities as well as unsecured NFS mount points. In normal mode, SAINT detects the vulnerabilities of fingerd, bootd, and rusersd and performs port scans on several well known TCP ports such as HTTP, FTP, Telnet, SMTP, UUCP, and NNTP, and UDP ports, such as DNS. Heavy mode is similar with normal mode except that many other uncommon ports are scanned as well.

1.2.5 Satan

Satan is a collection of C and Perl programs and is the previous version of SAINT. They are quite similar in purpose and design. The main difference between them is the particular vulnerabilities that they scan for. Like SAINT, Satan supports three levels of scanning: light, normal, and heavy. An example for the list of vulnerabilities scanning in the heavy mode is as follows,

- NFS export to unprivileged programs.
- NFS export via port mapper.
- NIS password file access.
- REXD access.
- TFTP file access.
- Remote shell access.
- Unrestricted NFS export.
- Unrestricted X Server access.
- Write-able FTP home directory.
- Several Sendmail vulnerabilities.
- Several FTP vulnerabilities.

Since Satan probes vulnerabilities using the same order as listed above, it can be identified based on the consistent pattern of network traffic that the program generates.

1.3 Privilege Escalation Attacks

Privilege escalation attacks are those attacks in which the intruder exploits a bug in a software application to gain access to resource that normally would have been protected from an application or user, resulting in an escalation or leverage of current privilege levels to carry out a malicious action with more privileges than intended by the application developer and system administrator. Known attacks in this type can be generally divided into two categories:

1. Vertical privilege escalation or User to Super-user: a lower privilege user with ordinary user account on a system exploits some flaws to assess functions or content reserved for higher privileged users or super (root) users.

2. Horizontal privilege escalation or Non-user to User: a normal user with ordinary account or without any account on a system exploits some vulnerability in the system in order to assess functions or content reserved for other normal users.

Some examples of well known privilege escalation attacks are illustrated in this section.

1.3.1 Buffer Overflow Attacks

A buffer is a contiguous allocated chunk of memory, such as an array or a pointer in C language. Generally, there are no automatic bounds checking on the buffer. Buffer overflow occurs when a program or process tries to store more data in a buffer than it is intended to hold. Since buffers are created to store a finite amount of data, the extra information has to go somewhere, leading an overflow into adjacent buffers, and thus corrupting and overwriting the valid data held in them. Buffer overflow attacks exploit this vulnerability and place the code that the attacker tries to execute in the buffer's overflowing area. The attacker then overwrite the return address of functions so it points back to the buffer and execute the intended code to trigger specific actions, such as spawning a shell with root permissions, damage the user's files, change data, or disclose confidential information.

A well known buffer overflow attack was discovered in Microsoft Outlook and Outlook Express in 2000. Due to a programming flaw made by Microsoft, attackers are able to execute any type of code they desired on the victim computers by simply sending an e-mail message. Unlike the other typical email viruses, users cannot protect themselves by not opening attached files because the program's message header mechanism has an implementation flaw that made it possible for senders to overflow the area with extraneous data and the process will be activated once the email recipient downloads the message from the server. Some other well known buffer overflow attacks for privilege escalations include Sendmail that overflows a buffer in the MIME decoding routine of the sendmail (SMTP) service on Linux machines and IMAP that exploits a bug in authentication code of the login transaction of IMAP service on Linux machines.

Typical countermeasures for buffer overflow attacks consists of writing of secure code, stack execute invalidation, secured compiler tools and dynamic run-time checks. However, none of these can solve completely the problem of buffer overflow because of the traditional framework supplied by C programming language and poor programming practices by software developer.

1.3.2 Misconfiguration Attacks

Each security system needs to be configured by the administrator for some parameters to reflect a part of security policy it enforces and to ensure that the system provides the functionality that the users need. This usually means turning on several options. The desired features work well after the administrator hits the right option. However, a problem might occur when the administrator forgets to deactivate those options when they are unnecessarily needed after a while. Any misconfiguration or weak configuration can be used by intruders either to skip a security barrier or to find out about a security breach. As a result, misconfigurtation or missing patch has become one of the most significant vulnerabilities the enterprises face recently and a prediction shows that misconfiguration attacks will account for 70% of successful WLAN attacks through 2009.

Some well known examples of misconfiguration attacks are Dictionary and FTP-Write. In the Dictionary (also known as brute-force) attack, an attacker knows about a user-name and makes repeated guessing attempts for the password from a list of possible passwords. If the administrator does not change the default username and password, guessing the possible passwords will become very easy. The Dictionary attack can be detected and prevented by setting up a maximum number of failed login attempts for each service or optionally inserting some delay between two consecutive login tries. The other misconfiguration attack, FTP-Write attack, exploits the anonymous account that is a common login mode provided by FTP services. If the anonymous FTP root directory or its subdirectories are owned by the FTP account or are in the same group as the FTP account and they are not write protected, an attacker will be able to add files like *rhosts* to gain local access to the system. By monitoring anonymous FTP accounts and checking for any attempts to create files in the FTP root folder, we can easily detect this kind of intrusions.

1.3.3 Race-condition Attacks

Processors work in the fashion of one discrete step a time. In the modern operating systems, multi tasks are implemented by quickly swapping over one or more time slices. Moreover, hardware or software interrupts can pre-empt other processes. A race condition occurs when the output and/or result of the process is unexpectedly and critically dependent on the sequence or timing of other specific competing instructions.

A well known example of is the old Unix login attack, in which when a new login process is created, there exists a short time gap that the new process is running at priority (kernel or root) mode and has not yet been switched to the normal user mode. At this time, if the human user repeatedly poked at the escape key while logging in, it is possible that the change from root to user will be prevented, allowing the human completing access to the entire system. In the old Unix login attack, its occurrence is totally dependent on whether the escape key processing occurred before or after the switch to normal user mode.

Some other places for race condition attacks involve the opening and validating of a shell or batch file, running a subprogram, checking a password or verifying a user name. In some operating systems, initial checking is made to ensure that the shell or batch file is safe. Once confirmed, the file is turned over to another process to be run. During this brief time window, the attacker might have an opportunity to substitute a different file for the one that has been validated, thus allowing free execution of commands that should be prevented from running.

The first line of defense for race condition attacks is to have good software writing practices, such as to be aware of what are atomic and non-atomic operations in application program macros, shell scripts, and locally written or user written programs. In addition, the system end users should always pay attentions to the security updates that patch race condition holes.

1.3.4 Man-in-the-Middle Attacks

Man-in-the-Middle (MITM) attack is a form of active eavesdropping in which the attacker controls the entire conversation between victims by making the independent connection with each victim, relaying messages between victims and making victims believe that they are talking directly to each other over a private connection. In order to conduct a successful MITM attack, the attacker must be able to intercept all messages going between the two victims, inject new ones and impersonate each endpoint to the satisfaction of the other. Although most cryptographic protocols or some form of endpoint authentication mechanisms can prevent MITM attacks, they occur straightforwardly in many circumstances, such as the attack against users on a public wireless access point conducted by the owner.

A typical example of MITM attack is illustrated as follows,

Suppose Mike wants to have a conversation with Jack. In order to start this communication, Mike must ask Jack for his public key. A MITM attack occurs if the third party man, Bob, can intercept the public key sent from Jack to Mike. In this case Bob is able to eavesdrop on the conversation by sending a forged message to Mike that claims to be from Jack including its own public key instead. Mike who believes this public key to be Jack's then encrypts his message with Bob's key and sends the enciphered message back to Jack. Again, Bob intercepts the message, deciphers it, stores a copy, and reenciphers it using the public key Jack originally sent to Mike. When Jack receives the newly enciphered message, he believes that it comes from Mike. In this attack example, any private information of Mike and Jack might be theft by Bob, and thus making the privilege escalation possible.

Strong encryption mechanism is the best countermeasure against man-in-the-middle attacks, such as using SSH instead of Telnet, using file encryption mechanism (e.g. PGP or Entrust), or session checksums, to name a few.

1.3.5 Social Engineering Attacks

Social Engineering is an attack method in which an attacker attempts to mislead a victim by aggressive persuasion or using other interpersonal skills to divulge confidential information for accessing to a protected critical information system. The social engineering attack can be divided into two categories, namely physical and psychological. Typical examples in the physical category include areas in the workplace and the trash dump. Typical examples for psychological category include a pretended persuasion by telephone or online communications.

In the workplace, the attacker can gain authentication information by simply standing in a place and watching an employee typing his password or simply asking the employee for the information under a pretense that it is needed to repair the system bugs. In trash dumpsters, the attacker can collect a huge amount of information including potentially credit union phone books, policy manuals, organizational charts, employee lists, system manuals, printouts of sensitive data or login names and passwords, and outdated hardware.

Another popular methods conducted by social engineering attacks are through phone and online communications. The attackers can simply make a call to Call Centers or Help Desks and pretend that they are calling from inside the credit union. By playing tricks on the phone system or operator, a smart attacker can imitate someone in a position of authority or relevance and gradually pull information out of the user or the smart attacker may masquerade as a legitimate user who needs a password reset. Usually most of employees in Call Centers and Help Desks tend to just answer questions and go on to the next phone call since they are minimally trained in the area of security, thus creating a huge security hole in this case.

The social engineering attacks conducted by online communications contain a broad category. The most popular one is email phishing. The email phishing attack appears to come from a legitimate source requesting information verification in which the email usually contains a link to a fraudulent web page with proper logos and content that looks rather legitimate and requests user to enter everything from contact information to username and password.

In general, automatic detection of social engineering attacks is difficult because they are not vulnerabilities or bugs in the system. No matter how much effort you spend on security technology and devices, the weakest link in any security system is usually the human factor. As a result, the best way to prevent social engineering attacks is the continuous training of users about possible spoofing they might come across with.

1.4 Denial of Service (DoS) and Distributed Denial of Service (DDoS) Attacks

Denial of service (DoS) attacks aim to interfere with the normal operation of network services by flooding, exhausting and overwhelming the resources of the targeted network or host. The resources may be network bandwidth, router's packet forwarding capacity, name servers, memory/computing power on servers, or operating systems' data structures. During DoS attacks, attackers usually generate large amounts of nonsense traffic such as incomplete TCP connections, malformed IP packets, bots-generated requests to web pages and some other carefully crafted methods, causing the service or program to cease functioning or prevent others from making use of the service or program.

Distributed denial of service (DDoS) attacks are developed in a distributed fashion. In real networks, the intended victims of DoS attacks are usually powerful servers with fast network connections. The DoS attacker, however, has only limited computational and network resources in most cases. As a result, in order to conduct a successful DoS attack against a powerful victim server, the smart attacker distributes and propagates the attack script over multiple intermediate hosts. These intermediate hosts are called zombies or bots in the hacker community. The computational capability for each zombie might be just as limited as the attacker's own host. The aggregation with a well organized structure for all zombies resources, however, is enough to overwhelm powerful servers with very fast connections.

Most of distributed network attacks exploit the security, configuration, or software flaws on the zombie hosts in order to control them for the purpose of distributed attacks. To organize an effective distributed attack which is usually difficult to be detected and prevented, the attacker can apply a wide variety of topologies, communication patterns and attack strategies based on some existing characteristics, such as the anonymity, ease of deployment and availability of intermediate hosts. As a result, standard definitions and shared taxonomy about the distributed network attacks are necessary in order to conduct an effective analysis about them. Some examples of the taxonomy for classifying distributed network attacks include [34, 65].

1.4.1 Detection Approaches for DoS and DDoS Attacks

The detection of DoS and DDoS attacks has received less attention than intrusion detection in the academic literature. Some existing intrusion detection systems such as Snort [63] apply signatures of well known DoS and DDoS attacks for identify them. Signatures are modeled and created though the analysis of each individual attack in order to uniquely label the malicious traffic. Others monitor the changes in the normal behavior of host and network and any deviation will be detected and reported as an attack. Existing systems, e.g. Bro [57], apply such as a way to detect

DoS and DDoS attacks based on the (statistical) changes in the normal behavior of applications and protocols.

A high traffic volume near the target server might be an indication of DDoS attacks. Such an example is illustrated by Lu and Traore in [48], in which a novel traffic-based metrics named *IPTraffic* was first proposed through studying the basic principle of DDoS attacks. An outlier detection algorithm based on Gaussian mixture model (GMM) is then used to analyze the value of *IPTraffic* and make intrusion decisions according to the outlier detection result. The proposed method was evaluated on a live networking environment and experimental results show that the approach not only can detect DDoS attacks effectively but also provide an efficient response to these attacks. However, due to the traffic spike, a high traffic is not merely enough for an evidence of DDoS attacks. Such a method is proposed by Lakhina et al. in [45], in which traffic patterns are first modeled in a high dimensional space and then principal component analysis is used to determine the linear subspace of normal traffic patterns. The major limitation of this approach is that it is non-adaptive and cannot be generalized. For example, when a web server that has small traffic becomes a high traffic web site, the approach will report an alert and flag it as an anomaly even though no DDoS attack has occurred. An improvement for this approach thus appears to rely on a combination of the abnormally high traffic volumes detection near the target server with some rules that determine whether the corresponding traffic actually constitutes an attack or just simply a traffic spike by checking the traffic content.

Instead of indicating DoS and DDoS attacks near the victim target, some approaches attempt to detect the attack patterns near the sources of the traffic (e.g. a zombie or a bot). Such a typical example is proposed by Mirkovic et al. in [51]. The detection near the source has many benefits such as providing a potential to block the DDoS traffc completely out of the network, preventing the target victim system being infected or reducing the impact of DDoS attacks on the entire network. However, a high error rate might limit the application of this method in reality since the false filtering against traffic generated from sources will have collateral damages to the innocent customers.

Whether near source or near target detection approaches for the detection of DDoS attacks, traffic features, metrics or patterns are always necessary for distinguishing DDoS attacks from regular traffic. In [30], Gil et al. propose a Multi-Level Tree for Online Packet Statistics, called MULTOPS, for identifying attacks by exploiting the correlation of incoming and outgoing packet rates at different levels of subnet prefix aggregation. Network devices with MULTOPS can detect ongoing bandwidth consumption DoS attacks based on the significant, disproportional difference between packet rates going to and coming from the victim or the attacker. Considering a typical anomaly on network traffic. The DDoS behavior is also detected by a set of traffic statistical models such as changes in the number of TCP SYN packets as compared to the TCP FIN (RST) packets [78], the Kolmogorov complexity of traffic content [29] and spectral analyses of traffic as it traverses links [33]. Some other works on DoS and DDoS detection can be found in [23, 41, 62, 67, 59, 60, 55, 15, 66].

1.4.2 Prevention and Response for DoS and DDoS Attacks

The prevention and response for DoS and DDoS attacks aim to provide guaranteed access to the resources, localizing the attackers and reducing the intensity of the attack. In order to achieve these they are usually conducted in a systematic fashion (i.e. they might happen most likely in the location of near-source host, near-target server or core system devices). The early approaches in core network devices rely on rules that block anomalous traffic from being proceeded further. Examples include Ingress/egress filtering [27, 2] and RPF (reverse path forwarding) check [25], in which packets with spoofed IP addresses will be prevented from being transmitted. More recently, the pushback protocol [35] and distributed firewall [36] are implemented to intervene in the malicious traffic started by DDoS attacks. By using pushback mechanism, the router near the victim server drops malicious packets and is responsible to deliver packets to the location where the attack occurs, so that the sources can take countermeasures against DDoS attacks accordingly. The major limitation of this method is that it cannot mitigate the denial-of-service on the target host, but merely reduce the work load on the router instead. The distributed firewall is closely related to pushback mechanisms. Its main advantage is that packets will be dropped in the end of destination and thus there is no bandwidth consumption on intermediate links for it. Some other prevention and response approaches conducted on core include [53, 40, 73].

Located at the near target victim servers, many attempts have been made to identify attack hosts and stop malicious traffic flows. Several techniques, generically called IP traceback, have been proposed to trace IP packets from the destination back to their sources in spite of IP spoofing. Although attack signatures could be characterized via this way, a large scale deployment over the Internet is required to effectively locate sources of the attack. Considering the trust level among different Internet authorities, it does not seem to happen in practice. More information on DDoS traceback can be found in [79, 26, 64, 69, 68, 74, 22, 17, 18].

Mirkovic et al. propose in [51] a system called D-WARD located at the source network router (either LAN or border router), which can autonomously detect and delete DDoS flows originating at that network. Although this approach seems to be an attractive countermeasure against DDoS attacks, as we discussed before, the false filtering on the traffic source will generate a serious collateral damage to the normal customers.

Completely free from DDoS attacks by deploying systems on individual locations is difficult, a combination of local responses and cooperative inter-domain responses is therefore proposed to solve effectively the flooding DoS and DDoS problem. In [49], Mahajan et al. propose an aggregate congestion control and a pushback technique to identify and throttle attack flows. Pushback plays a role on reacting aggregate upstream until the congestion actually happens. Moreover, the detection of traffic aggregation is only based on the destination IP addresses. Some other example on cooperation prevention and response against DDoS attacks include [61, 39, 76, 54, 37, 77, 76, 58, 43].

1.4.3 Examples of DoS and DDoS Attacks

In this section a few examples of real well known DoS or DDOS attacks are explained. Most of them are used to consume the uplink bandwidth or server bandwidth.

- **TCP-SYN Flood:** The idea behind SYN Flood attack is to abuse the TCP connection establishment process. Normal TCP connection establishment involves a three-way handshake process. Firstly, the client sends request packets with SYN bit to the server. Secondly, the server allocates a TCP control block to prepare to receive the next packet and sends a reply packet with SYN/ACK bits to the client. At this point, the server remains in half-open state. Thirdly, the client sends packets with ACK bit to the server. After the server receives packets from the client, a normal TCP connection is established. SYN Flood attack generates a large number of half-open TCP connections to fill up the TCP control block in order to exhaust the available resources. As such, the target host becomes unable to accept any more incoming TCP connections. This creates a denial of service for legitimate requests. Although TCP-SYN flood attack is a quite old attack, it is still very popular. Sending packets from highly distributed sources or with spoofed IP addresses makes devising a countermeasure difficult. Some existing tools that can execute TCP-SYN flood attacks include Phatbot/Agobot [3], TFN2K [4], Stacheldraht [5], Trinity [6], TFN [7] and Shaft [8]. A similar attack with TCP-SYN flood is TCP-ACK flood attack in which an attacker sends one SYN and multiple ACKs with a spoofed source IP address to overload the server. This attack can be simply filtered by a SPI firewall since the flooding packets do not belong to an established TCP connection. An example of existing tools to execute TCP-ACK flood attack is Mstream [9].
- **ICMP/UDP Flood Attack:** UDP and ICMP are stateless protocols, by which UDP or ICMP packets can be transmitted between two machines at higher rates. A large number of packets with UDP and ICMP protocol directed to the server can cause it overload due to massive responses. The IP spoofing makes it hard to be traced and stopped, but appears to be a decreasing threat with the usage of egress filtering. Some existing executing UDP and ICMP flood attack tools include SDBot/SpyBot [10] and Trinoo [11].
- **Ping of Death:** An attacker sends an ICMP echo request packet containing a very large amount of information, such as oversized data to a target host. The kernel buffer of the target host will then be overflowed if it attempts to respond to this ICMP request. As a result, the host will crash following this attack. Ping of death belongs to the category of fragment packet attack that usually sends packets with bad length or offsets. Currently, most operating systems and firewalls are able to handle and drop such malformed packets. Trinity is a typical tool for this kind of attacks.
- **Smurf:** A smurf attack is carried out by using ICMP protocol. In normal conditions, source host A sends an echo request message to destination host B and then B makes an echo reply message to A. When a smurf attack occurs, host A

spoofs the IP address by using host C and then sends an echo request message to a broadcast address so that the victim host C will receive all echo reply messages. As a result, links and routers to host C may get clogged by flooding traffic, and C cannot receive requests from other users. The smurf attack can be easily detected by observing a traffic behavior in which a large number of echo replies is sent to a certain system with no echo request originating from the victim system. A typical tool to execute the smurf attack is TFN2K.

- **Process Table:** The process table exploits the vulnerability that network services will allocate a new process for each incoming TCP/IP implementation. It is possible that the process table of a target host will be filled with multiple instantiations of network servers, and thus other commands cannot be executed on the target host. Many Unix services such as smtp, imap, and finger are vulnerable to this type of attack. In order to avoid this attack, vulnerable services must have resistances to rapid-consecutive requests when system load exceed over a certain level.

- **UDPStorm:** During the UDPStorm attack, an attacker generates a never-ending data stream between two UDP ports in the same or different hosts. As a result, the host cannot offer services to other users and the network may be congested or slowed down. Modeling behaviors of such an attack is rather easy and can be fully prevented using a gateway that blocks IP-spoofed packets.

- **Syslogd:** This attack exploits an implementation flaw in syslogd of Solaris v2.5 server. The syslogd daemon does a DNS lookup on the source IP address of an incoming message. In case no IP address is found to match a valid DNS record, the syslogd service will stop with a Segmentation Fault error message. Similar with syslogd attack, Teardrop attack also exploits flaws in the implementation of IP protocol in the process of re-assembly of overlapping IP segments. The teardrop attack crashes a system using an unusual fragmentation of IP packets that will cause a complete crash of a machine (blue screen) or a loss of network connectivity on vulnerable machines. The attacker sends two or more fragments that cannot be reassembled properly by manipulating the offset value of the packet and causes the victim's computer to reboot or halt its activities. Updating operating systems using security patches can effectively prevent this type of attack.

- **Mailbomb:** As a typical example of DoS attacks in application level, Mailbomb attacks overflow the queue of SMTP server or the quota on an individual's mailbox by sending enormous number of mail messages to a mail server (e.g. SMTP or POP). The detection of mailbomb attack is rather subjective, and totally depends on the server configurations like the allowed number or rate of incoming mails for a particular user or group of users, history of average mail service usage, quota size, and so forth.

- **Apache2:** An attacker sends a request containing a lot of HTTP headers to the target Apache web servers. The server will use an increasing amount of CPU time to process these headers and thus may deny service to other users and eventually crash due to running out of memory. The detection of this attack is rather easy because a typical HTTP request usually includes at most 20 headers and any deviation far beyond this limit is anomalous.

The above examples show that the craft of DoS and DDoS attacks can be very different, ranging from abusing or overusing a legitimate feature of the protocol or system (e.g. Mailbomb and Smurf), constructing malformed packets that throw off the TCP/IP stack implementation (e.g. Teardrop and Ping of Death) or exploiting flaws in existing implementations of applications (e.g. Apache2 and Syslogd). Moreover, the newly appeared DDoS attacks become more and more intelligent, such as the flash crowds using http "get" and "request" on the web server, in which it is very difficult to distinguish between traffic generated by real normal users and malicious traffic generated by bots or zombies since they behave similarly.

1.5 Worms Attacks

Computer worms replicate themselves from system to system without the use of a host file and perform malicious actions such as using up the computer's resources and shutting the system down. In contrast to viruses that require the spreading of an infected host file, worms exist as separate entities and do not attach themselves to other files.

The Morris worm is one of the first computer worms distributed via the Internet [70]. The basic idea behind Morris worm and the recent frequently launched worm attacks on the Internet is to target vulnerabilities in daemon processes of important network services through exploiting the static buffer overflow. Computer worms have become one of the most serious threats to the current Internet since the appearance of the first worm. In 2001, the Nimda and Code Red rapidly propagated through Internet and made more than 250,000 servers infected according to the Computer Emergency Response Team (CERT) [12]. More information about Nimda and Code Red can be found in [13] and [14]. Some examples of recent worms include Slammer, Blaster and Nachi.

1.5.1 Modeling and Analysis of Worm Behaviors

The traditional epidemic models are applied to model the spread of the Internet worms and to analyze their magnitude by some researchers. In [38], Joukov et al. investigate the existing worms and propose some methods to contain worms. In [52], Moore et al. apply simulation methods to study the spread behaviors of CodeRed and related worms. With a large number of machines infected by the worms, various scenarios involving content blocking and address blacklisting are simulated. Instead of proposing particular detection techniques for worm containment on the public Internet, they assume that the detection and dissemination of detection results will take a fixed amount of time. Accordingly, the containment is then carried out through either blocking infected IP addresses or creating signatures that prevent any further propagation of the worm from containment devices. The simulation results show that containing some types of worms is extremely difficult, if not impossible, under reasonable assumptions because no response time will be fast enough to protect against widespread epidemic. Some other approaches for the defensibility of large scale-free networks against malicious rapidly self-propagating code like worms include [16, 21].

The magnitude of the worm threats is analyzed by Staniford et al. [72], in which they use a traditional epidemic model to study the spread of the Code Red right after the original Code Red incident in 2001. It is claimed and urged that a well-engineered Internet active worm could play a significant role in warfare between nations and the development of a National Center for Disease Control (NCDC) analog for virus-based and worm-based threats to each nation's cybersecurity is necessary.

1.5.2 Detection and Monitoring of Worm Attacks

The main goal of this subject is to detect and stop Internet worms in their early stages of activity. In [81], Zou et al. propose a system architecture for monitoring worm, which consists of a Malware Warning Center (MWC) and distributed monitors. The basic idea behind the proposed system is monitoring ingress/egress scans to unused addresses/ports at access points of networks and then the collected information is aggregated at a central point for analysis. The Kalman filter is used to estimate the spreading parameters of the worm dynamically. More information about simulation results of the system can be found in [81]. The other similar worm monitoring system is presented by Berk et al. [19], which is based on the collection of ICMP Destination Unreachable messages generated by routers for packets to non-existent IP addresses. Such ICMP data are actually the same data as the data collected by the ingress scan monitoring in [81]. When encountering packets to unused IP addresses the routers of local networks can either send ICMP messages to the monitoring system in [19] or send such information to the MWC in [81].

A distributed worm detection architecture, called Netbait, is proposed by Brent et al. [20]. Netbait is a query processing system on intrusion detection system (IDS) data, in which probe information collected by local IDSs on a geographically distributed set of cooperating machines is aggregated. The information stored on Netbait can be shared at the global level through a distributed query processing architecture using SQL statements. By querying and aggregating data from many nodes, ISPs and network administrators could have different viewpoints on the ongoing infection and then build blacklists automatically to identify infected machines. To deploy such a distributed system on the real networks, a certain level of trusty and coordination is necessary. This is not always the case, however, due to the trust level among different Internet authorities. As a result, serious concerns still remain about the real scalability of the system. Some other approaches on this subject can be found in [31, 72].

1.5.3 Worms Containment

The goal of worm containment is to disrupt the on-going spread of a worm either on end systems or in the network infrastructure after it is identified. In [71], Staniford investigates the containment of random scanning worms (e.g. Code Red, Slammer, or Blaster) on a large-scale enterprise network. It is claimed that the worm containment could be highly effective in preventing scanning worm infections under the circumstance that the density of vulnerabilities on the network is below a critical threshold. Above that threshold, worms can spread and infect the enterprise globally, but containment may still limit that infection to a certain level. It is argued that recent worms are predominantly random scanning worms and thus most worms occurring on the last three years could be easily containable.

In [75], Toth et al. propose a system to detect and respond to worms propagation based on the connection history recorded by each host on networks. A central monitoring station collects all connection information and then builds a connection graph for analyzing suspicious patterns that are likely to be indicative of a worm activity. Patterns that indicate the spread of worms have to meet some particular properties, such as same vulnerability is repeatedly exploited at different hosts, the destination node of a certain connection opening a similar connection with same port and same payload to another host after a short period of time or a compromised host intending to locate new victim hosts by connecting to the services at random IP addresses. Once worms are detected the firewall rules deployed at the edge of network will be activated through broadcasting.

Instead of obtaining a quick system response for preventing the propagation of worms, a resilient infrastructure is proposed by Williamson to slow down the attacks automatically and buy time for a human response [80]. The proposed virus throttling limits the rate of allowed connections to new hosts. Considering the errors might be made the system delays the connections that are destined for new hosts rather than dropping them. The more uncorrelated the traffic is the more it will be delayed. According to Williamson, occasional detection errors result in small delays, virus-like behaviors, however, will be delayed. Generally, the rate of connections to new machines is always less than a certain allowed rate, thus ensuring that viruses can only spread slowly and reducing the spreading of a worm by up to an order of magnitude finally, if deployed universally.

In [46], LaBrea attempts to slow down the growth of TCP-based worms by deploying probes to unallocated addresses and placing such connections in a persistent state virtually. The thread used to initiate the probe will be blocked and therefore the worm's rate of infection will be reduced. Modifying a worm code can easily circumvent this approach [52].

1.5.4 Examples of Well Known Worm Attacks

We discuss in this section the characteristics of some well known worm attacks appeared recently with a large-scale outbreak in Internet and affecting a large number of systems and services.

- **Blaster:** Also known as Lovsan, the Blaster worm spread on computers with Windows XP and Windows 2000 operating systems in August 2003. The worm exploits the buffer overflow vulnerability in the DCOM RPC service and is coded to start a SYN flood port 80 of website windowsupdate.com. As a result Microsoft shut down the update site temporarily in order to minimize potential damages by the worm. The worm outbreak is curbed at a later time by a patch released by Microsoft.
- **Nachi:** The Nachi worm exploits a vulnerability in the Microsoft RPC service. Different with the Blaster worm, Nachi helps the customer downloading and installing security patches from Microsoft website which seems no harm is caused. It, however, affects the network traffic, reboots the infected system without operator's consent. In August 2003, the outbreak of Nachi infected the ATM machines of two main financial institutions, triggered banks' IDSs to disconnect many ATMs from the network. The after effect is just equivalent to a successful DoS attack.
- **Slammer:** The Slammer worm started in January 2003 infected 75000 victims in just 10 minutes and is considered as one of the fast-propagating Internet worms. It exploits two buffer overflow flaws in Microsoft SQL Server and then replicates itself by sending packets to randomly-generated IP addresses seeking more probable victim hosts. The worm makes a dramatic slowdown on Internet traffic because: 1) many routers are collapsed by the bombardment traffic load generated from infected servers; and 2) most Internet bandwidth is consumed by routers when they attempt to update their routing tables at the time they crash or the crashed ones come back on.

1.6 Routing Attacks

Routing attacks exploit flaws and vulnerabilities in the design and implementation of routers. A common routing attack is a protocol specific break-in that targets operations of routing information exchange. Most sophisticated attacks or substantial DoS attacks are originally based on the routing attacks against the IP routing infrastructure. Since replacing the current insecure routing infrastructure is not always possible, a complementary approach relies on the detection of routing attacks and execution of appropriate countermeasures [28]. There are two common protocols that are widely used in the implementation of Internet routers namely open shortest path first (OSPF) protocol and border gateway protocol (BGP).

OSPF is perhaps the most widely used link-state hierarchical Interior Gateway Protocol (IGP) routing algorithm in which the shortest path tree is calculated using a method based on Dijkstra's algorithm. A link state database is constructed to maintain the tree image of network topology in each router and identical copies of the database will be periodically updated by flooding on all routers in each OSPF aware area. A natural successor to the RIP (Routing Information Protocol), OSPF is less vulnerable to external attacks because it does not use TCP or UDP but uses IP directly and thus negates the need for TCP or UDP functions.

BGP is a core routing protocol of the Internet and works by maintaining a table of IP networks that designate network reachability both inside an Autonomous System (AS, is a collection of IP networks under control of a single entity) as well as outside an AS. BGP is a path vector protocol and does not use traditional IGP metrics. Routing decisions are made based on path, network policies or rules.

1.6.1 OSPF Attacks

Some examples of OSPF insiders attacks are discussed in [24] for the purpose of evaluating a real-time protocol-based intrusion detection system, which include Seq++ attack, Maximum Age attack and Maximum Sequence Number attack.

- **Seq++:** During a seq++ attack, the hacker receives a link state advertisement (LSA) instance, modifies the link state metric, increases the LSA sequence number by 1, and recalculates both the LSA and OSPF checksums before the modified LSA is re-injected into the routing system. Other routers will consider the modified LSA as a fresher due to its increased sequence number. The changed LSA is finally propagated back to its originator and then the originator should fight back (according to the protocol) with a new LSA including correct link status information and a fresher sequence number. If in this case the attacker keeps on generating seq++ LSAs, the network topology will become unstable.
- **Maximum Age:** In contrast to seq++ attack, the maximum age attack modifies the LSA age to Maximum Age (i.e. 1 hour) and then re-injects it into the routing system. The modified LSA will make all routers drop the corresponding LSA from their network topology tables. Similarly, the originator of the dropped LSA will receive the MaxAge LSA finally and fight back accordingly with a new LSA containing correct link status information and a fresher sequence number. In case the attacker carries on generating Maximum Age LSAs, the attack could make an unstable network topology.
- **Maximum Sequence Number:** Different with the seq++ and maximum age attack, maximum sequence number attack sets the LSA sequence number to Maximum Sequence Number (7FFFFFFFh). According to the protocol the originator will drop the LSA with the maximum sequence number and then flood a new LSA containing correct link status information with the smallest sequence number: 80000001h. If the OSPF protocol is implemented properly, an unlimited generation of such a LSA with maximum sequence number therefore lead an

unstable network topology. In case dropping the MaxSeq LSA is missed in the router, the MaxSeq LSA will stay in every router's topology table for one hour before it reaches its Maximum Age.

1.6.2 BGP Attacks

According to [56], the main objectives of a typical BGP attack usually include blackholing, redirection, subversion and instability. Blackholing makes a prefix unreachable from a large portion of the Internet. Redirection enforces traffic flowing to a particular network taking a different path and then reaching a compromised destination. Subversion can sniff and modifying data when the traffic is forced to pass through a certain link. Instability can trigger route dampening in upstream routers and therefore cause connectivity outages. Blackholing, redirection and instability can be easily achieved when a compromised router modifies, drops, or introduces fake BGP updates since in this case other routers obtain incorrect view of the network conditions and topology.

There are 7 common mechanisms that BGP attackers usually like to use, namely false updates and prefix hijacking, de-aggregation, contradictory advertisements, update modifications, advertent link flapping, instability and congestion-induced BGP session failures. During false updates and prefix hijacking an AS announces or originates an invalid route or prefix that it does not actually have. De-Aggregation breaks up an address block into a number of specific longer prefixes with higher preferences and as a result, the attacker can announce fake routes preferred over the legitimate routes to that network. Generally contradictory advertisement is a legitimate interdomain traffic engineering technique in which different routing announcements are sent by the same AS to different BGP peers. The attacker can exploit it by redirecting traffic to the malicious router itself or to another AS, resulting in congestion in that AS. In update modifications a compromised router redirects traffic to make trouble for the origin AS. It is difficult to detect this attack because business relationships and policies between AS and/or service providers are kept confidential and will not be released to the third party. Through the advertent link flapping a compromised router advertently flaps a route to a victim address block in a fashion that neighboring BGP speakers dampen those routes. Therefore, the victim network will stay unreachable during the time period of route dampening. Instability can be caused by many factors, such as a number of timeout BGP sessions due to link congestion, router reboots, or repeatedly physical link failures, and routing or policy changes due to the MinRouteAdver timer and the way BGP exploring alternate paths. Instability attacks are usually conducted by exploiting one or more hijacked routers. The congestion-induced BGP session failures exploit an implementation flaw that the heavy congestion carrying BGP peering sessions in links will lead to a slowdown for TCP based BGP sessions. As a result many of these sessions will be eventually aborted, causing thousands of routes to be withdrawn. When BGP sessions are backed up again, routers have to exchange full routing tables, thus creating large amounts of BGP traffic and causing significant routing convergence delays.

References

1. Common Vulnerabilities and Exposures (CVE). Available on: http://www.cve.mitre.org/, February 2009.
2. SANS Institute, Egress filtering v 0.2. Available on: http://www.sans.org/y2k/egress.htm, February 2009.
3. Phatbot. Available on: http://www.lurhq.com/phatbot.html, February 2009.
4. TFN2K. Available on: http://packetstormsecurity.org/distributed/TFN2k-Analysis-1.3.txt, February 2009.
5. Stacheldraht. Available on: http://packetstormsecurity.org/distributed/stacheldraht.analysis, February 2009.
6. Trinity. Available on: http://packetstormsecurity.org/advisories/iss/iss.09-05-00.trinity, February 2009.
7. TFN. Available on: http://www.cert.org/incident-notes/IN-99-07.html-tfn, February 2009.
8. Shaft. Available on: http://packetstormsecurity.org/distributed/shaft-analysis.txt, February 2009.
9. Mstream. Available on: http://packetstormsecurity.org/distributed/Mstream-Analysis.txt, February 2009.
10. Sdbot. Available on: http://www.sophos.de/virusinfo/analyses/w32sdbotblw.html, February 2009.
11. Trinoo. Available on: http://packetstormsecurity.org/distributed/.analysis.txt, February 2009.
12. Cert advisory ca-2001-26 nimda worm. Available on: http://www.cert.org/advisories/CA-2001-26.html, May 2009.
13. Dynamic graphs of the nimda worm. Available on: http://www.caida.org/dynamic/analysis/security/nimda/, March 2009.
14. The spread of code red worm (crv2). Available on: http://www.caida.org/research/security/code-red/coderedv2_analysis.xml, June 2009.
15. A. Akella, A. Bharambe, M. Reiter, and S. Seshan, *Detecting DDoS attacks on ISP networks*, Proceedings of the Workshop on Management and Processing of Data Streams, 2003.
16. R. Albert, H. Jeong, and A. Barabasi, *Error and attack tolerance in complex networks*, Nature **406** (2000), 387–482.
17. H. Aljifri, M. Smets, and A. Pons, *IP traceback using header compression*, Computers & Security **22** (2003), no. 2, 136–151.
18. S.M. Bellovin, M. Leech, and T. Taylor, *ICMP traceback messages*, (2000).
19. V. Berk, G. Bakos, and R. Morris, *Designing a framework for active worm detection on global networks*, Proceedings of the IEEE International Workshop on Information Assurance (Darmstadt, Germany), 2003.
20. N. Brent, G. Lee, and H. Weatherspoon, *Netbait: a distributed worm detection service*, Tech. Report IRB-TR-03-033, Intel Research Berkeley, September 2003.
21. L. Briesemeister, P. Lincoln, and P. Porras, *Epidemic profiles and defense of scale-free networks*, Proceedings of the 2003 ACM workshop on Rapid malcode, ACM New York, NY, USA, 2003, pp. 67–75.
22. H. Burch and B. Cheswick, *Tracing anonymous packets to their approximate source*, Proceedings of the USENIX Large Installation Systems Administration Conference (New Orleans, USA), 2000, p. 319327.
23. J. Cabrera, L. Lewis, X. Qin, W. Lee, R. Prasanth, B. Ravichandran, and R. Mehra, *Proactive detection of distributed denial of service attacks using mib traffic variables - a feasibility study*, Proceedings of the 7th IFIP/IEEE International Symposium on Integrated Network Management (Seattle, WA), 2001, pp. 609–622.

24. Ho-Yen Chang, S. Felix Wu, and Y. Frank Jou, *Real-time protocol analysis for detecting link-state routing protocol attacks*, ACM Transactions on Information and System Security (TIS-SEC) **4** (2001), no. 1, 1–36.
25. CISCO, *Understanding unicast reverse path forwarding*, Available on: http://www.cisco.com/web/about/security/intelligence/unicast-rpf.html, June 2009.
26. D. Dean, M. Franklin, and A. Stubblefield, *An algebraic approach to IP traceback*, ACM Transactions on Information and System Security (TISSEC) **5** (2002), no. 2, 119–137.
27. P. Ferguson and D. Senie, *RFC2267: Network Ingress Filtering: Defeating Denial of Service Attacks which employ IP Source Address Spoofing*, RFC Editor United States (1998).
28. S. Fischer-Hbner and K. Brunnstein, *Combining verified and adaptive system components towards more secure computer architectures*, Proceedings of the International Workshop on Computer Architectures to Support Security and Persistence of Information (Bremen, Germany), May 1990, pp. 1–7.
29. Simson Garfinkel and Gene Spafford, *Practical unix and internet security*, OReilly and Associates, Sebastopol, CA, USA, 1996.
30. T. Gil and M. Poletto, *Multops: A data-structure for bandwidth attack detection*, Proceedings of the USENIX Security Symposium (Washington, DC), 2001, p. 2338.
31. Ajay Gupta and R. Sekar, *An approach for detecting self-propagating email using anomaly detection*, Proceedings of Recent Advances in Intrusion Detection (RAID) (Pittsburgh, PA, USA), Lecture Notes in Computer Science, Springer-Verlag Heidelberg, September 2003, pp. 55–72.
32. S. Hansman and R. Hunt, *A taxonomy of network and computer attacks*, Computers & Security **24** (2005), no. 1, 31–43.
33. X. He, C. Papadopoulos, J. Heidemann, and A. Hussain, *Spectral characteristics of saturated links*, Tech. report, University of Southern California, 2000.
34. A. Hussain, J. Heidemann, and C. Papadopoulos, *A framework for classifying denial of service attacks*, Proceedings of the 2003 conference on Applications, technologies, architectures, and protocols for computer communications, ACM New York, NY, USA, 2003, pp. 99–110.
35. J. Ioannidis and S. Bellovin, *Implementing pushback: Router-based defense against ddos attacks*, Proceedings of the Network and Distributed Systems Security Symposium (San Diego, California), 2002, pp. 79–86.
36. S. Ioannidis, A.D. Keromytis, S.M. Bellovin, and J.M. Smith, *Implementing a distributed firewall*, Proceedings of the 7th ACM conference on Computer and communications security, ACM New York, NY, USA, 2000, pp. 190–199.
37. Cheng Jin, Haining Wang, and Kang G. Shin, *Hop-count filtering: an effective defense against spoofed ddos traffic*, Proceedings of the 10th ACM conference on Computer and communication security (CCS) (Washington D.C., USA), 2003, pp. 30–41.
38. N. Joukov and T. Chiueh, *Internet worms as internet-wide threats*, Tech. Report RPE report, TR-143, Department of Computer Science, Stony Brook University, September 2003, http://www.ecsl.cs.sunysb.edu/tr/TR143-nikolaiRPE.pdf.
39. Charlie Kaufman, Radia Perlman, and Bill Sommerfeld, *Dos protection for udp-based protocols*, Proceedings of the 10th ACM conference on Computer and communication security (CCS) (Washington D.C., USA), 2003, pp. 2–7.
40. A.D. Keromytis, V. Misra, and D. Rubenstein, *SOS: An architecture for mitigating DDoS attacks*, IEEE Journal on Selected Areas in Communications **22** (2004), no. 1, 176–188.
41. S.S.O. Kim, A.L.N. Reddy, and M. Vannucci, *Detecting Traffic Anomalies at the Source through aggregate analysis of packet header data*, Proceedings of the IEEE Computer Networking Symposium, 2004.
42. William L. Konigsford, *A taxonomy of operating-system security flaws*, Tech. Report UCID-17422, Lawrence Livermore Laboratory, 1976.
43. G. Koutepas, F. Stamatelopoulos, and B. Maglaris, *Distributed management architecture for cooperative detection and reaction to ddos attacks*, Journal of Network and Systems Management **12** (2004), no. 1, 73–94.
44. Ivan Victor Krsul, *Software vulnerability analysis*, Ph.D. thesis, Purdue University, West Lafayette, IN, USA, 1998.

45. A. Lakhina, M. Crovella, and C. Diot, *Diagnosing Network-Wide Traffic Anomalies*, ACM SIGCOMM, 2004, pp. 219–230.
46. T. Liston, *Welcome to my tarpit: The tactical and strategic use of LaBrea*, Dshield. org White paper (2001).
47. D.L. Lough, *A taxonomy of computer attacks with applications to wireless networks*, Ph.D. thesis, Virginia Polytechnic Institute and State University, Blacksburg, VA, USA, 2001.
48. W. Lu and I. Traore, *An unsupervised approach for detecting ddos attacks based on traffic based metrics*, Proceedings of IEEE Pacific Rim Conference on Communications, Computers and Signal Processing (Victoria, BC), 2005, pp. 462–465.
49. R. Mahajan, S. Bellovin, S. Floyd, J. Ioannidis, V. Paxson, and S. Shenker, *Controlling high bandwidth aggregates in the network*, ACM Computer Communication Review **32** (2002), no. 3, 62–73.
50. Christey S.M. Mann, D.E., *Common vulnerabilities and exposures*, Tech. report, The MITRE Corporation, 1999.
51. J. Mirkovic, G. Prier, and P. Reiher, *Attacking ddos at the source*, Proceedings of the 10th IEEE International Conference on Network Protocols (Paris, France), 2002, pp. 312–321.
52. D. Moore, C. Shannon, G. Voelker, and S. Savage, *Internet quarantine: Requirements for containing self-propagating code*, Proceedings of The 22nd Annual Joint Conference of the IEEE Computer and Communications Societies (INFOCOM 2003), April 2003.
53. J.T. Moore, J.K. Moore, and S. Nettles, *Predictable, Lightweight Management Agents*, Lecture notes in computer science (2002), 111–119.
54. William G. Morein, Angelos Stavrou, Debra L. Cook, Angelos D. Keromytis, Vishal Misra, and Dan Rubenstein, *Using graphic turing tests to counter automated ddos attacks against web servers*, Proceedings of the 10th ACM conference on Computer and communication security (CCS) (Washington D.C., USA), 2003, pp. 8–19.
55. P. Mutaf, *Defending against a denial-of-service attack on tcp*, Proceedings of Recent Advances in Intrusion Detection (RAID) (Purdue, IN, USA), 1999.
56. O. Nordstrom and C. Dovrolis, *Beware of BGP Attacks*, Communication Review **34** (2004), no. 2, 1–8.
57. Vern Paxson, *Bro: a system for detecting network intruders in real-time*, Computer Networks **31** (1999), no. 23-24, 2435–2463.
58. T. Peng, C. Leckie, and R. Kotagiri, *Defending against distributed denial of service attacks using selective pushback*, Proceedings of the 9th IEEE International Conference on Telecommunications (Beijing, China), 2002.
59. _____, *Detecting distributed denial of service attacks by sharing distributed beliefs*, Proceedings of the 8th Australasian Conference on Information Security and Privacy (Wollongong, Australia), 2003.
60. _____, *Detecting reflector attacks by sharing beliefs*, Proceedings of the IEEE 2003 Global Communications Conference (Globecom 2003), Communications Security Symposium (San Francisco, California, USA), 2003.
61. _____, *Protection from distributed denial of service attack using history-based ip filtering*, Proceedings of the IEEE International Conference on Communications (ICC) (Anchorage, Alaska, USA), 2003, pp. 482–486.
62. _____, *Proactively detecting ddos attack using source ip address monitoring*, Proceedings of the Networking 2004 (Athens,Greece), 2004.
63. Martin Roesch, *Snort-lightweight intrusion detection for networks*, Proceedings of LISA'99: 13th USENIX Systems Administration Conference (Seattle, Washington), 1999, pp. 229–238.
64. D. Schnackengerg, H. Holliday, R. Smith, K. Djahandari, and D. Sterne, *Cooperative intrusion traceback and response architecture (citra)*, Proceedings of The DARPA Information Survivability Conference and Exposition II, DISCEX'01 (Anaheim, CA, USA), vol. 1, 2001, pp. 56–68.
65. Clay Shields, *What do we mean by network denial of service*, Proceedings of the 2002 IEEE Workshop on Information Assurance and Security (West Point, N.Y.), 2002.

66. C. Siaterlis, B. Maglaris, and P. Roris, *A novel approach for a distributed denial of service detection engine*, Proceedings of HP Open View University Association Workshop (HPOVUA) (Purdue, IN, USA), 2003.

67. Christos Siaterlis and Basil Maglaris, *Towards multisensor data fusion for dos detection*, Proceedings of the 2004 ACM symposium on Applied computing (Nicosia, Cyprus), 2004, pp. 439 – 446.

68. A.C. Snoeren, *Hash-based IP traceback*, Proceedings of the 2001 conference on Applications, technologies, architectures, and protocols for computer communications, ACM New York, NY, USA, 2001, pp. 3–14.

69. D. Song and A. Perrig, *Advanced and authenticated marking schemes for ip traceback*, Proceedings IEEE Infocomm (Anchorage, Alaska), 2001.

70. E. Spafford, *The internet worm: crisis and aftermath*, Communications of the ACM **32** (1989), no. 6, 678–687.

71. S. Staniford, *Containment of scanning worms in enterprise networks*, Journal of Computer Security **85** (2004), 99.

72. S. Staniford, V. Paxson, and N. Weaver, *How to Own the internet in your spare time*, Proceedings of the 11th USENIX Security Symposium (Washington, DC), 2002.

73. A. Stavrou, D.L. Cook, W.G. Morein, A.D. Keromytis, V. Misra, and D. Rubenstein, *WebSOS: an overlay-based system for protecting web servers from denial of service attacks*, Computer Networks **48** (2005), no. 5, 781–807.

74. Dan Sterne, Kelly Djahandari, Brett Wilson, Bill Babson, Dan Schnackenberg, Harley Holliday, and Travis Reid, *Autonomic response to distributed denial of service attacks*, Proceedings of Recent Advances in Intrusion Detection (RAID), Lecture Notes in Computer Science, Springer-Verlag Heidelberg, 2001, pp. 134–149.

75. T. Toth and C. Kruegel, *Connection-history based anomaly detection*, Proceedings of IEEE Workshop on Information Assurance and Security (West Point, NY), 2002.

76. U.K. Tupakula and V. Varadharajan, *A controller agent model to counteract dos attacks in multiple domains*, Proceedings of the IFIP/IEEE Eighth International Symposium on Integrated Network Management, 2003, pp. 113–116.

77. Marcus Tylutki and Karl Levitt, *Mitigating distributed denial of service attacks using a proportional-integral-derivative controller*, Proceedings of Recent Advances in Intrusion Detection (RAID) (Pittsburgh, PA, USA), Lecture Notes in Computer Science, Springer-Verlag Heidelberg, 2003, pp. 1–16.

78. H. Wang, D. Zhang, and K.G. Shin, *Detecting SYN flooding attacks*, Proceedings of the Twenty-First Annual Joint Conference of the IEEE Computer and Communications Societies (INFOCOM), vol. 3, 2002.

79. X. Wang and D.S. Reeves, *Robust correlation of encrypted attack traffic through stepping stones by manipulation of interpacket delays*, Proceedings of the 10th ACM conference on Computer and communications security, ACM New York, NY, USA, 2003, pp. 20–29.

80. M. M. Williamson, *Resilient infrastructure for network security*, Proceedings of the ACSAC workshop on Application of Engineering Principles to System Security Design (Bostom, MA, USA), 2002.

81. Cliff Changchun Zou, Lixin Gao, Weibo Gong, and Don Towsley, *Monitoring and early warning for internet worms*, Proceedings of the 10th ACM conference on Computer and communication security (Washington D.C., USA), ACM Press, October 2003, pp. 190–199.

Chapter 2
Detection Approaches

The basic principle of intrusion detection is based on the assumption that intrusive activities are noticeably different from normal ones and thus are detectable [16]. Many intrusion detection approaches have been suggested in the literature since Anderson's seminal report [5]. Traditionally these approaches are classified into three categories: misuse detection, anomaly detection and specification-based detection. Anomaly based intrusion detection approaches are dedicated to establishing a model of the data flow that is monitored under normal conditions without the presence of any intrusive procedures. In contrast, misuse detection approaches aim to encode knowledge about patterns in the data flow that are known to correspond to intrusive procedures in form of specific signatures. In specification based detection approaches, security experts predefine the allowed system behaviors and thus events that do not match the specifications are labeled as attacks. In this chapter we discuss these different approaches in detail and summarize some representative examples in each category.

2.1 Misuse Detection

The study of misuse detection began with Anderson's report in 1980. Intrusions are detected by matching actual behavior recorded in audit trails with known suspicious patterns. While misuse detection is fully effective in uncovering known attacks, it is useless when faced with unknown or novel forms of attacks for which the signatures are not yet available. Moreover, for known attacks, defining a signature that encompasses all possible variations of the attack is difficult. Any mistakes in the definition of these signatures will increase the false alarm rate and decrease the effectiveness of the detection technique.

Figure 2.1 illustrates a typical misuse detection model. The model consists of four components: namely, data collection , system profile , misuse detection and response. Data are collected from one or many data sources including audit trails, network traffic, system call trace, etc. Collected data are transferred into a format

A.A. Ghorbani et al., *Network Intrusion Detection and Prevention: Concepts and Techniques*,
Advances in Information Security 47, DOI 10.1007/978-0-387-88771-5_2,
© Springer Science + Business Media, LLC 2010

that is understandable by the other components of the system. The system profile is used to characterize normal and abnormal behaviors. The profiles characterize what a normal subject behavior should be and what operations the subjects typically would perform or do not perform on the objects. The profiles are matched with actual system activities and reported as intrusions in case of deviations.

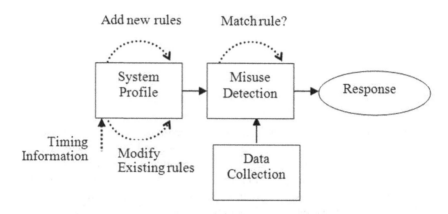

Fig. 2.1 A typical misuse detection system

Four classes of techniques are commonly used to implement misuse detection, namely pattern matching, rule-based techniques, state-based techniques, and data mining. We discuss in detail these techniques and sample systems in the rest of this section.

2.1.1 Pattern Matching

Pattern matching based intrusion detection approaches are commonly used in the network based intrusion detection systems in which attack patterns are modeled, matched and identified based on the packet head, packet content or both. Attack patterns could also be established in host-based intrusion detection systems through concatenating the words representing the system calls in a system audit trail. With the continual emerging of new types and varied forms of attacks the number of signatures is constantly growing, thus making the pattern matching more expensive in terms of the computational cost. In order to address this limitation, Abbes et al. propose a method combining a novel protocol analysis approach with traditional pattern matching to improve the performance of pattern matching when looking for attack signatures [1]. The protocol analysis checks patterns in specific parts of the packet rather than in the entire payload and it is implemented based on the construction of a decision tree. The biggest advantage of this approach is that it can reduce the search space for patterns that results in a fast search. Moreover, the approach has the potential to reduce the number of false positives since patterns are matched only in the extracted protocol fields. The performance evaluation of pattern matching based intrusion detection approaches is studied by Kreibich and Crowcroft [6], in which a workload model is proposed to provide reasonably accurate estimates compared to real workloads. The model attempts to emulate a traffic mix of different applications, reflecting the characteristics of each application and the way these applications interact with the system. The model has been implemented as part of a traffic generator that can be extended and tuned to reflect the needs of different scenarios.

2.1.2 Rule-based Techniques

Rule-based expert system is one of the earliest techniques used for misuse detection. Expert systems encode intrusive scenarios as a set of rules, which are matched against audit or network traffic data. Any deviation in the rule matching process is reported as an intrusion. Examples of rule-based systems include MIDAS (Multics Intrusion Detection and Alerting System) [65], IDES (Intrusion Detection Expert System) [53], and NIDES (Next-generation Intrusion Detection Expert System) [3, 4].

2.1.2.1 MIDAS

MIDAS was designed and developed by the National Computer Security Center (NCSC) to monitor intrusions for NCSC's networked mainframe, Dockmaster. It uses and analyzes audit log data by combining the expert system technology with statistical analysis. MIDAS uses the Production Based Expert System Toolset (P-BEST) [51] in discriminating and implementing the rule base, which is written in LISP language.

The structure of the rules in the P-BEST rule base includes two layers. The first (lower) layer is used to match certain types of events such as number of user logins, and then fires new events by setting up a particular threshold of suspicion. Rules in the second (higher) layer process these suspicions and decide whether the system should raise an alert or not. Figure 2.2 illustrates an example of MIDAS rule. The rule defines an intrusion scenario involving some unusual login time. It determines whether the time when the user logins is outside normal hours or not. The rule also illustrates that an unusual behavior does not necessarily stands for an intrusion.

defrule unusual_login_time *states*
    if there exists a login_entry
       such that user *is* userid *and*
       time_stamp *is* login_time *and*
       (unusual_login_time userid login_time)
    then
       remember a user_login_anomaly
       such that user *is* userid *and*
       time_stamp *is* login_time

Fig. 2.2 Unusual login time rule

2.1.2.2 IDES

IDES is one of the early implementation of the basic ideas and notions underlying intrusion detection. The IDES model results from Denning's seminal paper [16], which provides a mathematical codification of intrusion detection mechanisms. The model is based on the assumption that normal interactions between subjects (e.g. users) and objects (e.g. files, programs, or devices) can be characterized, and also that users always behave in a consistent manner when they perform operations on the computer system. These usages can be characterized by computing various statistics and correlated with established profiles of normal behaviors. New audit records are verified by matching known profiles for both subjects and their corresponding groups. Deviations are then flagged as intrusions. To improve the detection rate, IDES monitors the subject depending on whether the activity happens on an *on* or *off* day since user activities on different day types are usually different. For example, activities for normal users on a working day may be abnormal on an off-working day.

IDES uses P-BEST to describe its rule base consisting of two types of rules: generic rules and specific rules. Generic rules can be used for different target systems and specific rules are strictly dependent on the operating system and the corresponding implementation. IDES architecture consists of three main components, namely audit database, profiles database and the system security officer (SSO) user interface.

2.1.2.3 NIDES

NIDES, the successor of IDES, is the acronym for the Next-generation Intrusion Detection Expert System. NIDES is a hybrid intrusion detection system consisting of a signature-based expert system component as well as a detection component based on statistical approaches. The expert system improves the old IDES version by encoding more known intrusion scenarios and updating the P-BEST version used. The detection component based on statistical approaches is based on anomaly detection. In these approaches over 30 criteria are used to establish normal user profiles including CPU or I/O usage, command used, local network activity, system errors, etc.

The NIDES system is highly modularized with well-defined interfaces between components. Compared with the IDES, NIDES has higher detection rate since it includes two complementary detection components: intrusions missed by one component maybe caught by the other one.

2.1.2.4 Limitations of Rule-based Techniques

Using rule-based techniques for misuse detection, quite often the burden of extending the rule-base as new intrusion scenarios are discovered falls on the shoulder of the security officer. Moreover, developing intrusion scenarios is not an easy task and requires a certain level of expertise and security insight and awareness. In addition, determining the relations between rules is difficult. When many related rules are included in an expert system, correctness of rules is difficult to verify due to the interactions among these rules. Consequently, in practical settings, most of the rule bases are outdated and quickly become obsolete.

2.1.3 State-based Techniques

State-based techniques detect known intrusions by using expressions of the system state and state transitions. State models simplify the specification of patterns for known attacks and can be used to describe attack scenarios easier than rule-based languages such as P-BEST. In state-based techniques, activities contributing to intrusion scenarios are defined as transitions between system states, and thus intrusion scenarios are defined in the form of state transition diagrams. Figure 2.3 depicts a generic state diagram; a node represents a system state, and an arc stands for an action.

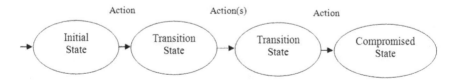

Fig. 2.3 Generic state transition diagram

The state of the system is a function of users or processes. Intrusion scenarios defined by the state transition diagram include three types of states, namely initial state, transition state and compromised state. An initial state refers to the beginning of the attack, while a compromised state stands for the successful completion of the attack. Transition states correspond to the successive states occurring between an initial state and a compromised state. An intrusion occurs if and only if a compromised state is finally reached. In the following section, we present two examples of state-based techniques, namely the state transition analysis tool proposed by Ilgun and colleagues [31, 32], and the IDIOT system based on colored petri-nets proposed by Kumar et al. [43, 41, 42, 40].

2.1.3.1 UNIX State Transition Analysis Tool (USTAT)

The UNIX State Transition Analysis Tool (USTAT) is based on the assumption that all attackers start from an initial state where they possess limited authorization to access a target system, and then after completing some operations on the target system, they acquire some previously unauthorized capabilities. USTAT is a mature prototype implementation of the state transition analysis technique for intrusion detection. It monitors the system state transition from safe to unsafe by representing all known vulnerabilities or intrusion scenarios in the form of a state transition diagram.

In USTAT, over 200 audit events are represented by ten USTAT actions, such as read(file_var), modify_owner(file_var), where the parameter file_var stands for the name of certain files. Known attacks are modeled as a sequence of state transitions that lead from an initial limited authorization state to a final compromised state. An inference engine in USTAT maintains a state transition table and determines whether the current action will cause a state transition to its successor state by matching the next state with the state transition table. Once the next new state is matched to the final state of the transition table, the intrusion alarm is raised.

USTAT is a host-based intrusion detection based on the State Transition Analysis Technique. Some other members of STAT family described in [84] include: NetSTAT is designed for real-time state-transition analysis of network data. WebSTAT and logSTAT are two other STAT family members that operate at the application level. Both of them apply STAT analysis to the events information stored in log files. WebSTAT parses the logs produced by Apache web servers, and logSTAT uses UNIX syslog files as input. Other examples for the STAT approach include [83, 79, 80, 82, 81].

Two additional assumptions underly the state transition analysis technique. First, intrusive behavior must have a visible effect on the system state, and second, this visible effect must be recognizable without using any external knowledge outside the system itself. Not all possible intrusions, however, satisfy these assumptions. For instance, passive listening of broadcast network traffic violates these assumptions. As a result, this technique carries the potential of missing a lot of intrusions that are either not recorded by the audit trail or not represented by state transition diagrams.

2.1.3.2 Colored Petri-nets

IDIOT, the acronym of Intrusion Detection In Our Time, is a state-based misuse detection system which uses pattern matching techniques based on the colored petri-nets (CPN) model. Intrusion scenarios are encoded into patterns in IDIOT, and incoming events are verified by matching them against these patterns. In the CPN model used in the implementation of IDIOT, a guard represents an intrusive signature context and the vertices represent system states. The selected CPN model is referred to as colored petri automata (CPA). The CPA defines a strict declarative specification of intrusions and specifies what patterns need to be matched instead of how to match them.

Figure 2.4 illustrates a simple example of CPA describing the following intrusion scenario: if the number of unsuccessful login attempts exceeds four within one minute report an intrusion. The combination of arrows and vertical bar stands for a transition between system states. For example, the transition from states S1 to S2 occurs when there is a token in S1; this stands for an unsuccessful login attempt. The time of first unsuccessful login attempt is saved in the token variable T1. The transition from S4 to S5 happens if there is a token in S4. The time difference between this and the first unsuccessful login attempt should be more than one minute, otherwise the system state is transferred to the final state S5, in which an alarm will be generated.

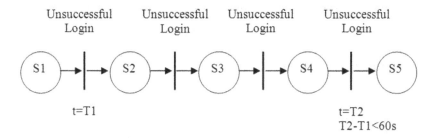

Fig. 2.4 Example of CPA illustrating four failed login attempts within one minute

It is suggested that this technique has several advantages. First, since the intrusion signatures are written in a system independent script, they can be exchanged across different operating systems and different audit logs. Second, the IDIOT system achieves an excellent real-time performance; only 5-6% CPU overhead was reported when it scanned for 100 different patterns. Third, multiple event sessions can be processed independently and then corresponding detection results are analyzed together to make the final decision.

The main limitation of this technique is that it can only detect known vulnerabilities. Also, translating known intrusions into patterns is not always easy. In addition, strict declarative expression about the intrusive patterns leads to a potential problem, that is, sophisticated attackers can easily bypass the detection system by changing their attack strategies.

2.1.4 Techniques based on Data Mining

In recent years, data mining techniques have been applied to network and host audit data for building misuse detection models [48, 49, 47]. In this case, intrusion detection is considered as a data analysis process, in which data mining techniques are used to automatically discover and model features of user's normal or intrusive behaviors. It is reported that three types of algorithms are particularly useful for mining audit data, namely classification, link analysis and sequence analysis.

Classification algorithms such as decision tree generate classifiers by learning based on a sufficient amount of normal or abnormal audit data. New audit data are labeled as either normal or abnormal according to the classifier. Link analysis determines the relation between fields in the audit database records and normal profiles are usually derived from these relations. Sequence analysis is used to find sequential patterns in audit data and embed these patterns into intrusion detection models.

Data mining based techniques performed very well in detecting known attacks during the 1998 DARPA intrusion detection competition. However, just like other misuse detection techniques, they operated fairly poorly on detecting new attacks. In addition, applying data mining techniques requires labeling the training data set, which makes the detection process error-prone, costly and time consuming.

2.2 Anomaly Detection

Different from misuse detection, anomaly detection is dedicated to establishing normal activity profiles for the system. It is based on the assumption that all intrusive activities are necessarily anomalous. Anomaly detection studies start by forming an opinion on what the normal attributes for the observed objects are, and then decide what kinds of activities should be flagged as intrusions and how to make such particular decisions.

A typical anomaly detection model is illustrated in Figure 2.5. It consists of four components, namely data collection, normal system profile, anomaly detection and response. Normal user activities or traffic data are obtained and saved by the data collection component. Specific modeling techniques are used to create normal system profiles. The anomaly detection component decides how far the current activities deviate from the normal system profiles and what percentage of these activities should be flagged as abnormal. Finally, the response component reports the intrusion and possibly corresponding timing information.

The primary advantage of anomaly detection is its capability to find novel attacks; as such it addresses the biggest limitation of misuse detection. However,

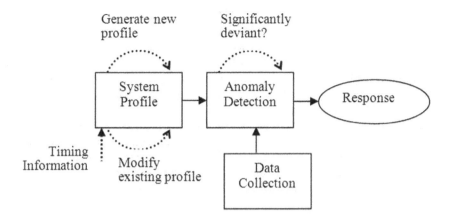

Fig. 2.5 A typical anomaly detection system

due to the assumptions underlying anomaly detection mechanisms, their false alarm rates are in general very high. Specifically, the main reasons for this limitation include the following:

1. The user's normal behavior model is based on data collected over a period of normal operations; intrusive activities missed during this period are likely to be considered as normal behaviors.
2. Anomaly detection techniques can hardly detect stealthy attacks because this kind of attacks are usually hidden in large number of instances of normal behaviors. Moreover, the types of parameters used as inputs of normal models are usually decided by security experts. Any mistake occurring during the process of defining these parameters will increase the false alarm rate and decrease the effectiveness of the anomaly detection system.

As a result, the design of the detection methods and the selection of the system or network features to be monitored are two of the main open issues in anomaly detection.

Many anomaly detection techniques have been proposed in the literature. These range from advanced statistical models to artificial intelligence and biological models based on human immune systems. Although it is difficult to classify these techniques we can divide them into four categories based on previous surveys on anomaly detection systems [7, 46, 35, 56, 27, 55, 72]. These include advanced statistical models, rule-based models, learning models, biological models, and signal processing techniques based models.

2.2.1 Advanced Statistical Models

Denning proposed in a seminal paper the earliest theoretical characterization of anomaly detection. Her detection framework, which is based on basic statistical analysis, consists of eight components: subjects, objects, audit records, statistical metrics, statistical models, profiles and profile templates, anomaly records and activity rules. A subject could be a user, a process, or system itself. The object is the receptor of actions and could be entities such as files, programs and messages. Audit records are m-tuples that represent a set of actions performed by subjects on objects. Once an event generator creates the audit records, the statistical model matches it with the appropriate profile and then makes decisions regarding the profile update, the abnormal behavior checking, and the report of detected anomalies. The activity profile includes various of variables measuring the behavior of the system based on predefined statistical metrics. The basic idea in Denning's model appear with little modification in many intrusion detection systems [40], such as Haystack [70], NIDES [3, 4] and EMERALD [61]. We provide an overview of these systems in the rest of this section.

2.2.1.1 Haystack

The haystack system was designed and implemented for the detection of intrusions in a multi-user Air Force computer system [70]. Statistical techniques are used to detect anomalous activities. A set of features such as the amount of I/O, CPU utilization, number of file accesses are observed and then the normal range of values for these features are defined. Activities falling outside these ranges are reported as intrusions.

Haystack is one of the earliest anomaly detection systems based on statistical models. It uses a very simple statistical model in which each feature is assigned a weight by the SSO. The main weakness of Haystack is that no test is conducted to verify if the weight value is sensitive to intrusion patterns and furthermore no explanation is given as to how the weight value is assigned. Moreover, the underlying assumption that features are statistically independent is usually not satisfied in practice.

2.2.1.2 NIDES

As indicated in the earlier section, NIDES includes a statistical anomaly detector as well. The audit information collected consist of user names, names of files accessed, elapsed user CPU time, total number of files opened, number of pages read from secondary storage, identities of machines onto which user has logged, etc. Statistics are computed from the collected audit information. NIDES stores only statistics related to frequencies, means, variances or covariance of measures instead of the total audit data. Given measures in NIDES, if the point in the m-space of measures is far away from the expected value, the corresponding event represented by the point is considered anomalous.

2.2.1.3 EMERALD

The Event Monitoring Enabling Responses to Anomalous Live Disturbances (EMER-ALD) is an environment for anomaly and misuse detection. It consists of a signature analysis component and a statistical profile-based anomaly detection component. The anomaly detector is based on the statistical approach where the events are labeled as intrusive if they are largely deviant from the expected behavior. In EMER-ALD more than 30 different criteria including CPU and I/O usage, commands used, local network activity, and system errors are used to build these expected user profiles. An EMERALD monitor is either passive through reading activity logs or network packets or active via probing for gathering a normal event. The analytical results can be exchanged asynchronously between different client monitors operated on different layers (e.g. domain layer, enterprise layer, etc.) [58]. Moreover, each monitor has an instance of the EMERALD resolver, a countermeasure decision engine fusing the alerts from its associated analysis engines and invoking response handlers to counter malicious activities.

More recently a lot of intrusion detection approaches based on statistical models have been proposed. Most of them model system or network behaviors on different input sources such as the application level anomaly detection approaches proposed by Kruegel et al. [39] in which sources of data are application log files, the user level anomaly detection approach presented by Lane [44] in which sources of data are UNIX command data sets collected from real human users under normal working conditions, the network level anomaly detection methods proposed by Bradford [9, 10], Thatton [75] and Siris [69] in which network flow and SNMP data are used for identifying traffic anomalies.

2.2.2 Rule based Techniques

Several anomaly detection models proposed in the literature were implemented using rule-based techniques. We present in this section four examples of such models, namely Wisdom & Sense, NSM, TIM and NADIR.

2.2.2.1 Wisdom & Sense (W&S)

Wisdom & Sensor is a unique approach to anomaly detection, which consists, as the name indicates, of two components: wisdom and sense [78]. The wisdom component consists of a set of rules describing normal behaviors of the system based on historical audit data. About 10,000 records per user are read from the file in order to create the rules. The sense component is an expert system based on the previous rules, which verifies whether the subsequent audit data violates the rule base or not. The system security officer is then alerted when the sense detects some anomalous behavior. In the implementation of W&S, the Figure of Merit (FOM) metric is used to compute an anomalousness score for each thread. The FOMs values for several events are summed and compared against a threshold. When the sum value is above the threshold, corresponding events are flagged as anomalies by the system.

2.2.2.2 Network Security Monitor (NSM)

Network Security Monitor (NSM) is a rule-based intrusion detection system targeting anomalous network activities. It is the first intrusion detection system using network traffic directly as the primary source of data [28]. All network traffic passing through a broadcast LAN are observed by NSM. Since network traffic is based on standard protocols such as TCP/IP, telnet, SMTP, etc., the traffic information on heterogeneous hosts is based on a consistent format.

Network traffic profiles are created by generating connection vectors derived from the network data. Host vectors and connection vectors are the main input to the expert system in NSM. The expert system illustrates the data-path with which systems are expected to communicate and the specifications of higher-level application layer protocols. Intrusions are decided according to analysis results of the expert system. The final result reported to the SSO consists of a connection vector and corresponding suspicion level. The suspicion level measures the likelihood that a particular connection represents some intrusive behaviors.

2.2.2.3 Time-based Inductive Machine (TIM)

Time-based Inductive Machine (TIM) models user's normal behavior patterns by dynamically generating activity rules using inductive generalization [73]. TIM discovers normal behavior patterns in a sequence of events instead of a single event. Each rule represents a model that can predict the next event from a given sequence of events. If user's behavior matches with previous event sequences and the actual next event is not included in the predicted event sets, the user's behavior is considered as intrusive. The major limitation of TIM is that the rules only model adjacent events. When many applications are executed at the same time, events occurring in one application may be interleaved with events occurring in other applications, in which case the rules generated by TIM may not accurately identify user's normal behaviors. Moreover, events that cannot match any previous event sequences in the training data set always fire an intrusion alarm, which most likely may correspond to some false alert.

2.2.2.4 NADIR

NADIR (Network Anomaly Detection and Intrusion Reporter) was developed at Los Alamos National Laboratory to monitor their internal computer networks [33, 29]. It collects audit information from three different kinds of service nodes, namely network security controller, common file system and security assurance machine. Network security controller provides user authentication and access control; common file system stores the data, and security assurance machine records attempts to degrade the security level of the data. The audit information collected for each event include a unique user ID associated with the subject, the date and time of the event, an accounting parameter, the error code, a flag indicating whether the corresponding action is successful or not, and the description of the event.

Individual user profile is computed on a weekly basis from the audit database. The user profiles are compared with a set of expert system rules in order to detect possible deviations in users' behaviors. The expert rules are mainly derived from the security policies and the statistical analysis of previous audit logs. Each rule is assigned a level-of-interest. If the corresponding sum of level-of-interest for a user is too big the intrusion alarm is raised.

2.2.3 Biological Models

Several anomaly detection models inspired from biological principles have been proposed in the literature. One of the earliest works in this area was authored by Forrest et al. They studied the analogy between human immune system's capability of distinguishing *self* from *nonself* and intrusion detection system [24, 22, 23, 18, 85]. In the human systems, T cells are created in the thymus and then a censoring process happens. If T cells bind with proteins or peptides (sub-units of proteins), then they will be transferred because they bind with themselves (*self*). Some T cells that do not bind with proteins are released to monitor the foreign material (*nonself*) of the body. A hypothesis is that those T cells that bind with foreign materials will then be removed from human systems.

When applying the *self-nonself* technique to intrusion detection, behaviors of the system are viewed as a string. This string is divided into sub-strings of equal length k. *Self* contains some of the possible 2^k strings. The rest of the sub-strings $2^k - self$ or the complement of *self* is called *nonself*. *Nonself* contains some detector strings, which are of length and does not exist in the collection of *self*. In the practical implementation, current behaviors of the system are first divided into sub-strings of length k and then are periodically compared with detector strings in *nonself*. A match indicates a possible intrusion or an unexpected change.

Nonself can be generated through various ways. A typical implementation for this is to randomly generate strings of length k, and then remove any string that is part of the collection of *self*. Consequently, a sub-string that is not in *self* is used as a detector and is added to *nonself*. The size of *nonself* determines the effectiveness

of detecting anomalous behaviors; the larger the size of *nonself* the more likely
intrusion will be detected.

Forrest et al. point out that perfect matching between strings is rare. Thus, they
define a partial matching rule: Given any two strings p and q, expression $match(p,q)$
is true if p and q match in at least r contiguous locations. For example, considering
two strings x and y, where $x = CEFGOPRTSY$ and $y = BABSOPRTTZ$, with $r >$
4, $match(x,y)$ is false, but with $r < 5$, $match(x,y)$ is true. Since perfect matching
is rare, the partial matching rule increases the likelihood of detecting anomalous
behaviors.

Another interesting biological method for intrusion detection proposed by Yu et
al. is based on the DNA sequence [89]. Yu et al. define DNA sequences for a computer system based on the knowledge that the DNA characterizes the make up of
human body and that any anomaly in tissues can be reflected in a particular DNA
sequence. Any change in the behavior patterns of the computer system may be traced
to the change of DNA sequences that can be either normal or abnormal. A standard
back-propagation neural network was used to train normal DNA sequences for network traffic, and then a UDP Flood attack was successfully detected based on the
DNA sequence for normal network traffic. Although encouraging, this preliminary
result needs to be extended in order to define a more complete DNA scheme for
computing systems.

More recently, Ahmed and Traore proposed the use of behavioral biometric for
detecting masqueraders [2]. Biometrics has so far been used only for authentication
not for intrusion detection. The framework proposed by Ahmed and Traore uses
mouse and keystroke dynamics both of which are behavioral biometrics that can
be collected passively and checked dynamically. The results reported in [2] seem
encouraging.

2.2.4 Learning Models

Learning models incorporate learning capabilities in intrusion detection process,
using artificial leaning techniques. In recent years, learning techniques have been
widely used in anomaly detection since the self-learning techniques can automatically form an opinion of what the subject's normal behavior is. According to
whether they are based on supervised or unsupervised learning techniques we divide the anomaly detection schemes into two categories: unsupervised and supervised. Supervised anomaly detection establishes the normal profiles of systems or
networks through training based on labeled data sets. In contrast, unsupervised
anomaly detection attempts to detect intrusions without using any prior knowledge
of attacks or normal instances. The main drawback of supervised anomaly detection
is the need of labeling the training data, which makes the process error-prone, costly
and time consuming, and difficult to find new attacks. Unsupervised anomaly detection addresses these issues by allowing training based on unlabeled data sets and
thus facilitating online learning and improving detection accuracy. Unsupervised

anomaly detection is relatively new compared with supervised anomaly detection schemes. We discuss both approaches in the rest of this section.

2.2.4.1 Supervised Anomaly Detection

In order to illustrate supervised anomaly detection techniques we summarize in the following section two of the proposed approaches, namely neural network and evolutionary approaches based on genetic algorithms.

Using Neural Network

Hyperview is an early attempt for intrusion detection using neural network, which consists of two components [15]. The first component is an expert system, which monitors audit trails for known intrusion signatures. The second component uses neural network to learn user behaviors; it then fires an alarm when there is a deviation between current behaviors and learnt behaviors. The use of neural network in Hyperview assumes that the audit data consist of multivariate time series, since user behavior exhibits a dynamic process executing an ordered series of events. In the implementation of Hyperview, a recurrent network is used for training and the time series are mapped with the neural network. The output is then selected as the next input to the system until the training process is terminated.

Another example of intrusion detection system using neural network is proposed by Ghosh [25]. A back-propagation network is used for training. In the practical implementation, Ghosh uses the program internal state and the input program as the input of back-propagation networks. The experimental results show that this approach increases the performance of anomaly detection by randomly generating data as anomalous input. However, choosing input parameters is not easy. Any mistake in input data will increase the false alarm rate. In addition, how to initialize the weights remains unclear.

The recent work on applying neural networks for detecting network anomalies is illustrated by Lei and Ghorbani in [50], in which a novel approach for detecting network intrusions is presented based on a competitive learning neural network. The self-organizing map (SOM) has been applied in anomaly detection for several years and it implicitly prepares itself to detect any aberrant network activity by learning to characterize the normal behaviors. However, the SOM has a significant shortage that is the number of neurons affects the network's performance. Increasing the number of output nodes will increase the resolution of the map, but the computation time will dramatically increase. As a result, Lei and Ghorbani proposed an efficient clustering algorithm based on the competitive neural networks. Experimental evaluations showed that the proposed approach obtained a similarly accurate detection rate as the SOM does, while using only one forth of the computation time of the SOM.

Using Genetic Algorithm

The genetic algorithm is an iterative search technique based on the theory of Darwinian evolution applied to mathematical models. It operates on a population of individuals in which each individual is a potential solution to a given problem. After the initial population is randomly generated the algorithm circularly evolves the population through three basic operators: selection operator, crossover operator and mutation operator until the best individual is obtained.

Genetic Algorithm as an Alternative Tool for Security Audit Trails Analysis (GASSATA) is one of the earliest attempts for using genetic algorithm (GA) for intrusion detection [57]. In GASSATA, Me defines an n-dimensional hypothesis vector H, where $H_i = 1$ if attack i is taking place according to the hypothesis, otherwise $H_i = 0$. As a result, the intrusion detection becomes the problem of finding the H vector that maximizes the product $W \times H$, subject to the constraint $(AE \times H)_i \leq O_i$; where W is a n-dimensional weight vector, AE is an attacks-events matrix, and O is the observed n-dimensional audit trail vector. Each individual in the population corresponds to a particular H vector. The fitness function is defined as follows,

$$Fitness = \sum_{i=1}^{n} W_i \times I_i \qquad (2.1)$$

Where I_i stands for an individual. The experimental evaluation showed that GA for intrusion detection had a low false alarm rate and the likelihood of detecting misuse behaviors was 0.996. However, the major limitation of GASSATA is that it cannot locate attacks precisely.

Another attempt using GA for intrusion detection is made by Chittur [13]. Chittur uses a certainty formula C_i to classify whether a record is an intrusive behavior or a normal behavior. C_i is defined as follows,

$$C_i(x) = \sum_{j=1}^{n} \Re_{ij} \times x_j \qquad (2.2)$$

Where $\Re_{ij}$ is the Ephemeral Random Constant-based coefficient for attribute x_j, and n is the number of attributes. A threshold value for C_i is established and any certainty value exceeding this threshold value is classified as a malicious attack.

The following fitness function is used:

$$F(\delta_i) = \frac{\alpha}{A} - \frac{\beta}{B} \qquad (2.3)$$

Where δ_i refers to the individual; α means the number of correctly detected attacks; and, A stands for the number of total attacks; β refers to the number of false positives and B is the total number of normal connections. The range of the fitness value is from -1 to 1. A high detection rate $\frac{\alpha}{A}$ and a low false positive rate $\frac{\beta}{B}$ will yield a high fitness value for an individual.

The experimental results show that GA successfully generates an accurate empirical behavior model from the training data. However, the major limitation of this approach is that an improper threshold value might easily lead to a high false alarm rate in detecting new attacks.

More efforts using GA for intrusion detection are made in [26, 8, 12]. Gomez et al. propose a linear representation scheme for evolving fuzzy rules using the concept of complete binary tree structures. GA is used to generate genetic operators for producing useful and minimal structure modifications to the fuzzy expression tree represented by chromosomes. However, the training process in this approach is computationally very expensive and time consuming. Bridges and Vaughn employ GA to tune the fuzzy membership functions and select an appropriate set of features in their intelligent intrusion detection system. Balajinath and Raghavan use GA to learn individual user behaviors. Active user behaviors are predicted based on past observed user behaviors which can be used for intrusion detection. The training process for both approaches is, however, time consuming.

Crosbie and Spafford propose a framework combining genetic programming (GP) and agent technology for detecting anomalous behaviors in a system [14]. Autonomous agents are used to detect intrusions using log data of network connections. Each autonomous agent is used to monitor a particular network parameter. Autonomous agents whose predication is correct are assigned a higher weight value to decide whether a session is intrusive or not. There are a number of advantages to having many small agents instead of a single large one. However, communications among so many agents lower the detection efficiency. Moreover, an improper primitive for each agent will make the training time long.

2.2.4.2 Unsupervised Anomaly Detection

Several unsupervised learning techniques for anomaly detection have been proposed in recent years. Clustering and outlier detection based techniques are among the most popular approaches suggested so far.

Lankewicz et al. author one of the earliest works in the literature [45]. Specifically, they propose a model applying pattern recognition to the characterization of individual users. The profiles computed with this model can be used for anomaly detection, particularly at the host level. A key aspect of their approach consists of using a variant of k-nearest-neighbor clustering algorithm for data compression and cluster discovery. According to them, this would facilitate real-time detection. Unfortunately, even though the main goals sought by the authors consist of improving detection efficiency and achieving real-time detection, it is not clear whether their model can achieve these goals, since no evaluation data are actually provided.

Staniford et al. propose a *portscan* detector, which is particularly effective against stealthy scans [71]. They propose an architecture that combines an anomaly sensor with a correlator. Firstly, the anomaly sensor computes an anomaly score for packets. Secondly, based on the anomaly scores the correlator uses simulated annealing to cluster packets into activities that are similar. This architecture is similar to ours, particularly since our IP weight metrics play the same role as their anomaly score. Our model, however, is broader and targets a wider range of network attacks, while their model focuses only on *portscan*. As indicated by the authors, formal experiments to measure the detection performance of their model have yet to be completed.

Another early attempt to unsupervised anomaly detection is presented by Eskin [20]. A mixture probability distribution model D is proposed to identify anomalous behaviors. Eskin assumes that each element in the model falls into one of two cases: elements are either anomalous with small probability (λ) or are normal with majority probability $(1 - \lambda)$. D is thus composed by normal distribution M and alternate distribution A according to the probability λ, giving $D = (1 - \lambda) \times M + \lambda \times A$. EM algorithm is used to estimate D. This method shows a strong ability to detect intrusive system calls when the amount of anomalous system calls consists of less than 5% of the total data. However, it has high false alarm rate when the number of anomalies is much larger than the number of normal instances in the data set.

Portnoy et al. extended the unsupervised anomaly detection approach suggested by Eskin [62]. They use a simple distance-based metrics and a simple variant of single-linkage to cluster the unlabeled data. In order to identify intrusions, they make the following assumptions:

1. The number of normal data instances largely outnumbers the number of intrusions.
2. The data instances include two clusters: intrusive cluster and normal cluster.

The direct consequence of these two assumptions is that normal instances are expected to form larger clusters compared to intrusive ones. And thus, large clusters will be flagged as normal, while small clusters will be considered intrusive. After testing their methodology using 1999 KDDCUP intrusion detection data set, they report an average detection rate of 40-55% with a 1.3-2.3% false positive rate.

Three clustering algorithms are later suggested to improve the accuracy of clustering-based detection in [21]. The first algorithm calculates the density of points near the data point being analyzed. If this point does not belong to a dense region, it will be considered an anomaly. The second algorithm calculates the sum of all the distances to the k-nearest neighbors. If the sum is greater than a threshold, the data point is flagged as an anomaly. The third algorithm is based on the support vector machine paradigm [64]. It solves convex optimization problems to classify the lower regions of support in a probabilistic distribution. Two different data sets are used to evaluate these algorithms and the evaluation result shows that the clustering algorithms have strong ability to detect anomalies. Although the evaluation results are promising, more experiments need to be done with different data sets.

Another well known clustering algorithm for network-based anomaly detection is Y-means [87]. Y-means is a clustering heuristic for intrusion detection which is based on the K-means algorithm and other related clustering algorithms, and overcomes two shortcomings of K-means, namely number of clusters dependency and degeneracy.

Similar with Y-means, a new unsupervised anomaly detection framework for network intrusions is proposed by Lu and Traore in [52], in which a new clustering algorithm named I-means and new anomalousness metrics named IP Weights are included. I-means is an evolutionary extension of k-means algorithm that is composed by a revised k-means algorithm and an evolutionary approach to mixture resolving, which estimates automatically the number of clusters for a set of data. IP Weights allow the automatic conversion of regular packet features into a 3-dimensional numerical feature space, in which the clustering takes place. Intrusion decisions are made based on the clustering result. The offline evaluation with a subset of 1998 DARPA intrusion detection data set shows that the system prototype detects 18 types of attacks out of a total of 19 network attack types; and an online evaluation in a live networking environment shows the system obtains a strong runtime efficiency, with response times falling within a few seconds ranges.

Yamanishi et al. propose an online unsupervised outlier detection approach for network intrusion detection [88]. Their model uses a finite probabilistic mixture model to represent the network data. An online discounting learning algorithm is used to learn the probabilistic model. Based on the learned model, a score is generated for the data, with a high score indicating an outlier. Intrusion detection in this case consists of identifying outliers and reporting them as intrusions. Evaluation of the model is performed using a subset of 1999 KDDCUP intrusion detection data set and reveals detection ratios ranging between 55% to 82%.

There are several other works that attempt to achieve unsupervised anomaly detection using techniques other than clustering or outlier detection. Examples of those include works by Sekar et al [66] and Shyu et al. [68]. Sekar et al. define state machine specifications of network protocols, augmented with statistical information that needed to be maintained to detect anomaly. They claim that the learning component in their method is robust enough to operate without human supervision and thus can be considered as unsupervised anomaly detection. However, they do not provide any experimental evaluation of these claims in their paper. Shyu et al. propose a novel anomaly detection scheme based on principle component classifier. They evaluate their algorithm using 1999 KDDCUP intrusion detection data. The experimental result shows that their approach has better performance than other approaches, such as LOF approach [11] and Canberra metrics [19]. Based on this robust result, they claim that their method would also work with unlabeled training data. However, they have not conducted any experimental evaluation to support this assertion.

2.3 Specification-based Detection

Specification-based detection approaches are neither misuse based, nor anomaly based since they use system behavioral specifications to detect attacks and premise that every well-behaved system execution shall conform to the specification of its intended behavior [77]. Instead of learning system behaviors, in specification-based systems the experts' knowledge determines the operating limits (threshold) of a system. Once the correct (or allowed) system behavior is specified. The events deviating from the specification would generate an alert [37].

Specification-based detection approaches focus on building specified behaviors based on the least privileged principle (or default deny principle). An execution sequence performed by the subject that violates the specification of programs will be considered as an attack. This approach, in theory, can detect unseen attacks that may be exploited in the future [38]. However, specifying the behavior of a large number of privileged programs running in real operating environments is a daunting and difficult task. Even though inductive logic programming is used to automatically synthesize specifications of programs in [36], rigorous validation of so many programs' specifications is still an open issue. Moreover, the formal methods community has been struggling with the same issue for decades without significant success. Hence, in spite of its appealing principles, specification-based detection still remains in infancy.

2.4 Hybrid Detection

Early research works on intrusion detection systems suggested that the intrusion detection capabilities can be improved through a hybrid approach consisting of both signature (misuse) detection as well as anomaly detection [54, 34, 61]. In such a hybrid system, the signature detection technique detects known attacks and the anomaly detection technique detects novel or unknown attacks. Typical recent research works for such a hybrid intrusion detection system are discussed in [76, 90, 60, 17, 30].

In [76], Tombini et al. applied an anomaly detection approach to create a list of suspicious items. Then a signature detection approach is used to classify these suspicious items into three categories, namely false alarms, attacks, and unknown attacks. The approach is based on an assumption that a high detection rate can be achieved by the anomaly detection component because missed intrusions in the first step will not be found by the follow-up signature detection component. Moreover, to make the system working well, it assumes the signature detection component has the potential to identify false alarms. Although the proposed hybrid system missed certain types of attacks, it do reduced the false alarm rate and increased the likelihood of examining most of the alerts.

Zhang et al. [90] proposed a hybrid IDS combining both misuse detection and anomaly detection components, in which a random forests algorithm was applied firstly in the misuse detection module to detect known intrusions. The outlier detection provided by the random forests algorithm is then utilized to detect unknown intrusions. Evaluations with the part of 1999 KDDCUP data set showed that their misuse detection module generated a high detection rate with a low false positive rate and at the same time the anomaly detection component has the potential to find novel intrusions. The whole hybrid system achieved an overall 94.7% detection rate with 2% false positive rate.

Peng et al. propose in [60] a two-stage hybrid intrusion detection and visualization system that leverages the advantages of signature-based and anomaly detection methods. It was claimed that their hybrid system could identify both known and novel attacks on system calls. However, evaluation results for their system were missed in the paper. The work is more like an introduction on how to apply multiple stage intrusion detection mechanism for improving the detection capability of IDS.

Similar with [90], Depren et al. [17] proposed a novel hybrid IDS system consisting of an anomaly detection module, a misuse detection module and a decision support system. The decision support system was used to combine the results of previous two detection modules. In the anomaly detection module, a Self-Organizing Map (SOM) structure was applied to model normal behavior and any deviation from the normal behavior will be classified as an attack. In the misuse detection module, a decision tree algorithm was used to classify various types of attacks. The final system was evaluated with the 1999 KDDCUP intrusion detection data set and experimental results showed that the proposed hybrid approach gave better performance over individual approaches.

Based on an idea of combining the advantages of low false positive rate of signature based IDS and the ability of anomaly detection system (ADS) for detecting new or unknown attacks, Hwang et al. proposed and reported a new experimental hybrid intrusion detection system (HIDS) in [30]. The ADS was built in HIDS, in which anomalies can be detected beyond capabilities of the well known signature based SNORT or Bro systems through mining anomalous traffic episodes from Internet connections. A weighted signature generation scheme was developed to combine ADS with SNORT through modeling signatures from detected anomalies. The HIDS scheme was evaluated with real Internet trace data mixed with 10 days of the 1999 DARPA intrusion detection data set. The obtained results showed HIDS achieves a 60% detection rate, compared with 30% and 22% detection rate acquired by the SNORT and Bro systems separately.

Instead of combining signature detection techniques and anomaly detection techniques, some other hybrid systems fuse multiple anomaly detection systems according to some specific criteria considering the detection capability for each anomaly detection technique is different. The main goal of such a hybrid system is to reduce the large number of false alerts generated by current anomaly detection approaches and at the same time keep an acceptable detection rate. Some examples of such research works are discussed in [86, 74, 59, 67, 63].

In [86], Xiang et al. proposed a multiple-level hybrid classifier utilizing a combination of tree classifiers and clustering algorithms. One of the most interesting ideas of this work is that they fuse both supervised learning (tree classifiers) and unsupervised learning (clustering) techniques. Although supervised learning technique needs a clear label for training, it was claimed in the paper that unsupervised learning might play an essential role on improving the detection rate. With the KDDCUP 1999 data set, they evaluated their approach and compared it with other popular approaches (i.e. MADAM ID and 3-level tree classifiers). Evaluation results showed that their hybrid approach was very efficient in detecting intrusions with an extremely low false negative rate of 3.37%, while keeping an acceptable level of false alarm rate of 9.1%.

Thames et al. proposed in [74] an intelligent hybrid IDS based on Bayesian Learning Networks and Self-Organizing Maps. Testing results with the 1999 KD-DCUP data set showed that such a hybrid system could achieve a significant improvement in classification accuracy compared to a non-hybrid Bayesian Learning approach when network-only data was used for classification. Although their detection results were promising, their intelligent system was sensitive to the training data they used because of the inherent limitation of learning systems. The authors discussed this limitation and proposed a possible solution addressing this issue in their future work.

Peddabachigari et al. proposed a hierarchical hybrid intelligent system model (DT-SVM) based on decision trees (DT) and support vector machines (SVM) techniques in [59]. It was assumed that combining the individual base classifiers and other hybrid machine learning paradigms can maximize the detection accuracy and minimize computational complexity. Evaluation results with part of the 1999 KDD-CUP data set showed that probing attacks could be detected with a 100% accuracy and moreover the hybrid DT-SVM approach improved and delivered equal performance for all the attack types when compared to a direct DT or SVM approach separately.

Shon and Moon proposed in [67] a new SVM approach (i.e. Enhanced SVM) by combining two existing SVM techniques, namely soft-margin SVM and one-class SVM, in order to provide unsupervised learning capability and to achieve a low false alarm rate. A set of additional techniques had been used to improve the performance of their approach, including creating normal packets profile with Self-Organized Feature Map (SOFM), filtering packets based on Passive TCP/IP Fingerprinting (PTF), selecting features using Genetic Algorithms (GAs) and using the flow of packets based on temporal relationships in data preprocessing. The experimental evaluation with DARPA intrusion detection data sets and a live data set captured from a real network showed that the proposed enhanced SVM approach obtained a low false positive rate similar to that of some real network IDS without requiring pre-labeled data.

Sabhnani and Serpen compared and evaluated nine well known pattern recognition and machine learning algorithm with the 1999 KDDCUP intrusion detection data set in [63]. Based on the performance for each algorithm, they selected three of them for obtaining an optimal detection result, including Multilayer Perceptron (MLP) for probing attacks, K-means for DoS attacks as well as U2R, and Gaussian classifier for R2L attacks. Evaluation results with the union of these three algorithms showed that the hybrid detection system could achieve a better performance than the 1999 KDD Cup's winner.

References

1. T. Abbes, A. Bouhoula, and M. Rusinowitch, *Protocol analysis in intrusion detection using decision tree*, Proceedings of International Conference on Information Technology: Coding and Computing (ITCC), vol. 1, 2004.
2. A.A.E. Ahmed and I. Traore, *Detecting computer intrusions using behavioral biometrics*, Third Annual Conference on Privacy, Security and Trust (PST), 2005.
3. D. Anderson, T. Frivold, and A. Valdes, *Next-generation intrusion detection expert system (NIDES): A summary*, SRI International, Computer Science Laboratory, 1995.
4. D. Anderson, T.F. Lunt, H. Javitz, A. Tamaru, and A. Valdes, *Detecting unusual program behavior using the statistical component of the Next-generation Intrusion Detection Expert System (NIDES)*, SRI International, Computer Science Laboratory, 1995.
5. J.P. Anderson, *Computer security threat monitoring and surveillance*, (1980).
6. S. Antonatos, K.G. Anagnostakis, and E.P. Markatos, *Generating realistic workloads for network intrusion detection systems*, ACM SIGSOFT Software Engineering Notes **29** (2004), no. 1, 207–215.
7. S. Axelsson, *Intrusion detection systems: A survey and taxonomy*, Tech. Report 99-15, Chalmers University of Technology, Department of Computer Engineering, 2000.
8. B. Balajinath and SV Raghavan, *Intrusion detection through learning behavior model*, Computer Communications **24** (2001), no. 12, 1202–1212.
9. P. Barford and D. Plonka, *Characteristics of network traffic flow anomalies*, Proceedings of the 1st ACM SIGCOMM Workshop on Internet Measurement, ACM New York, NY, USA, 2001, pp. 69–73.
10. Paul Barford, Jeffery Kline, David Plonka, and Amos Ron, *A signal analysis of network traffic anomalies*, Proceedings of the second ACM SIGCOMM Workshop on Internet measurment (Marseille, France), SIGCOMM: ACM Special Interest Group on Data Communication, ACM Press New York, NY, USA, 2002, pp. 71–82.
11. M.M. Breunig, H.P. Kriegel, R.T. Ng, and J. Sander, *LOF: identifying density-based local outliers*, ACM SIGMOD Record **29** (2000), no. 2, 93–104.
12. S.M. Bridges and R.B. Vaughn, *Fuzzy data mining and genetic algorithms applied to intrusion detection*, Proceedings of the Twenty-third National Information Systems Security Conference, National Institute of Standards and Technology, October 2000.
13. A. Chittur, *Model generation for an intrusion detection system using genetic algorithms*, High School Honors Thesis, Ossining High School in cooperation with Columbia University (2001).
14. M. Crosbie and E. H. Spafford, *Applying genetic programming to intrusion detection*, Proceedings of the 1995 AAAI Fall Symposium on Genetic Programming, November 1995.
15. H. Debar, M. Becker, and D. Siboni, *A neural network component for an intrusion detection system*, Proceedings of the 1992 IEEE Symposium on Security and Privacy, 1992, pp. 240–250.
16. DE Denning, *An intrusion-detection model*, IEEE Transactions on software engineering (1987), 222–232.
17. O. Depren, M. Topallar, E. Anarim, and M.K. Ciliz, *An intelligent intrusion detection system (IDS) for anomaly and misuse detection in computer networks*, Expert systems with Applications **29** (2005), no. 4, 713–722.
18. P. D'haeseleer, S. Forrest, and P. Helman, *An immunological approach to change detection: algorithms, analysis, and implications*, IEEE Symposium on Security and Privacy, IEEE COMPUTER SOCIETY, 1996, pp. 110–119.
19. S.M. Emran and N. Ye, *Robustness of canberra metric in computer intrusion detection*, Proceedings of the IEEE Workshop on Information Assurance and Security, West Point, NY, USA, 2001, pp. 80–84.
20. E. Eskin, *Anomaly detection over noisy data using learned probability distributions*, In Proceedings of the Seventeenth International Conference on Machine Learning (ICML'00), 2000, pp. 255–262.

21. E. Eskin, A. Arnold, M. Prerau, L. Portnoy, and S. Stolfo, *A geometric framework for unsupervised anomaly detection*, Applications of Data Mining in Computer Security (2002), 77–101.
22. S. Forrest, S. Hofmeyr, A. Somayaji, and T. Longstaff, *A sense of self for unix processes*, Proceedings of the 1996 IEEE Symposium on Security and Privacy (Los Alamitos, CA), IEEE Computer Society Press, 1996, p. 120128.
23. S. Forrest, S.A. Hofmeyr, and A. Somayaji, *Computer immunology*, Communications of the ACM **40** (1997), no. 10, 88–96.
24. S. Forrest, AS Perelson, L. Allen, and R. Cherukuri, *Self-nonself discrimination in a computer*, Proceedings of the Symposium on Research in Security and Privacy, 1994, pp. 202–212.
25. AK Ghosh, J. Wanken, and F. Charron, *Detecting anomalous and unknown intrusions against programs*, Proceedings of the 14th Annual Computer Security Applications Conference (ACSAC'98), 1998, pp. 259–267.
26. J. Gómez, D. Dasgupta, O. Nasraoui, and F. Gonzalez, *Complete expression trees for evolving fuzzy classifier systems with genetic algorithms*, Proceedings of the North American Fuzzy Information Processing Society Conference (NAFIPS-FLINTS), 2002, pp. 469–474.
27. M. Dacier H. Debar and A. Wespi, *A revised taxonomy for intrusion-detection systems*, Tech. report, IBM Research Report, 1999.
28. LT Heberlein, GV Dias, KN Levitt, B. Mukherjee, J. Wood, and D. Wolber, *A network security monitor*, Proceedings of the Symposium on Research in Security and Privacy (Oakland, CA), 1990, pp. 296–304.
29. J. Hochberg, K. Jackson, C. Stallings, JF McClary, D. DuBois, and J. Ford, *NADIR: An automated system for detecting network intrusion and misuse*, Computers and Security **12** (1993), no. 3, 235–248.
30. K. Hwang, M. Cai, Y. Chen, and M. Qin, *Hybrid intrusion detection with weighted signature generation over anomalous internet episodes*, IEEE Transactions on Dependable and Secure Computing (2007), 41–55.
31. K. Ilgun, *USTAT: A real-time intrusion detection system for UNIX*, Proceedings of the IEEE Symposium on Security and Privacy, 1993, pp. 16–28.
32. K. Ilgun, R.A. Kemmerer, and P.A. Porras, *State transition analysis: A rule-based intrusion detection approach*, IEEE transactions on software engineering **21** (1995), no. 3, 181–199.
33. KA Jackson, DH DuBois, and CA Stallings, *An expert system application for network intrusion detection*, Proceedings of the National Computer Security Conference, vol. 1, 1991.
34. Harold S. Javitz, A. Valdez, T. Lunt, and M. Tyson, *Next generation intrusion detection expert system (nides)*, Tech. Report SRI Technical Report A016, SRI International, March 1993.
35. A. Jones and R. Sielken, *Computer system intrusion detection: A survey*, Tech. report, Department of Computer Science, University of Virginia, Thornton Hall, Charlottesville, VA, September 2000.
36. C. Ko, *Logic induction of valid behavior specifications for intrusion detection*, Proceedings of IEEE Symposium on Security and Privacy, 2000, pp. 142–153.
37. Calvin Ko, Paul Brutch, Jeff Rowe, Guy Tsafnat, and Karl Levitt, *System health and intrusion monitoring using a hierarchy of constraints*, Proceedings of Recent Advances in Intrusion Detection, 4th International Symposium, (RAID 2001) (Davis, CA, USA) (W, L. M Lee, and A. Wespi, eds.), Lecture Notes in Computer Science, Springer-Verlag Heidelberg, October 2001, pp. 190–203.
38. Calvin Ko, Manfred Ruschitzka, and Karl Levitt, *Execution monitoring of security-critical programs in distributed systems: A specification-based approach*, Proceedings of IEEE Symposium on Security and Privacy, May 1997, pp. 175–187.
39. Christopher Kruegel and Giovanni Vigna, *Anomaly detection of web-based attacks*, Proceedings of the 10th ACM conference on Computer and communication security (Washington D.C., USA), ACM Press, October 2003, pp. 251–261.
40. S. Kumar, *Classification and detection of computer intrusions*, Ph.D. thesis, Purdue University, 1995.
41. S. Kumar and E. Spafford, *A pattern matching model for misuse intrusion detection*, Proceedings of the 17th National Computer Security Conference, 1994.

42. S. Kumar and E. Spafford, *A software architecture to support misuse intrusion detection*, Proceedings of the 18th National Information Security Conference, 1995.
43. Sandeep Kumar and Eugene Spafford, *An application of pattern matching in intrusion detection*, Tech. Report 94-013, Purdue University, Department of Computer Sciences, March 1994.
44. T. Lane, *Machine learning techniques for the computer security domain of anomaly detection*, Ph.D. thesis, Purdue University, August 2000.
45. L. Lankewicz and M. Benard, *Real-Time Anomaly Detection Using a Nonparametric Pattern Recognition Approach*, Proceedings of the 7th Annual Computer Security Applications Conference (ACSAC'91), 1991.
46. J. Lee, S. Moskovics, and L. Silacci, *A Survey of Intrusion Detection Analysis Methods*, 1999.
47. W. Lee, S. J. Stolfo, and K. W. Mok, *A data mining framework for building intrusion detection models*, Proceedings of the 1999 IEEE Symposium on Security and Privacy, May 1999, pp. 120–132.
48. W. Lee and S.J. Stolfo, *Data mining approaches for intrusion detection*, Proceedings of the 7th USENIX Security Symposium, 1998.
49. W. Lee, S.J. Stolfo, and K.W. Mok, *Mining audit data to build intrusion detection models*, Proceedings of the 4th International Conference on Knowledge Discovery and Data Mining, AAAI Press, 1998, pp. 66–72.
50. Z. Lei and A.A. Ghorbani, *Network intrusion detection using an improved competitive learning neural network*, Proceedings of the Second Annual Conference on Communication Networks and Services Research (Fredericton, NB, Canada), 2004.
51. U. Lindqvist and PA Porras, *Detecting computer and network misuse through the production-basedexpert system toolset (P-BEST)*, Proceedings of the IEEE Symposium on Security and Privacy, 1999, pp. 146–161.
52. W. Lu and I. Traore, *Unsupervised Anomaly Detection Using an Evolutionary Extension of K-means Algorithm*, International Journal on Information and Computer Security, Inderscience Publisher **2** (May, 2008), 107–139.
53. T. Lunt, R. Jagannathan, R. Lee, S. Listgarten, D. Eclwards, P. Neumann, H. Javitz, and A. Valdes, *IDES: The Enhanced Prototype. A Real-Time Intrusion Detection System*, Tech. report, Technical Report SRI Project 4 185-010, SRI-CSL-88, 1988.
54. T. F. Lunt, A. Tamaru, F. Gilham, R. Jagannathan, C. Jalali, P. G. Neumann H. S. Javitz, A. Valdes, and T. D. Garvey, *A real time intrusion detection expert system (ides)*, Tech. report, SRI International, Menlo Park, CA, February 1992.
55. Teresa F. Lunt, *Detecting intruders in computer systems*, Proceedings of the 1993 Conference on Auditing and Computer Technology, 1993.
56. J. McHugh, *Intrusion and intrusion detection*, International Journal of Information Security **1** (2001), no. 1, 14–35.
57. Ludovic Me, *Gassata, a genetic algorithm as an alternative tool for security audit trails analysis*, Proceedings of the 1st International Symposium on Recent Advances in Intrusion Detection (RAID'98) (Louvain-la-Neuve, Belgium), September 1998.
58. P. G. Neumann and A. Ph. Porras, *Experience with emerald to date*, Proceedings of First USENIX Workshop on Intrusion Detection and Network Monitoring (Santa Clara, California), IEEE Computer Society Press, April 1999, pp. 73–80.
59. S. Peddabachigari, A. Abraham, C. Grosan, and J. Thomas, *Modeling intrusion detection system using hybrid intelligent systems*, Journal of Network and Computer Applications **30** (2007), no. 1, 114–132.
60. J. Peng, C. Feng, and J. Rozenblit, *A hybrid intrusion detection and visualization system*, Proceedings of the 13th Annual IEEE International Symposium and Workshop on Engineering of Computer Based Systems (ECBS'06), 2006, pp. 505–506.
61. A. Ph. Porras and P. G. Neumann, *Emerald: Event monitoring enabling responses to anomalous live disturbances*, Proceedings of the National Information Systems Security Conference, 1997, pp. 353–365.

62. L. Portnoy, E. Eskin, and S.J. Stolfo, *Intrusion detection with unlabeled data using cluster-ing*, Proceedings of ACM CSS Workshop on Data Mining Applied to Security (DMSA'01), Philadelphia, PA, 2001, pp. 76–105.

63. M. Sabhnani and G. Serpen, *Application of machine learning algorithms to KDD intrusion de-tection dataset within misuse detection context*, International Conference on Machine Learn-ing, Models, Technologies and Applications, 2003, pp. 209–215.

64. B. Scholkopf, J.C. Platt, J. Shawe-Taylor, A.J. Smola, and R.C. Williamson, *Estimating the support of a high-dimensional distribution*, Neural computation **13** (2001), no. 7, 1443–1471.

65. M. Sebring, E. Shellhouse, M. Hanna, and R. Whitehurst, *Expert systems in intrusion detec-tion: A case study*, Proceedings of the 11th National Computer Security Conference, 1988, pp. 74–81.

66. R. Sekar, A. Gupta, J. Frullo, T. Shanbhag, A. Tiwari, H. Yang, and S. Zhou, *Specification-based anomaly detection: a new approach for detecting network intrusions*, Proceedings of the 9th ACM conference on Computer and communication security (CCS'02) (Washington D.C., USA), ACM Press, November 2002, pp. 265–274.

67. T. Shon and J. Moon, *A hybrid machine learning approach to network anomaly detection*, Information Sciences **177** (2007), no. 18, 3799–3821.

68. M.L. Shyu, S.C. Chen, K. Sarinnapakorn, and L.W. Chang, *A Novel Anomaly Detection Scheme Based on Principal Component Classifier*.

69. V.A. Siris and F. Papagalou, *Application of anomaly detection algorithms for detecting SYN flooding attacks*, Computer Communications **29** (2006), no. 9, 1433–1442.

70. S.E. Smaha, *Haystack: An intrusion detection system*, Aerospace Computer Security Applica-tions Conference, 1988., Fourth, 1988, pp. 37–44.

71. S. Staniford, J. Hoagland, and J. McAlerney, *Practical automated detection of stealthy portscans*, Journal of Computer Security **10** (2002), no. 1 and 2, 105–126.

72. A. Sundaram, *An introduction to intrusion detection*, Crossroads **2** (1996), no. 4, 3–7.

73. HS Teng, K. Chen, and SC Lu, *Adaptive real-time anomaly detection using inductively gener-atedsequential patterns*, Proceedings of the Symposium on Research in Security and Privacy (Oakland, CA), 1990, pp. 278–284.

74. J.L. Thames, R. Abler, and A. Saad, *Hybrid intelligent systems for network security*, Pro-ceedings of the 44th annual Southeast regional conference, ACM New York, NY, USA, 2006, pp. 286–289.

75. Marina Thottan and Chuanyi Ji, *Anomaly detection in ip networks*, IEEE Transactions on Signal Processing **51** (2003), no. 8, 148–166.

76. E. Tombini, H. Debar, L. Me, M. Ducasse, F. Telecom, and F. Caen, *A serial combination of anomaly and misuse IDSes applied to HTTP traffic*, Proceedings of the 20th Annual Computer Security Applications Conference (ACSAC'04), 2004, pp. 428–437.

77. Prem Uppuluri and R. Sekar, *Experiences with specification-based intrusion detection*, Pro-ceedings of Recent Advances in Intrusion Detection, 4th International Symposium, (RAID 2001) (Davis, CA, USA) (W, L. M Lee, and A. Wespi, eds.), Lecture Notes in Computer Science, Springer-Verlag Heidelberg, October 2001, pp. 172–189.

78. H. S. Vaccaro and G. E. Liepins, *Detection of anomalous computer session activity*, Pro-ceedings of the Symposium on Research in Security and Privacy (Oakland, CA), May 1989, pp. 280–289.

79. A. Valdes and K. Skinner, *Adaptive, model-based monitoring for cyber attack detection*, Lec-ture Notes in Computer Science (2000), 80–92.

80. G. Vigna, S.T. Eckmann, and R.A. Kemmerer, *The stat tool suite*, Proceedings of DISCEX 2000 (Hilton Head, SC), IEEE Press, January 2000, pp. 46–55.

81. G. Vigna and RA Kemmerer, *NetSTAT: A network-based intrusion detection approach*, Pro-ceedings of the 14th Annual Computer Security Applications Conference (ACSAC'98), 1998, pp. 25–34.

82. G. Vigna and R.A. Kemmerer, *NetSTAT: A network-based intrusion detection system*, Journal of Computer Security **7** (1999), no. 1, 37–71.

83. G. Vigna, W. Robertson, V. Kher, and R.A. Kemmerer, *A stateful intrusion detection system for world-wide web servers*, Proceedings of the Annual Computer Security Applications Conference (ACSAC 2003) (Las Vegas, NV), December 2003, pp. 34–43.

84. G. Vigna, F. Valeur, and R.A. Kemmerer, *Designing and implementing a family of intrusion detection systems*, Proceedings of the European Software Engineering Conference and ACM SIGSOFT Symposium on the Foundations of Software Engineering (ESEC/FSE 2003) (Helsinki, Finland), September 2003.

85. C. Warrender, S. Forrest, and B. Pearlmutter, *Detecting intrusions using system calls: alternative data models*, Proceedings of the 1999 IEEE Symposium on Security and Privacy, May 1999, pp. 133–145.

86. C. Xiang and S.M. Lim, *Design of multiple-level hybrid classifier for intrusion detection system*, Proceedings of the 2005 IEEE Workshop on Machine Learning for Signal Processing, 2005, pp. 117–122.

87. A.A. Ghorbani Y. Guan and N. Belacel, *Y-means : A clustering method for intrusion detection*, IEEE Canadian Conference on Electrical and Computer Engineering, Proceedings, 2003.

88. K. Yamanishi, J.I. Takeuchi, G. Williams, and P. Milne, *On-line unsupervised outlier detection using finite mixtures with discounting learning algorithms*, Data Mining and Knowledge Discovery **8** (2004), no. 3, 275–300.

89. B. Yu, E. Byres, and C. Howey, *Monitoring Controller's" DNA Sequence" For System Security*, ISA Emerging Technologies Conference, Instrumentation Systems and Automation Society, 2001.

90. J. Zhang and M. Zulkernine, *A hybrid network intrusion detection technique using random forests*, The First International Conference on Availability, Reliability and Security (ARES'06), 2006, pp. 262–269.

Chapter 3
Data Collection

Data collection is one of the most important steps when designing an Intrusion Detection System (IDS) and it influences the whole design and implementation process, and also the final detection result. Usually, the attacks target not only one individual computer but also aim for a group of hosts. As a result, some intrusions might
show an anomalous behavior at the network layer, while others could exhibit anomalous behaviors at the application layer. In order to cover various network intrusions
we need to monitor each layer on networks. Although ideally it is possible to design
and implement an IDS that can inspect a wide range of data extracted from both network and application layer, it is infeasible in practical due to two main reasons: one
is the diversity of the data, and the other one is the time and space resources that the
system has to consume for collecting and interpreting the data. Intrusion detection
systems collect data from many different sources, such as system log files, network
packets or flows, system calls and a running code itself. The place where the data are
collected decides the detection capability and scope of IDSs, i.e. a network based
IDS can not detect a User-to-Root attack, while an application based IDS is not able
to find a port scanning attack. In this chapter, we discuss the data collection in terms
of the different locus including host-based, network-based and application-based.

3.1 Data Collection for Host-Based IDSs

Host-based Intrusion Detection Systems (HIDSs) analyze activities on a protected
host by monitoring different sources of data that reside on that host, such as a log
file, system calls, file accesses, or the contents of the memory. A HIDS is usually a
software running on the protected host, and thus, the coverage of a HIDS is restricted
to only one machine. As a result, to protect the entire enterprise network, a HIDS
must be installed on each individual system within the internal network. There are
two main data sources that can be used for Host-Based detection, namely audit-
logs and system calls. Audit-logs stand for a set of events created by the Operating

A.A. Ghorbani et al., *Network Intrusion Detection and Prevention: Concepts and Techniques*,
Advances in Information Security 47, DOI 10.1007/978-0-387-88771-5_3,
© Springer Science + Business Media, LLC 2010

System (OS) for performing certain tasks, and system-calls represent the behavior of each user-critical application running on the OS.

3.1.1 Audit Logs

Auditing is a process operated by a host for detecting and recording security-related events. The records of such events are stored in the so-called audit log files, usually consisting of a record of all the running processes, the consumed memory, and the file-systems that these processes operate with. For example, in the Solaris OS platform, its Basic Security Module (BSM) can provide the function of log file creation, by recording security related events requested via the executing processes [6, 9, 11, 20, 40].

In [6], Biskup et al. identified three categories of audit data created by the Solaris OS, namely, host-based, network-based and out-of-band. The host-based data are derived from external sources located at different hosts and stored in the Host-Audit log file by the OS. The network-based data are derived from network information sources and are stored in the Net-Audit log file. The out-of-band data are derived from application sources and are stored in both Application-Audit and Accounting log files. The BSM Solaris system allows two types of log collection: 1) audit data streams could be written into the log files by the applications directly; and 2) the data is written into the log files using a third-party daemon (e.g. *syslogd* and *auditd*). *Syslogd* and *auditd* are two specialized daemons running on the Solaris OS to enrich the quantity and quality of data and then transfer them into the log-files. Both of them can receive event records directly from the Solaris OS and applications. As a part of SunSHIELD Basic Security Module, the *auditd* daemon provides security information about the initiator of each event for tracing back the acting subject in compliance with the Trusted Computer System Evaluation Criteria TCSEC [6, 21], while the *syslogd* daemon collects the audit regarding the classification of events and their priority.

Table 3.1 lists some examples of the programs that can be monitored by an HIDS, in which all of them belong to the SUID root programs running on the Unix servers. Based on these, Gosh et al. in [11] proposed three anomaly based methods (i.e., Elman Recurrent Neural Network, String Transducer, and State Tester) for detecting misuse of privileged-programs in real-time. Each method learns a normal profile for each privileged-program regarding the system calls generated by the BSM. During the detection phase, the modeled profile is compared against the current one and any deviation will be considered as an anomaly [11].

Similar with the work of Gosh et al. in [11], Zhang et al. proposed an anomaly based technique [40], in which they applied Support Vector Machines (SVM) to build the applications profile. To achieve the best performance when applying the above mentioned techniques, a high quality of training data is necessary. That is, an ideal training data for normal operations is not only attack free, but also it has to cover all possible states that the program may exhibit during normal operations.

admintool	allocate	aspppd	at	atd	atq	atrm	auditd
automountd	cardctl	chage	chfn	chkey	chsh	cron	crond
crontab	ct	cu	deallocate	dhcpcd	dos	eject	exrecover
fdformat	ff.core	ff.bcofig	fsush	gpasswd	gpm	hpnpd	untd
in kcms	inetd	kcms_calibrate	configure	kerbd	kerneld	kushd	klogd
kswapd	List_	lockd	login	lpd	lpq	lpr	lprm
m64config	devices	mkdevalloc	mkdevmaps	mount	newgrp	nispasswd	nmbd
nscd	mingetty	pageout	passwd	ping	procmail	ps	pt_chmod
pwdb rcp	nxterm	rdist	rdistd	rlogin	routed	rpcbind	rpciod
rpld	chkpwd	rusersd	rwhod	sacadm	sadmind	sendmail	smbd
sperl5.00404	rsh	sshd	su	suidperl	tcpd	timed	traceroute
umount	ssh1	userhelper	usernetctl	utmp_update	utmpd	uu	volcheck
vold	uptime	whodo	wu.ftpd	xlock	xscreensaver	xterm	Xwrapper
ypbind	w	zgv	yppasswd				

Table 3.1 An example of the list of programs

Consequently, a big challenge in this context is how to find and build up a good training data set for the anomaly detection. In order to address this issue, J. Kuri et al. proposed a signature-based approach that analyzes the sequence of log events and compares them against a database of signatures in [16]. The signature patterns are formed by concatenating the words appearing on the system calls in the audit trail. As a result, the intrusion detection problem becomes a multiple approximate pattern matching problem and a possible intrusion can be a substring of the current audit trial.

When applying audit logs based approach for intrusion detection, one big problem is we do not have a generic auditing mechanism designed specifically for intrusion detection. Collecting appropriate features from the log files, in most cases, is not possible. Moreover, different OS platform records different information into the log files and there is a lack of compatibility between them. In order to address this issue, Flack et al. proposes an auditing language that helps in defining semantic meaning for the intrusion-related events [9]. The new language formalizes the description of an audit log, thus improving the semantic accuracy of the IDSs that rely on the log files. Even though the information in a log file can be exploited by IDSs to detect intrusions, an intruder may also target them to gain some information about that system and all the users of it, raising another delicate issue related to data privacy (i.e. log files may be maliciously exploited by intruders). In [6], Biskup et al. propose a mechanism that inspects the personal data and replaces any private data by transaction-based pseudonyms. The pseudonyms are encrypted so that only audit analyzers are able to perform decryption and any unauthorized user attempting to access the log files will be given an encrypted data. Instead of encrypting only the private data, Schneier et al. propose in [30] an approach to encrypt the whole log file based on a secret key known by both untrusty hosts and trusted verification systems. Each record in the log file has been assigned a derived encryption key, thus making it possible to assign different encryption keys for different entries. In this case, even if the access to the protected log file is gained by the attacker he/she would have to know the derived keys for each Log entry as well [30].

3.1.2 System Call Sequences

System Call (SC) sequences have proved to be an effective information source in host-based intrusion detection. Any program in an OS must call some basic operations (i.e. system calls) in order to accomplish its task thus making it possible to model and characterize the behaviors of an application. The basic idea behind using system calls for intrusion detection is that if an anomaly exists in the application, it will also affect the way in which the application interacts with the OS. Usually, the normal application profile is built up based on learning techniques during the training phase and any error or attack behavior included in the training data will have a dramatic influencing on the performance of the HIDS. Some other challenges faced with HIDSs using system calls include the diversity of applications and the lack of similarity between them. Moreover, an apparent limitation of system calls based techniques is the application dependency on the OS. If the same application runs on two different OSs, its behavior at the SC level will be radically different.

In [10], Forrest et al. conducted a pioneer work of using the SC sequences to detect abnormal program behavior. The data sets that they collected at the University of New Mexico have become a standard test benchmark for several research projects and have been released to the public so that researchers can refer them to evaluate different HIDSs. As part of contributions in their computer immunology research project at the University of New Mexico, Forrest et al. proposed a method for detecting anomaly, in which normal is defined by short-range correlations in a process's system calls. The basic idea behind their approach is that the short SC sequences (i.e., $length \in [5, 11]$) made by a program during its normal executions are very consistent throughout different runs. Moreover, those sequences are proved to be very different from the normal execution of the program to the abnormal execution as well as from program to program. As a result, they built a database that contains a set of normal profiles of programs and any deviation of patterns when matched with the database will be labeled as the anomalies. In order to establish such a database, a sliding window of size k (where $k \in 5, 6, 11$) across the trace of system calls is applied to collect all the patterns in SC that are encountered during the training. For instance, consider $k = 3$ and the following sequence of SC [10]: *open, read, mmap, mmap, open, getrlimit, mmap, close*, during the training phase, as the window is slided over the sequence, for each SC all the next k calls in the encountered sequences are stored in a table (see Table 3.2). The normal profile of each process is defined by such a table. After training, the abnormal sequences not found in the training table indicate anomalies in the running process.

In [41], Li et al. propose an anomaly-based intrusion detection technique called ScanAID (Statistical Characteristics of N-grams for Anomaly-based Intrusion Detection). The ScanAID detects anomalies using the N-gram features of system call data. An N-gram is a sequence of SC with a specific length. In ScanAID, the absolute occurrence frequency of each N-gram is trained. Subsequently, the encountered sequences from the test data are compared to those in the normal database in the detection model. An anomaly value for each system call is computed based on the known absolute frequencies of the N-grams. Compared to the work in [10], extract-

call	position1	position2	position3
open	read	mmap	mmap
	getrlimit		close
read	mmap	mmap	open
mmap	mmap	open	getrlimit
	open	getrlimit	mmap
	close		
getrlimit	mmap	close	
close			

Table 3.2 The patterns extracted from a SC sequence using a sliding window of 3 calls

ing N-grams of system calls does not represent any significant improvement and also the reported results show that the performance has not been significantly improved.

In [14], Kruegel et al. claim that it is possible to create carefully crafted attacks containing system calls sequences that are similar with the normal system call patterns, and thus the IDSs can be easily fooled. Addressing this issue, Kruegel et al. apply only the SC arguments instead of finding relations between sequences of actions. The application specific profiles of the normal usage are learned and modeled during the training process. It is well known that the attack free training data is necessary to obtain the optimal detection performance. Given n arguments of a system call $s < a_1^s, a_2^s, \ldots, a_n^s >$, Kruegel et al. construct four different models for each argument of the system call. Each model analyzes a particular feature of the arguments and the final anomaly factor is computed based on these models. Table 3.3 illustrates the four features targeted by the IDS for each argument of a system call. In most cases a string argument of a system call represents the name of a particular entry into the file-system. As a result, their length usually does not exceed 100 characters and most of them are the human readable characters. In [14], Kruegel et al. apply the length of a string argument to approximate and detect any deviation from the normal behavior. As illustrated in Table 4.3, the second feature is based on the assumption that the characters in a string argument are not uniformly distributed, but occur with different distributions. This is reasonable because of the small number of human-readable characters (i.e., 256) that are letters, numbers, and a few special characters. During the training phase the IDS learns an *Idealized Character Distribution* and during the detection phase the learned distribution is applied as the normal profile and any deviation will be considered as a suspicious action. The third feature is the structural inference that is inspired by the fact that a program always accesses the files located in the program's home directory and its subdirectories. Therefore, a grammar can be extracted through analyzing the structure of the argument. Once the grammar is learned and modeled, any attempt in accessing files residing in different directories will be easily observable and consequently intrusions can be detected. The fourth feature is the token finder aiming at the numerical-attributes. The values of an attribute are either restricted to a set of numbers or follow a random pattern. The number of different values for each parameter is bound to some threshold that can be learned during the training. Consequently, at runtime, any new value of that argument is expected to belong to the set of normal identifiers, otherwise an anomaly is identified.

Number	Feature
1	String Length
2	String Character Distribution
3	Structural Inference
4	Token Finder

Table 3.3 The features used by Kruegel et al. for characterizing each application

A commercial product, called StormFront, is developed by OKENA to detect intrusions using SC [23]. The specification based profiles for each application running in the system is built base on SC, and each profile consists of rules regarding the client-server communication, the file system controls, registry controls, and the COM controls. Different with the above mentioned anomaly based techniques for host based intrusion detection, Ko et al. propose a specification-based system in which rules are defined to model the normal behavior of the applications [13]. The proposed System Health and Intrusion Monitoring (SHIM) architecture includes the host SHIM sensors and a centralized SHIM manager. Each SHIM sensor is deployed on a host, and is responsible for monitoring the applications and system call activities running on that particular system. The SHIM manager provides a single-point configuration functionality to operate all the deployed sensors in the network, collects the alert messages from all the sensors and allows the administrator to handle them. SHIM uses a hierarchy of constrains defined for the UNIX system that models the normal operation of the system by restricting the set of actions (i.e. system calls) that each security-critical application can execute. Consequently, SHIM does not only detect the attacks directly but also identifies the malicious manifestation of them.

Even though system-calls prove to be a good information source for intrusion detection at the application layer, they still face several limitations, including: (1) the big difference between different OSs at SC level makes the same application to behave very differently once it is deployed on two different OSs, (2) the number of applications existing in the current information systems makes the tracking and processing of system calls impracticable and thus this technique focuses mostly on application-critical programs, (3) the same application deployed on the same OS will behave differently from user to user, (4) the IDS will slow down the speed of that particular computer where the IDS system is operating due to the computational time and the amount of data that it has to process, and (5) for a large scale network, the maintenance of many host-based IDSs is hard to handle.

3.2 Data Collection for Network-Based IDSs

The Network-Based Intrusion Detection Systems (NIDS) collect and analyze data captured directly from the network. They usually work by capturing and examining the types and contents of packets or flows when they pass through the network. Relying on the location where the data is collected, a NIDS captures and analyzes the traffic within a subnet, a network, or between a network and the Internet. Traditionally, NIDSs ignore the payload of the packets due to the computational time, the vast diversity of protocols, and sometimes privacy issues. The payload stands for the data belonging to the Application Layer specification based on the TCP/IP protocol suite, and the header represents the data belonging to the transport, network, and link layers from the TCP/IP protocol suite [34].

3.2.1 SNMP

Developed by the Internet Engineering Task Force (IETF), the Simple Network Management Protocol (SNMP) defines how management information is exchanged between network management applications and management agents. In SNMP, Network Management Systems (NMSs) monitor the network status passively and provide information about the network traffic statistics. The SNMP based systems support variables including the traffic counts from different network activities. Although these variables cannot directly provide a traffic performance metric, they can be used to characterize network behavior and thus providing the potential for network anomaly detection [35].

NMSs and IDSs are usually operated independent of each other on the current network. IDSs are used to detect and respond to intrusions, while NMSs are applied to monitor the general performance of a network. A typical example of SNMP based intrusion detection is conducted by Qin et al. [29] in which they proposed a mechanism to merge NMSs and IDSs so that they can exchange their information, in order to enhance the security capabilities of NMSs as well as to improve the performance of IDSs as well. In the practical implementation, Qin et al. deployed a number of light-weight agents called ID agents to various network components. Since one individual IDS cannot cover all possible attacks to the network in an accurate and timely manner, multiple ID agents are used in their system in which each ID sensor specializes a certain category of intrusions. For instance, host-based ID agents can analyze BSM audit data, system call traces, or user shell command streams to monitor applications and user behaviors, while network ID agents may use packet data or SNMP data to identify the network level attacks, such as DDoS and probing attacks. MIB variables are also applied by Qin et al. to find network intrusions in the proposed system, e.g. the information from MIB II, such as *udpInErrors*, can be used to detect traffic based intrusions directly without inspecting network packets. More details regarding the MIB Detection Engine is discussed in [29]. According to Qin et al., 91 MIB variables are grouped into 18 sub-modules based on their defini-

tions. Once an anomaly for one of the variables is found in the sub-module, an alert
will be generated. In [29], RIPPER is used to build up a rule set for each MIB object
for predicting its normal values. The previous values of each MIB object are used
to predict the future values. After obtaining enough normal data from an MIB object, RIPPER then extracts a rule set for the prediction of future values. As a result,
an anomaly in the variable can be detected using this rule set. Experimental results
reported in [29] show the effectiveness of MIB Engine on detecting intrusions, such
as SYN Flood, UDP Flood, Ping Flood, and Mix Flood.

The other typical example of using SNMP data for anomaly detection is conducted by Thattan et al. [35] in which a statistical signal processing technique based
on abrupt change detection is applied for detecting network anomalies using SNMP.
Starting from a review of network anomalies, sources of network data, and network anomaly detection methods, Thattan et al. claim that network anomalies are
characterized by traffic related MIB variables expressing correlated abrupt changes.
Abrupt change detection for individual MIB variables are then carried out using a
technique based on generalized likelihood ratio (GLR). The obtained abnormality
indicator is a number between 0 and 1.

3.2.2 Packets

There are two common data sources for network-based intrusion detection systems,
namely network packets and flows. Packets are captured using flow capture engines
located at different critical points within the network. The data gathered from these
packets is then used to provide detailed network attack and performance information. *Tcpdump* is the most common tool for capturing network packets [1]. For flow-
based monitoring a traditional flow is defined by source-destination IP addresses,
source-destination port numbers and protocols. A typical open source tool for network flows monitoring is called *Flowscan* [2] that can group packets into flows
exported by routers.

In reality, the most common architecture of NIDS is to have a single packet or
flow capture engine that sends the captured data to a detection engine. The main advantages of this architecture are the simplicity in communications between the capture engine and the detection engine, and the low cost of manufacturing. Moreover,
since the communication between the capture engine and the detection engine does
not rely on the network there is no IP address needed for the NIDS. For different
network topologies, the main disadvantage of a single packet/flow capture engine
is the lack of adaptability, e.g. the engine cannot capture the data from two subnets
separated by a router. Consequently, the distributed NIDS is proposed to capture
data from different points on the network and at the same time keeping a single detection engine in the system. The packet/flow capture engines can also extract the
features from the network packets or flows and then send them to the processing
engine. This leads to the part of the computational load involved in the detection
process distributed between different capturing engines and thus making the dis-

tributed approach suitable for large scale communication networks. One of the most important steps when designing a NIDS is the feature selection since a good set of features may dramatically improve the detection performance of the NIDS.

Choosing a good set of features is not easy due to the diversity of protocols existing at the network layers and the amount of features extracted from each particular protocol. Current network intrusion detection research community does not provide such a complete feature set that can cover all the network-level intrusions, and researchers tend to focus on particular set of intrusions when it comes to detection scope, e.g., R2U, U2R, and DoS in [7, 17, 8], Horizontal, Vertical, and Block PortScanning for TCP and UDP in [33], Denial of Quality of Service in [18], Worms in [36, 5, 42], DDoS in [28, 22], TCP-SYN Flooding Attacks in [38], TCP-SYN Flood, UDP Flood, and ICMP Flood Attacks in [31]. Current NIDSs mainly focus on the features extracted based on IP, TCP,UPD and ICMP protocols. One simple way is to inspect and consider each field of a packet as a separate and independent feature. In [19], Mahoney et al. propose an approach, called *Packet header anomaly detection* (PHAD) to detect anomalies in the network based on 33 fields of the Ethernet, IP, TCP, ICMP, and UDP protocols. Table 3.4 illustrates some of the features used in [19]. The range of values of each packet header fields can be learned during the training process and thus an anomaly could be detected when out of range occurs. The evaluation results with the DARPA data set show that the PHAD system successfully detects 29 attack types from the total 59.

Number	Feature Description	Number	Feature Description
1	Ethernet Size	10	IP Source
2	Ethernet Destination	11	IP Destination
3	Ethernet Source	12	TCP Source Port
4	Ethernet Protocol	13	TCP Destination Port
5	IP header Length	14	UDP Source Port
6	IP Type of Service	15	UDP Destination Port
7	IP Length	16	UDP Length
8	IP Time To Live	17	ICMP Type
9	IP Protocol	18	ICMP Code

Table 3.4 Features extracted based on the analysis of each header-field

The other popular method to extract network features for intrusion detection is correlating several fields and packets from the protocols, e.g. the three-way-handshaking sequence of TCP protocols leads to a big variety of *connection features* that can be used for a better detection of the network attacks. Moreover, recent TCP attacks show a certain anomaly regarding the number of SYN, RST, and FIN flags of the TCP connection. As a result, *connection features* have been proposed recent literatures and can be divided into two main categories: *basic features* and *derived features* [7, 8, 3, 17].

Basic Features encapsulates all the attributes extracted from a TCP/IP connection. In [17], Lee et al. name *basic features* as *essential attributes* while they are called in the Knowledge Discovery and Data Mining competition (1999) [3] as *ba-*

sic features of an individual TCP connection. Most of these features, such as number of packets, number of data bytes, average Kb/s, duration, can only be computed after the TCP connection has been terminated, thus leading to a significant delay in detection process. Table 3.5 illustrates an example of basic features extracted based an individual TCP connection.

Number	Feature Description
19	Source IP
20	Destination IP
21	Duration of Connection
22	Connection Starting Time
23	Connection Ending Time
24	Number of packets sent from Source to Destination
25	Number of packets sent from Source to Destination
26	Number of packets sent from Destination to Source
27	Number of data bytes sent from Source to Destination
28	Number of data bytes sent from Destination to Source
29	Number of Fragmented packets
30	Number of Overlapping Fragments
31	Number of Acknowledgement packets
32	Number of Retransmitted packets
33	Number of Pushed packets
34	Number of SYN packets Number of FIN packets
35	Number of TCP header Flags
36	Number of Urgent packets

Table 3.5 Basic features of a TCP/IP connection

Derived features, called *traffic features* as well in [17], include features that are computed during a period of a time window interval, which measure the similarities and abnormalities between different TCP connections. There are two main types of window intervals, namely *time based* and *connection based* intervals. Features over a *time based* window interval can be used to detect fast attacks that happen within a short time period (e.g. Worm and DDoS attacks), while the features over a *connection based* interval (e.g. the latest k connections) have the potential to detect slow scanning attacks (e.g., one scan per minute; one scan per hour). Tables 3.6 summarize some of the most frequently used window-based features. Features from 39 to 50 (i.e. the same host features) in the Table are computed based on a certain source or destination IP, while features from 51 to 54 (the same service features) are computed based on a certain service.

The issue of feature selection for network-based IDSs is studied by in [27, 26, 25]. As well known, the design of a Network Intrusion Detection System (NIDS) is a delicate process which requires the successful completion of numerous design stages. The feature selection stage is one of the first steps that needs to be addressed, and can be considered among the top most important ones. If this step is not carefully considered the overall performance of the NIDS will greatly suffer, regardless of the detection technique, or any other algorithms that the NIDS is using.

Number	Feature Description	Time Based features	Connection Based features
37	No. of unique connections used by the same SrcIP as the current record	in the last Δ interval	in the last k connections
38	No. of unique connections used by the same SrcIP on the same DstPort as the current record	in the last Δ interval	in the last k connections
39	No. of unique connections used by the same SrcIP on different DstPort as the current record	in the last Δ interval	in the last k connections
40	No. of unique connections used by the same SrcIP as the current record that have SYN flag	in the last Δ interval	in the last k connections
41	No. of unique connections used by the same SrcIP as the current record that have RST flag	in the last Δ interval	in the last k connections
42	No. of unique connections that use the same DstIP as the current record	in the last Δ interval	in the last k connections
43	No. of unique connections that use the same DstIP on the same DstPort as the current record	in the last Δ interval	in the last k connections
44	No. of unique connections that use the same DstIP on different DstPort as the current record	in the last Δ interval	in the last k connections
45	No. of unique connections that use the same DstIP as the current record that have SYN flag	in the last Δ interval	in the last k connections
46	No. of unique connections that use the same DstIP as the current record that have RST flag	in the last Δ interval	in the last k connections
47	No. of unique Ports used by the same SrcIP to connect on the same DstIP and the same DstPort as the current record	in the last Δ interval	in the last k connections
48	No. of unique Ports opened on the sane DstIP by the same SrcIP as the current record	in the last Δ interval	in the last k connections
59	Number of unique connections that use the same service as the current packet	in the last Δ interval	in the last k connections
50	Number of unique connections that use the same service and have different DstIP as the current packet	in the last Δ interval	in the last k connections
51	Number of unique connections that use the same service as the current packet that have SYN flag	in the last Δ interval	in the last k connections
52	Number of unique connections that use the same service as the current packet that have RST flag	in the last Δ interval	in the last k connections

Table 3.6 Derived features

The most common approach for selecting the network features is to use expert knowledge to reason about the selection process. However, this approach is not deterministic, thus, in most cases researchers end-up with completely different sets of important features for the detection process. Furthermore, the lack of a generally accepted feature classification schema forces different researchers to use different names for the same (subsets of) features, or the same name for completely different ones. As a result, Onut and Ghorbani proposed in [26, 25] a Fuzzy Feature Evaluation Framework for Network Intrusion Detection, which focuses on mining the most useful network features for attack detection. They propose a new network feature classification schema as well as a mathematical feature evaluation procedure that helps to identify the most useful features that can be extracted from network packets.

The new network feature classification schema provides a better understanding, and enforces a new standard, upon the features that can be extracted from network packets, and their relationships. The classification has a set of 27 feature categories based on the network abstractions that they refer to (e.g., host, network, connection, etc). Also the proposed feature classification schema is used to select a comprehensive set of 671 features for conducting and reporting experimental findings.

The feature evaluation procedure provides a deterministic approach for pinpointing those network features that are indeed useful in the attack detection process. The procedure uses mathematical, statistical and fuzzy logic techniques to rank the participation of individual features into the detection process. According to Onut and Ghorbani, the experimental results, conducted on three different real-world network data sets, empirically confirm that the proposed feature evaluation model can successfully be applied to mine the importance of a feature in the detection process.

3.2.3 Limitations of Network-Based IDSs

The traditional centralized NIDSs tend to cause network latency and drop packets at high-speed networks due to the high volume of network traffic passing through. Kruegel et al. conducted a research on high-speed intrusion detection in [12]. Distributed agent-based systems such as the one reported in [12] are able to help distribute the processing effort among the networked systems, thus improving the chances to find intrusions that might be missed by a centralized network-based IDS. In addition to the speed limitations of NIDSs, Vigna et al. study the adaptability criteria that a capture engine must satisfy in [37]. They claim in the paper that no packet capture application can meet the requirement for intrusion detection and analysis. Based on this, they then define three main capabilities that a sophisticated packet capture application must have, namely (1) maintaining different traffic windows with different characteristics, such as window length, filters, and type of stored information, (2) dynamical modification and reconfiguration according to the current incident analysis process, and (3) supporting queries on the collected data during the incident response and analysis process. MNEMOSYNE is a system implemented by Vigna et al. with the above mentioned capabilities, which is built based on a library called *liblcap*, an extension of functionality of the well-known *libcap* library. MNEMOSYNE is able to maintain multiple windows of network traffic with different characteristics, and it can be remotely reconfigured on the run time. It also supports network traffic queries on the collected information.

Inline NIDSs are also limited by their false alerts, i.e. it might block legitimate traffic, thus leading collateral damage to the normal users. Moreover, a centralized NIDS deployed at the border of the network may be entirely failed against attacks launched from the internal network by an insider [24] or a compromised internal host (i.e., malicious outbound traffic).

Distributed NIDSs improve the performance of centralized NIDSs. They, however, still have some limitations. The communication between a data collection point and the processing (central) unit in a distributed NIDS is usually implemented as client-server architecture. The major drawback of this architecture is the need for a stable connection between client and server, which makes it impracticable for heavy traffic networks, highly distributed problems, as well as in poor quality links [12]. Moreover, the client-server architecture employs a protocol agreed by both client and server side, forming a static interface between the two sides and thus consuming a high cost of recoding the application and the additional workload for establishing the connection between the two sides. In order to address this issue, Helmer et al. propose an agent-based implementations of network IDSs [44], in which *Lightweight* agents are used for intrusion detection. A *Lightweight* agent is a special type of agent that accomplishes its tasks using minimal code, and carrying only its primary features in the network. As a result, it is smaller, simpler, and faster to transport a Client-Server connection or standard agents.

Due to the large number of traffic data produced in a network, most current NIDSs analyze only the header of the network packets or flows and totally miss the application payload in order to obtain a high speed processing of traffic data. However, in case the high level application attack does not exhibit any anomalous behavior on the network layer, it will remain undetectable to the NIDS. Another extreme is the NIDSs using only the payload information in order to detect application-level attacks. In contrast, these NIDSs, however, are blind to any network-level attack.

3.3 Data Collection for Application-Based IDSs

The Application-based intrusion detection systems examine and analyze the log files of a specific application for detecting the application-specific attack targeting the monitored application. A typical example of application based intrusion detection is by Kruegel et al. [15], in which they use web logs as the source of data and concentrate only on web-based attacks against web-servers. The detection engine is based on the obtained profiles of the web queries for each server side program and the whole IDS analyzes the parameters of encountered GET requests passed to the server-side program. Although there are a lot of information that can be extracted from the header of an HTTP request, their study only uses the parameters that a GET request has. A similar idea is also exploited in [14] by Kruegel et al. when analyzing the attributes of each system call.

In reality, a typical query string for a GET request can be illustrated as a string "*GET* = *dir1* = *dir2* = *dir3* =*file:pl?arg1* = *value1&arg2* = *value2*", the string is used to pass parameters (i.e., parameters are identified by leading "?" character) to the server-side program. During the training phase, the normal profile of each HTTP attribute is learned as a function of a set of properties, namely *length* of the attribute, *character distribution*, *structure* of an argument, *tokens*, *presence/absence* of a argument, and *order* in a HTTP query. For more details about these properties see [15].

3.4 Data Collection for Application-Integrated IDSs

The application-integrated based IDSs uses embedded detectors in the program code itself. Different with all the previously discussed IDSs that function independently from the applications they attempt to protect, an Application-Integrated IDS uses a module tightly coupled with the application to extract the desired information. As a result, the communication between the application and IDS is less vulnerable to desynchronization. Furthermore, an application-integrated IDS needs in-depth knowledge about the expected behavior of the application. Due to the tight connection and the in-depth knowledge of the application-integrated IDS, its response to an attack against specific application is very specific and fast at the same time.

A typical example of application-integrated IDSs is developed by Soman et al. [32], in which all the Java applications a thread-level auditing mechanism for JikesRVM (i.e., a high performance JVM for server applications) and a signature based IDS are used to monitor all java applications. Each Java thread running under JikeRVM is related to a unique system identifier (SID) and a user identifier (UID). The SID enables the auditing system to identify a specific thread and the UID enables the auditing system to uniquely identify each user using JAVA. The audit-logs are generated based on four critical event categories generated by an application at running time, namely, (1) *Class Events* which are generated every time when a thread loads a class, (2) *System Call Events* which are generated every time when by the use of SC a thread accesses the network communication, I/O files, and the system memory, (3) *JNI Events* which manipulates the Host's file-system, the process memory and other resources directly, and (4) *Thread Interaction Events* that are encountered whenever two threads interact by invoking methods that could harm the normal behavior of a thread (i.e., suspend, interrupt, stop, and kill). The other typical example of an application-integrated IDS is developed by Almagren et al. [4], in which they monitors each request and interaction of the Apache server with the external users. The behavior of a Web server is well defined and each request is processed in several stages. At the end of each stage, the proposed IDS is able to provide feed-back to the server regarding the current operation status. There are two main advantages for integrating applications into IDSs, namely, (1) the IDS has the capability to access all of the internal information that is not reported to outside and has possibly not be encrypted yet, and (2) the IDS is able to monitor the user sessions through the web server itself and all the response or feedback to the applications is handled at the end of each stage.

The main disadvantage of application-integrated IDSs is that they are limited to a certain application domain and therefore each single type of application needs to be monitored by an IDS [4]. Moreover, any additional IDS process running on the same host as the monitored service will slow down the system [4, 39]. To address these limitations, Welz et al. propose a common *interface* to monitor all the applications [39]. The *interface* is a set of library calls and any security related events through calling the appropriate methods from the *interface* will be reported. In a more detail, Welz et al. define three different information types, namely *Credentials* (i.e., data about the identity of the application), *Domain Specific Information* (i.e., data dependable on the domain in which the application operates), and *Domain Independent Information* (i.e., data that remains unchanged across multiple application domains). In their system, the actions taken by each application are rated by the programmer based on the impact on the confidentiality and integrity of data. Therefore, an IDS concentrate only upon events that exhibit a medium and high degree of threat to the integrity of the application. The concepts proposed in the paper have also been implemented for a number of applications such as: Apache server, two experimental FTP servers, login, to name a few.

3.5 Hybrid Data Collection

Hybrid intrusion detection systems receive data from many different sources and it is expected that a hybrid system has the potential to detect sophisticated attacks that involve multiple hosts or networks with the information from multiple sources. Moreover, an IDS integrating different kinds of information is able to increase its detection rate and reduce false alarm rate at the same time. A typical example of using hybrid data collection is proposed by Qin et al. [29], consisting of three detection modules, namely, *Signature Engine*, *Profile Engine* and *MIB Engine*. The first two engines collect and use the data source such as BSM or network raw packets, the *MIB Engine*, on the other hand, collects the data from MIB objects. The final detection results are correlated by *ID Correlators* in order to discover the nature of the intrusions.

References

1. TCPDUMP, Available on: http://www.tcpdump.org/, September 2008.
2. FlowScan,a   network   analysis   and   reporting   tool,   Available   on: http://net.doit.wisc.edu/ plonka/FlowScan/, October 2008.

3. KDD Cup 1999. Available on: http://kdd.ics.uci.edu/databases/kddcup 99/kddcup99.html, Ocotber 2007.
4. M. Almgren and U. Lindqvist, *Application-integrated data collection for security monitoring*, Lecture Notes in Computer Science (2001), 22–36.
5. V. Berk, G. Bakos, and R. Morris, *Designing a framework for active worm detection on global networks*, Proceedings of the IEEE International Workshop on Information Assurance (Darmstadt, Germany), 2003.
6. Joachim Biskup and Ulrich Flegel, *Transaction-based pseudonyms in audit data for privacy respecting intrusion detection*, Proceedings of Recent Advances in Intrusion Detection (RAID), Lecture Notes in Computer Science, Springer-Verlag Heidelberg, October 2000, pp. 28–48.
7. P. Dokas, L. Ertoz, V. Kumar, A. Lazarevic, J. Srivastava, and P.N. Tan, *Data mining for network intrusion detection*, Proceedings of the NSF Workshop on Next Generation Data Mining, 2002, pp. 21–30.
8. L. Ertoz, E. Eilertson, A. Lazarevic, P.N. Tan, P. Dokas, V. Kumar, and J. Srivastava, *Detection of novel network attacks using data mining*, Proceedings of the Workshop on Data Mining for Computer Security (DMSEC), 2003.
9. Chapman Flack and Mikhail J. Atallah, *Better logging through formality applying formal specification techniques to improve audit logs and log consumers*, Proceedings of Recent Advances in Intrusion Detection (RAID), Lecture Notes in Computer Science, Springer-Verlag Heidelberg, October 2000, pp. 1–16.
10. S. Forrest, S. Hofmeyr, A. Somayaji, and T. Longstaff, *A sense of self for unix processes*, Proceedings of the 1996 IEEE Symposium on Security and Privacy (Los Alamitos, CA), IEEE Computer Society Press, 1996, p. 120128.
11. Anup K. Ghosh, Christoph Michael, and Michael Schatz, *A real-time intrusion detection system based on learning program behavior*, Proceedings of Recent Advances in Intrusion Detection (RAID), Lecture Notes in Computer Science, Springer-Verlag Heidelberg, October 2000, pp. 93–109.
12. G. Helmer, J.S.K. Wong, V. Honavar, L. Miller, and Y. Wang, *Lightweight agents for intrusion detection*, The Journal of Systems & Software **67** (2003), no. 2, 109–122.
13. C. Ko, *System health and intrusion monitoring (shim): project summary*, Proceedings of the DARPA Information Survivability Conference and Exposition II, DISCEX'03, vol. 2, April 2003, pp. 202–207.
14. C. Kruegel, D. Mutz, F. Valeur, and G. Vigna, *On the detection of anomalous system call arguments*, Proceedings of the 8th European Symposium on Research in Computer Security (ESORICS) (Gjovik, Norway), LNCS, Springer-Verlag, October 2003, pp. 326–343.
15. Christopher Kruegel and Giovanni Vigna, *Anomaly detection of web-based attacks*, Proceedings of the 10th ACM conference on Computer and communication security (Washington D.C., USA), ACM Press, October 2003, pp. 251–261.
16. Josu Kuri, Gonzalo Navarro, Ludovic M, and Laurent Heye, *A pattern matching based filter for audit reduction and fast detection of potential intrusions*, Proceedings of Recent Advances in Intrusion Detection (RAID), Lecture Notes in Computer Science, Springer-Verlag Heidelberg, October 2000, pp. 17–27.
17. W. Lee, S. J. Stolfo, and K. W. Mok, *A data mining framework for building intrusion detection models*, Proceedings of the 1999 IEEE Symposium on Security and Privacy, May 1999, pp. 120–132.
18. V.A. Mahadik, X. Wu, and D.S. Reeves, *Detection of Denial-of-QoS Attacks Based On χ 2 Statistic And EWMA Control Charts*, (2002).
19. J. McHugh, *Intrusion and intrusion detection*, International Journal of Information Security **1** (2001), no. 1, 14–35.
20. CC Michael and A. Ghosh, *Simple, state-based approaches to program-based anomaly detection*, ACM Transactions on Information and System Security (TISSEC) **5** (2002), no. 3, 203–237.
21. Computer Security Center (NCSC), *Audit in trusted systems*, July 1987, Library no. S-228 470.

22. S. Noh, C. Lee, K. Choi, and G. Jung, *Detecting distributed denial of service (ddos) attacks through inductive learning*, Lecture Notes in Computer Science (2003), 286–295.
23. OKENA, *Stormsystem*, August 2002, Cisco acquired Okena in 2003.
24. TH Ong, CP Tan, YT Tan, and C. Ting, *SNMSShadow Network Management System*, Proceedings of the Second International Workshop on Recent Advances in Intrusion Detection, 1999.
25. I.V. Onut, *A Fuzzy Feature Evaluation Framework for Network Intrusion Detection*, PhD Thesis, Faculty of Computer Science, University of New Brunswick (2008).
26. I.V. Onut and A. A. Ghorbani, *A Feature Classification Scheme For Network Intrusion Detection*, International Journal of Network Security **5** (2007).
27. I.V. Onut and A.A. Ghorbani, *Toward a feature classification scheme for network intrusion detection*, Proceedings of The Fourth Annual Conference on Communication Networks and Services Research, 2006.
28. T. Peng, C. Leckie, and R. Kotagiri, *Proactively detecting ddos attack using source ip address monitoring*, Proceedings of the Networking 2004 (Athens,Greece), 2004.
29. X. Qin, W. Lee, L. Lewis, and JBD Cabrera, *Integrating intrusion detection and network management*, IEEE/IFIP Network Operations and Management Symposium (NOMS), 2002, pp. 329–344.
30. B. Schneier and J. Kelsey, *Secure audit logs to support computer forensics*, ACM Transactions on Information and System Security (TISSEC) **2** (1999), no. 2, 159–176.
31. Christos Siaterlis and Basil Maglaris, *Towards multisensor data fusion for dos detection*, Proceedings of the 2004 ACM symposium on Applied computing (Nicosia, Cyprus), 2004, pp. 439 – 446.
32. S. Soman, C. Krintz, and G. Vigna, *Detecting malicious Java code using virtual machine auditing*, Proceedings of the Twelfth USENIX Security Symposium, 2003, pp. 153–167.
33. S. Staniford, J. Hoagland, and J. McAlerney, *Practical automated detection of stealthy portscans*, Journal of Computer Security **10** (2002), no. 1 and 2, 105–126.
34. W.R. Stevens, *TCP/IP illustrated (vol. 1): the protocols*, Addison-Wesley Longman Publishing Co., Inc. Boston, MA, USA, 1993.
35. Marina Thottan and Chuanyi Ji, *Anomaly detection in ip networks*, IEEE Transactions on Signal Processing **51** (2003), no. 8, 148–166.
36. T. Toth and C. Kruegel, *Connection-history based anomaly detection*, Proceedings of IEEE Workshop on Information Assurance and Security (West Point, NY), 2002.
37. G. Vigna and A. Mitchell, *Mnemosyne: Designing and implementing network short-term memory*, Proceedings of the 8th IEEE International Conference on Engineering of Complex Computer Systems (ICECCS) (Greenbelt, MD), IEEE Press, December 2002, pp. 91–100.
38. H. Wang, D. Zhang, and K.G. Shin, *Detecting SYN flooding attacks*, Proceedings of the Twenty-First Annual Joint Conference of the IEEE Computer and Communications Societies (INFOCOM), vol. 3, 2002.
39. M. Welz and A. Hutchison, *Interfacing trusted applications with intrusion detection systems*, Lecture notes in computer science (2001), 37–53.
40. Zonghua Zhang and Hong Shen, *Online training of svms for real-time intrusion detection*, Proceedings of the 18th International Conference on Advanced Information Networking and Applications (AINA), vol. 1, March 2004, pp. 568–573.
41. L. Zhuowei, A. Das, and S. Nandi, *Utilizing statistical characteristics of N-grams for intrusion detection*, Proceedings of the International Conference on Cyberworlds, 2003, pp. 486–493.
42. Cliff Changchun Zou, Lixin Gao, Weibo Gong, and Don Towsley, *Monitoring and early warning for internet worms*, Proceedings of the 10th ACM conference on Computer and communication security (Washington D.C., USA), ACM Press, October 2003, pp. 190–199.

Chapter 4
Theoretical Foundation of Detection

We have seen in previous chapters that both misuse detection and anomaly detection rely on statistical models of the two classes: normal and intrusion. Thus, in order to obtain these models, we can apply two approaches: manual definition and machine learning. Manual definition is usually used by signature-based detection, in which knowledge about the characteristics of known attacks is modeled manually. However, this approach is time-consuming and can only be performed by experienced experts, leading to high development and signature updating costs. Alternatively, machine learning can construct the required models automatically based on some given training data. A motivation for this approach is that the necessary training data is already available or that it can be at least acquired more easily compared to the effort required to define the model manually. With the growing complexity and the number of different attacks, machine learning techniques that allow building and maintaining anomaly detection system (ADS) with less human intervention seem to be the only feasible approach for realizing next generation IDSs.

4.1 Taxonomy of Anomaly Detection Systems

The idea of applying machine learning techniques for intrusion detection is to automatically build the model based on the training data set. This data set contains a collection of data instances each of which can be described using a set of attributes (features) and the associated labels. The attributes can be of different types such as categorical or continuous. The nature of attributes determines the applicability of anomaly detection techniques. For example, distance-based methods are initially built to work with continuous features and usually do not provide satisfactory results on categorical attributes.

The labels associated with data instances are usually in the form of binary values, i.e. normal and anomalous. In contrast, some researchers have employed different types of attacks such as DoS, U2R, R2L and Probe rather than the anomalous label. This way learning techniques are able to provide more information about the types of anomalies. However, experimental results show that current learning techniques are not precise enough to recognize the type of anomalies.

Since labeling is often done manually by human experts, obtaining an accurate labeled data set which is representative of all types of behaviors is quite expensive. As a result, based on the availability of the labels, three operating modes are defined for anomaly detection techniques:

1) Supervised Anomaly Detection: supervised methods, also known as classification methods, need a labeled training set containing both normal and anomalous samples to build the predictive model. Theoretically, supervised methods provide better detection rate compared to semi-supervised and unsupervised methods since they have access to more information. However, there exist some technical issues which make these methods be as not accurate as they are assumed to be. The first one is the lack of a training data set that covers all the legitimate areas. Furthermore, obtaining accurate labels is very challenging and the training sets usually contain some noises which results in higher false alarm rates. As examples of supervised learning methods we can name Neural Networks, Support Vector Machines (SVM), k-Nearest Neighbors, Bayesian Networks, and Decision Trees.

2) Semi-supervised Anomaly Detection: Semi-supervised learning falls between unsupervised learning (without any labeled training data) and supervised learning (with completely labeled training data). Generally speaking, semi-supervised methods employ unlabeled data in conjunction with a small amount of labeled data. As a result, they highly reduce the labeling cost, while maintaining the high performance of supervised methods.

In the area of anomaly detection, however, semi-supervised learning methods assume that the training data has labeled instances for only the normal class. This way, they are more practicable than supervised methods to operate in real networks since they do not require any labels for the anomaly class. One-class SVM is one of the most well-known classifiers of this type which makes a discriminative boundary around the normal instances, and any test instance that does not fall within the learned boundary is declared as anomalous. Although the typical approach in semi-supervised techniques is to model the normal behavior, there exist a limited number of anomaly detection techniques that assume availability of the anomalous instances for training [16, 39, 15, 27]. Such techniques are not wildly used since it is almost impossible to obtain a training set which covers every possible anomalous behavior.

3) Unsupervised Anomaly Detection: unsupervised techniques do not require training data. Instead, this approach is based on two basic assumptions [48]. First, it assumes that the majority of the network connections represent normal traffic and that only a very small percentage of the traffic is malicious [60]. Second, it is expected that malicious traffic is statistically different from normal traffic [38]. Based on these two assumptions, data instances that build groups of similar instances and appear very frequently are supposed to represent normal traffic, while instances that appear infrequently and are significantly different from the majority of the instances are considered to be suspicious.

While supervised methods are very dependent on the labeled training data which is usually error-prone, time consuming and costly, unsupervised learning techniques avoid such complications by not using the labeled training data and any prior knowledge of attacks or normal instances, but partitioning the data into normal operations and anomalies based on statistical models. Applying such techniques to the problem of anomaly detection is one of the possible avenues of being able to build large, reliable anomaly detection systems without the need for extensive and costly manual labeling of instances.

In addition to the types of training sets, anomaly detection methods can be categorized based on the method they use to report the anomalies. Typically, there are three types of output to report the anomalies namely scores, binary labels, and labels.

1) Scores: in this technique, anomaly detectors will assign a numeric score to each instance which indicates how likely it is that the test instance is anomaly. The advantage of this technique is that the analyst can rank the malicious activities, set a threshold to cut off the anomalies, and select the most significant ones. Bayesian networks such as Naive Bayes are good examples of this kind of methods in which they provide the administrator with the calculated probabilities.

2) Binary Labels: some of the anomaly detection techniques such as Decision Trees are not able to provide scores for the instances; instead they label the test instances as either anomalous or normal. This approach can be considered as the special case of labeling techniques.

3) Labels: anomaly detection techniques in this category assign a label to each test instance. In this approach, usually there is one label for normal traffic, normal. For the anomalies, however, there are plenty of labels showing the types of anomalies. For example, some methods apply the labels normal, DoS, Probe, U2R, and R2L to show the general category of the detected attacks. Most of the non-scoring learners such as Decision Tress methods can be applied for this purpose. The only requirement is that there should be enough samples from each class of labels.

Regardless of label availability and reporting method, anomaly detection systems can be also classified based on the machine learning techniques they use. In the rest of this chapter, we study the significant machine learning techniques have been applied for the sake of anomaly detection.

4.2 Fuzzy Logic

Imagine a word that is not colored only in black and white, ruled not only by right and wrong or true and false, imagine the grey color and the reality of not being absolutely right or merely wrong and then you will find yourself in the fuzzy word. Fuzzy logic extends traditional logic, enabling it to handle approximations and linguistic variables. For example, one can say "It might be raining in the afternoon". In this statement "might" can be interpreted as "there is a 50% probability of raining in the afternoon".

Before starting with the fuzzy inference the concept of fuzzy logic has to be be studied and some expressions have to be defined.

Fuzzy Membership Function $\mu_A(x)$: This function is an indication of the degree of membership for an element of the universe X to a fuzzy subset A. This function can associate every x member of the function domain with a degree of membership in the set A. The above expression can be demonstrated in the mathematical way as shown in below:

$$\mu_A(x) : A \longrightarrow [0\ \ 1], \tag{4.1}$$

where X is called universe and A is a fuzzy subset of X. This expression can be displayed in another way as well:

$$\mu_A(x) = Degree(x \varepsilon A) \quad where \quad \mu_A(x) \quad is \quad defined \quad as \quad 0 \le \mu_A(x) \le 1 \tag{4.2}$$

The fuzzy set with discrete elements is presented in the following way [21]:

$$A(a_1/x_1, a_2/x_2, a_3/x_3, \ldots, a_n/x_n), \tag{4.3}$$

where $a_i = \mu_A(x_i)$ is the mapping function that maps the input numerical elements a_i into their fuzzy equivalence x_i.

The concept of the fuzzy inference was first introduced by Lotfi Zadeh in 1965 [72]. In his theory he had considered a fuzzy set as a probability density function. This function was mapping a number of elements from the linguistic variables on a number between 0 and 1. This number is an indication of our belief on the membership of that element in the fuzzy set.

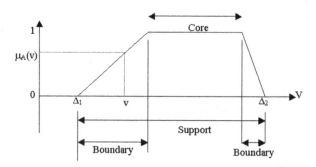

Fig. 4.1 Fuzzy membership function

Fuzzy membership functions of a variable represent the degrees of similarity of its different values to imprecisely defined properties (i.e., linguistic terms) [19]. The core of a membership function for a fuzzy set A, $core(A)$, is defined as those elements of the universe, v, for which $\mu_A(v) = 1$. The core represents full membership in fuzzy set A. Non-membership in the fuzzy set A is defined by Δ_1 and Δ_2, i.e., $\mu_A(v) = 0$ for $v \leq \Delta_1$ and $v \geq \Delta_2$. The boundaries of a membership function are decided by $0 < \mu_A(v) < 1$. The area of a boundary shows the intermediate degrees of membership. The support of a membership function for a fuzzy set A, $supp(A)$, is defined as $0 < \mu_A(v) \leq 1$. Figure 4.1 illustrates the regions for the core, support, and boundaries of a typical fuzzy set.

4.2.1 Fuzzy Logic in Anomaly Detection

The application of fuzzy logic for computer security was first proposed by Hosmer in 1993 [35]. Later, Dickerson et al [18] proposed a Fuzzy Intrusion Recognition Engine (FIRE) for detecting malicious intrusion activities. In the reported work the anomaly based Intrusion Detection System (IDS) is implemented using both the fuzzy logic and the data mining techniques. The fuzzy logic part of the system is mainly responsible for both handling the large number of input parameters and dealing with the inexactness of the input data.

There are three fuzzy characteristics used in this work: COUNT, UNIQUENESS and VARIANCE. The implemented fuzzy inference engine uses five fuzzy sets for each data element (LOW, MEDIUM-LOW, MEDIUM, MEDIUM-HIGH and HIGH) and appropriate fuzzy rules to detect the intrusion. In their report authors have not indicated how they have derived their fuzzy set. The fuzzy set is a very important issue for the fuzzy inference engine and in some cases genetic approach can be implemented to select the best combination. The proposed system is tested using data collected from the local area network in the college of Engineering at Iowa State University and results are reported in this paper. The reported results are descriptive and not numerical; therefore, it is difficult to evaluate the performance of the reported work.

4.3 Bayes Theory

Conditional probability $P(A|B)$ is used for calculating the probability of A once the condition B is present. However, in the real world applications it is the other way around, i.e. one needs to know about the conditional probability $P(B|A)$ for B once its evidence A is present. In other words, in the real world applications it is necessary to find the probability for a hypothesis H from the probability of its evidence E. This type of probability is usually called Posteriori Probability. Generally speaking, the conditional probability progresses in time but the posteriori probability will advance in opposite direction in time. One can also say that it will advance in past or history of the events. The solution to this problem was initially introduced by 18th century British mathematician called Thomas Bayes and ever since it is called Bayes theory. In this theory, goal is to calculate the probability of a given hypothesis H considering its sign or evidence E already exists. The H can be assumed to be a sampled column feature vector and noted as $\mathbf{x} = \{x_1, x_2, \ldots\}$. In the following text the E (Evidence) and the C(Class) sign can be replaced (where $C = \{c_1, c_2, \ldots\}$), if it makes it easier for the reader to understand the concept. The formula to calculate this probability is presented in below:

$$P(H|E) = \frac{P(H) * P(E|H)}{P(E)}, \qquad (4.4)$$

where $P(E|H)$ is the conditional probability of the evidence E once the hypothesis H is in hand. P(H) is the probability of the hypothesis H. P(E) is the probability of the evidence E. $P(H|E)$ is the posteriori probability of the hypothesis H once the evidence E is available.

4.3.1 Naive Bayes Classifier

A Naive Bayes classifier is a simple probabilistic classifier based on applying Bayes' theorem with strong independence assumptions [63]. Depending on the precise nature of the probability model, Naive Bayes classifiers can be trained efficiently in a supervised learning approach. In many practical applications, parameter estimation for Naive Bayes models uses the method of maximum likelihood, i.e. one can work with the Naive Bayes model without believing in Bayesian probability or using any Bayesian methods. A simple Naive Bayes probabilistic model can be expressed as follows:

$$P(C|F_1, F_2, ..., F_n) = \frac{1}{Z}P(C)\Pi_{i=1}^{n}P(F_i|C), \qquad (4.5)$$

where $P(C|F_1, F_2, ..., F_n)$ is the probabilistic model over a dependent class variable C with a small number of outcomes or classes, conditional on several feature variables F_1 through F_n; Z is a scaling factor dependent only on $F_1, \ldots, F_n$, i.e., a constant if the values of the feature variables are known. A Naive Bayes classifier combines the probabilistic model with a decision rule that aims to maximize a posterior, thus the classifier can be defined using the following function:

$$Classify(f_1, f_2, \ldots, f_n) = argmax_c P(C = c)\Pi_{i=1}^{n}P(F_i = f_i|C = c) \qquad (4.6)$$

4.3.2 Bayes Theory in Anomaly Detection

In [7], Barbara et al propose a pseudo-Bayes estimator based on Naive Bayes probabilistic model in order to enhance an anomaly detection system's ability for detecting new attacks while reducing the false alarm rate as much as possible. They indicate in the paper that the work is the continuation of an ongoing research based on an anomaly detection system called Audit Data Analysis and Mining (ADAM) [6]. ADAM applies mining association rules techniques to detect abnormal events in network traffic data first, and then abnormal events are classified into normal instances and abnormal instances. After this, the number of false alarms is greatly reduced because the abnormal associations that belong to normal instances will be filtered out. However, a major limitation of ADAM is that the classifier is limited by training data, i.e. it cannot recognize the normal instances and the attacks appeared in the training data. As a result, they construct a Naive Bayes classifier to classify the instances into normal instances, known attacks and new attacks. One advantage of pseudo-Bayes estimators is that no knowledge about new attacks is needed since the estimated prior and posterior probabilities of new attacks are derived from the information of normal instances and known attacks. Detection results reported in [7] are satisfactory but this assertion totally depends on their testing environment. Problem arises according to Barbara et al., i.e. "To better evaluate the performance of pseudo-Bayes estimator, we pick a set of attacks that behave very differently, while for the attacks that share some similarities, we only select one candidates to represent the rest". Since a basic assumption for the Naive Bayes theory is that the parameters are conditional independent; once the behavior of the anomalies are similar, the proposed classifier will misclassify the attacks as they are evident in the reported results.

4.4 Artificial Neural Networks

Inspired from known facts about how the brain works, researchers in the area of artificial intelligence (AI) have developed computational models which exhibit performance somewhat comparable to that of the brain. Artificial neural networks (ANNs) are adaptive parallel distributed information processing models that consists of: (a) a set of simple processing units (nodes, neurons), (b) a set of synapses (connection weights), (c) the network architecture (pattern of connectivity), and (d) a learning process used to train the network.

In the following subsections we discuss the important aspects of these components. The topics and amount of information presented here are chosen mainly based on their relevance to later sections and chapters.

4.4.1 Processing Elements

The processing element is the basic building block of artificial neural networks. There exist a large number of biological neuron-like processing elements in ANNs. The processing element, which we will refer to as a node or a unit hereafter, performs all the necessary computing. Nodes vary in terms of the structure and functions they perform. They are responsible for all the computations that are taking place locally inside the network. They can possess local memory in order to carry out localized information processing operations. Generally, the computations consist of multiplication, summation, and nonlinear mapping operations.

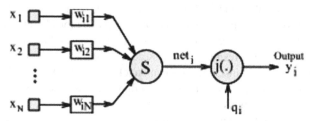

Fig. 4.2 A typical node

There are three types of nodes: (a) *input* nodes which receive data from outside; (b) *hidden* nodes whose input and output signals remain within the network itself; and (c) *output* nodes which send data out of the network. Figure 4.2 shows a schematic of a typical node.

Each node receives input from itself or other sources and computes an output which in turn is sent to other nodes (See Figure 4.3). The output of a node (node signal) can be given by a functional relationship $\varphi_w(x)$. The subscript w used in the functional relationship indicates that the output of a node is a function of weighted input x. We drop this subscript hereafter.

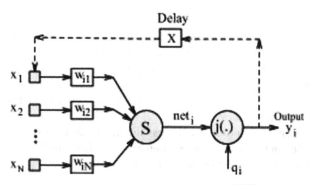

Fig. 4.3 A single node with feedback loop; Ξ is the *time-delay* operator

Every node i has also an extra input, x_0, which is set to a fixed value θ_i with connection weight label w_{i0}, and is referred to as a node's bias (see Figures 4.3 and 4.4).

A node can be either a static node or a dynamic node:

- A *static* node simply applies a squashing function, φ, on the weighted sum of its inputs, as

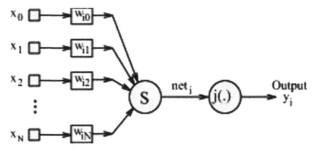

Fig. 4.4 A typical node; x_0 is set to threshold value θ_i

$$net_i(n) = \sum_{j=0}^{N} w_{ij}x_j(n) \qquad (4.7)$$

and

$$y_i(n) = \varphi(net_i(n)), \qquad (4.8)$$

where N is the number of inputs (i.e., the output signals of the units having connections to the ith unit), and $net_i(n)$ is the overall excitation of unit i at time n and we will refer to it as *net input*.

The *net input* is simply the inner product of the input vector $x = [x_0, x_1, \ldots, x_N]$ with the weight vector $w_i = [w_{i0}, w_{i1}, \ldots, w_{iN}]^T$, which shows the degree of agreement of directions between x and w_i. Note that x_0 is reserved for the threshold value, $\theta_i \in \Re$. The effect of the squashing function φ is to limit the neuron's output to some finite value.

- A *dynamic* node computes its *net input* using one of the following equations

a) Node with local activation value feedback

$$net_i(n) = w_{ii}net_i(n-1) + \sum_j w_{ij}x_j(n). \qquad (4.9)$$

b) Node with local output value feedback. Figure 4.3 depicts a node with local output value feedback. A delay element is incorporated into this architecture.

$$net_i(n) = w_{ii}y_i(n-1) + \sum_j w_{ij}x_j(n). \qquad (4.10)$$

The common choices of the activation function φ used for static as well as dynamic nodes are as following:

- Binary Threshold function,

$$\varphi(net_i) = \begin{cases} 1 \text{ if } net_i > 0 \\ 0 \text{ otherwise} \end{cases} \qquad (4.11)$$

- Piecewise Linear function,

$$\varphi(net_i) = \begin{cases} 1 & \text{if } net_i \geq \frac{1}{2} \\ net_i & +\frac{1}{2} > net_i > -\frac{1}{2} \\ 0 & net_i \leq -\frac{1}{2} \end{cases} \tag{4.12}$$

- Sigmoid function,

$$\varphi(net_i) = \frac{1}{1 + e^{-\lambda net_i}}, \tag{4.13}$$

where λ is the gain (sharpness) parameter of the sigmoid function. The function assumes values in the continuous range (0,1). Other alternatives in this category are $\tanh(\lambda net_i)$ and Gaussian function $e^{-(\lambda net_i)^2}$, which can assume a continuous range of values from $(-1, +1)$ and $(0, 1)$, respectively.

4.4.2 Connections

Neurons are interconnected to each other via synapses (links). Each *connection* is a unidirectional link that takes care of the flow of information between two neurons. The strength or weakness of a connection is dependent on the local biochemical environment of that connection [69], which in turn is determined by the progressive modification through the course of the learning process.

Artificial neural networks can be viewed as directed graphs. The nodes are located at the intersection of directed links. Associated with each link is a weight that influences and modulates the amount of information passing between nodes. Weights can be either positive or negative. A connection with a positive weight is called an excitatory connection and that with a negative weight is referred to as inhibitory connection. The pattern of connectivity represents what the network is representing at any time.

A connection weight, w_{ij}, is modified as follows

$$w_{ij}(n+1) = w_{ij}(n) + \eta \, \delta_j(n) x_j(n), \tag{4.14}$$

where η is the learning rate, and δ_j is the learning signal (also called local gradient) of the jth node.

The learning signal, δ, which we call delta hereafter, is generally a function of a connection weight and input signal. That is, for jth node

$$\delta_j = f(x_j, w_j),$$

where x_j, w_j are the input and weight vectors of the jth node, respectively. In the case of supervised learning the desired output, d, is also a factor in computing the learning signal [2]. That is, for jth node

$$\delta_j = f(x_j, w_j, d_j).$$

4.4.3 Network Architectures

The artificial neural networks fall into two main categories: (a) *Feedforward* networks, and (b) *Recurrent* networks. They are briefly described in the following subsections.

4.4.3.1 Feedforward networks

The feedforward networks can be considered as computational devices consisting of a set of interconnected nodes organized in one or more layers. In this architecture no feedback connections are allowed. Thus, *feedforward* networks can be pictorially described as a directed acyclic graph as depicted in Figure 4.5.

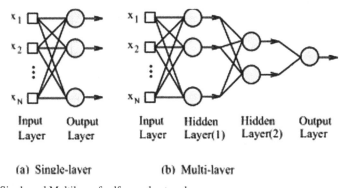

Fig. 4.5 Single and Multilayer feedforward networks

Figure 4.5(a) shows a single-layer feedforward network. In this type of network, there is an input layer of source nodes that projects onto an output layer. The output layer is the only layer in this model that consists of computational nodes. A linear associative memory, by which an input vector is associated with an output vector, is an example of single-layer feedforward network.

Figure 4.5(b) shows a multilayer feedforward network (also called a multilayer perceptron, MLP). Multilayer feedforward networks are networks made of layers of units with nonlinear activation functions. The units of the network are organized in several layers, namely an input layer, one or more hidden layer(s), and an output layer. The outputs of one layer feed the inputs of the following layer through weighted connections. Networks with as few as two layers are capable of universal approximation from one finite dimensional space to another [34].

4.4.3.2 Recurrent networks

The recurrent networks are feedforward networks with feedback loops. Feedforward networks are suitable for static information processing whereas recurrent networks are suitable for spatio-temporal information processing [33]. The dynamic properties of recurrent neural networks make them universal approximators of dynamical systems.

There are two types of recurrent neural networks: discrete time recurrent neural networks and continuous time ones. Figure 4.6(a) illustrates a recurrent network without hidden nodes and without self-feedback loops. Note that the *time delay* operator causes the recurrent networks of nonlinear nodes to perform nonlinear dynamic behavior.

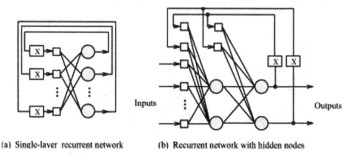

(a) Single-layer recurrent network   (b) Recurrent network with hidden nodes

Fig. 4.6 Single and Multilayer recurrent networks

Figure 4.6(b) shows a recurrent network with hidden units. The extra input layer nodes, one for each hidden layer node and/or output layer node, are recurrent nodes. The feedback of the network is handled by the recurrent nodes.

4.4.4 Learning Process

Learning is the process of finding an optimal or near optimal pattern of connectivity for the neural network (i.e., an optimal or near optimal set of weights) so that the network can have a desired response to a specific input signal. There are many different iterative methods used to adapt the weights to an optimum point according to some optimality criteria. The existing learning algorithms can be divided into two main categories:

• **Supervised learning** in which the learning process is supervised by a teacher who presents input vectors (patterns) with matching (desired) outputs. In supervised learning, nodes are considered as adaptive elements. Their connection strengths are adjusted depending on the input signals they receive, their actual output values, and the associated teachers responses. A variation to this is the *reinforcement* learning algorithm in which a quantitative measure of comparison between actual output and the desired output of a network is used to train the network.

- **Unsupervised learning** wherein the learning is to discover significant patterns or features in the input data without supervision. There is no teacher to provide the desired output signals nor are there any reward or punishment to be used in the process of learning.

With proper choice of the connection weights, number of units, external inputs, outputs, training strategies, and other parameters, one should be able to devise classes of ANNs to perform virtually any computation [17]. Hornik et al. proved that every well behaved function can be approximated by a neural network with just one hidden layer.

4.4.5 Artificial Neural Networks in Anomaly Detection

Multilayer perceptron (MLP) [71] is one of most commonly used neural network classification algorithms. Authors in [66] apply MLP for detecting attacks in the KDD CUP 99 data set. Their architecture consists of a three layer feed-forward neural network: one input, one hidden, and one output layers. Unipolar sigmoid transfer functions are used for each neuron in both the hidden and the output layers with slope value of 1.0. The learning algorithm used is stochastic gradient descent with mean squared error function. There are a total of 41 neurons in the input layer (41-feature input pattern), and 5 neurons (one for each class) in the output layer. Detection results reported in [66] show that 88.7% Probe attacks are detected with a 0.4% FAR, 97.2% DoS attacks are detected with a 0.3% FAR, 13.2% U2R attacks are detected with a 0.05% FAR, and 5.6% R2L attacks are detected with a 0.01% FAR. In [9], Bivens et al. use a multilayer perceptron combined with self-organizing maps for classifying intrusions and is fairly representative of such approaches.

Self-Organizing Map (SOM) [41] is another neural network model for analyzing and visualizing high dimensional data. By applying a competitive unsupervised learning technique, an SOM extracts structural information from high dimensional data and provides a low-dimensional (2-D or 3-D) visualization in form of a topology preserving map. This means that data instances that are near each other in the high-dimensional input space are mapped to nearby units in the topological map.

Self-Organizing Map has recently become very popular for implementing both network-based and host-based anomaly detection systems [23, 62, 50, 44, 26, 58]. The major reason for their popularity is certainly their capability to provide also visualization of the high-dimensional data. However, the quality of the produced clustering used for labeling the data seems to be not significantly better compared with other approaches.

Zhong et al. have evaluated the suitability of SOM for clustering in a network intrusion detection scenario against other algorithms [74]. Their results show that SOM are a very fast approach comparable with K-Means but in contrast to K-Means the computation time of the algorithm scaled sub-linearly with the number of clusters. Experimental results reported in [73] also showed that SOM are computational attractive even if K-Means seems to perform a little better.

Another neural network approach that is applied in anomaly detection is Adaptive Resonance Theory (ART) nets [12]. Similar to SOM single units in an ART net represent cluster units and associated weight vectors are matched against given training data.

However, the selection of the Best Matching Unit is based on relative similarity instead of absolute difference (as in SOM) between the given data instance and the weight vector. In ART nets the number of clusters has not to be predefined, however, the behavior of the net can indirectly be influenced by tuning a vigilance parameter. Similar to other clustering techniques, determining an accurate value for this parameter seems to be difficult and requires several experimental tests.

An approach called Unsupervised Neural Net based Intrusion Detector (UNNID) that utilizes two different types of unsupervised ART nets (ART-1 and ART-2) for network anomaly detection is described in [3]. The authors also present results of an experimental evaluation using the KDD Cup 99 data set. Although the approach is not directly compared with any other approach for benchmarking, the reported results seem to be promising (detection rates of about 90% in combination with false alarm rates of 1-2%).

However, because only a relatively small subset of the KDD Cup 99 data set has been used for the experiments, further evaluations seem to be necessary to judge the actual capabilities of ART nets for anomaly detection. Moreover, the authors do not provide information about the time complexity of the algorithms.

4.5 Support Vector Machine (SVM)

The basic idea of SVM is to increase dimensionality of the samples so that they can be separable. Therefore, despite the usual trend toward dimensionality reduction, in SVM the dimensionality is actually increased. The idea is to find a hyper-plane to place samples from the same class inside it (in the high dimensional space this may look like a hyper-volume). As Hastie in his book [31] indicates: "Generally linear boundaries such a polynomial in enlarged space achieve better training class separation and translate to nonlinear boundaries in the original space".

Assume the original samples are in the $\mathbf{x}$ space and they are transformed (dimensionality enlargement) to the $\mathbf{y}$ space, where $\mathbf{y} = \phi(\mathbf{x})$. In addition, suppose we have some hyperplane which separates the positive from the negative examples (a "separating hyperplane") provided by:

$$\mathbf{w}^T \mathbf{x} + b = 0 \qquad (4.15)$$

where $\mathbf{x}$ is an input vector (sample set) and $\mathbf{w}$ is the weight vector (to be adjusted) and b is a bias value. The distance between the closest data point to the hyperplane is called *Margin of Separation* and it is denoted by ρ. The goal is to maximize this margin. The hyperplane that is doing this separation is the optimal hyperplane. Assuming that d_i is the desired respond (output value) the +1 or -1 values show the linearly separable classes.

$$\mathbf{w}^T \mathbf{x}_i + b \geq 0 \ for \ d_i = +1$$
$$\mathbf{w}^T \mathbf{x}_i + b < 0 \ for \ d_i = -1$$
(4.16)

where $\mathbf{x}_i$ is the pattern for the ith example. Therefore the optimal discriminant hyperplane will be:

$$g(\mathbf{x}) = \mathbf{w}_o^T \mathbf{x} + b_o$$
(4.17)

where the optimal hyperplane will be:

$$\mathbf{w}_o^T \mathbf{x} + b_o = 0$$
(4.18)

Haykin [32] also suggests that:

$$\mathbf{x} = \mathbf{x}_p + r \frac{\mathbf{w}_o}{|\mathbf{w}_o\|}$$
(4.19)

where $\mathbf{x}_p$ is the normal projection of the $\mathbf{x}$ onto the optimal hyperplane, and r is the desired algebraic distance." r will be positive if $\mathbf{x}$ is placed on the positive side of the hyperplane and negative once it is placed on the negative side of the hyperplane. The value for r can be calculated as follows:

$$r = \frac{g(\mathbf{x})}{\|\mathbf{w}_o\|}$$
(4.20)

Considering the above, it is clear that the pair $(\mathbf{w}_o, b_o)$ have to be selected such that they support the following constraints:

$$\mathbf{w}_o^T \mathbf{x}_i + b_o \geq 0 \ for \ d_i = +1$$
$$\mathbf{w}_o^T \mathbf{x}_i + b_o \leq 0 \ for \ d_i = -1$$
(4.21)

Data points such as (x_i, d_i) that satisfy one of the aforementioned equations (with equality signs) are called support vectors. For the same reason, this system is called *Support vector Machine*. In this system, the separation margin ρ is calculated in the following way:

$$\rho = 2r = \frac{2}{\|\mathbf{w}_o\|}$$
(4.22)

In this system, the cost function is defined to be $\Phi(\mathbf{w}) = \frac{1}{2}\mathbf{w}^T \mathbf{w}$. The training goal is to minimize this function. Using the Lagrange Multipliers α_i, an objective function can be derived:

$$Q(\alpha) = \sum_{i=1}^{N} \alpha_i - \frac{1}{2} \sum_{i=1}^{N} \sum_{j=1}^{N} \alpha_i \alpha_j d_i d_j \mathbf{x}_i^T \mathbf{x}_j; \qquad \alpha_i \geq 0$$
(4.23)

The following constraints apply to the above equation:

$$\sum_{i=1}^{N} \alpha_i d_i = 0 \tag{4.24}$$

$$\alpha_i \geq 0 \qquad for\ i = 1, 2, \ldots, N \tag{4.25}$$

Once the optimized α_o is found, it can be substituted in the $\mathbf{w} = \sum_{i} = 1^{N} \alpha_i d_i \mathbf{x}_i$ and result will yield:

$$\mathbf{w}_o = \sum_{i=1}^{N} \alpha_{0,\,i} d_i \mathbf{x}_i \tag{4.26}$$

Consequently, the optimized bios values can be calculated using the following formula:

$$b_o = 1 - \mathbf{w}_o^T \mathbf{x}^{(s)} \qquad for\ d^{(s)} = 1 \tag{4.27}$$

Given the feature vector $\varphi(\mathbf{x}_i)$ for the corresponding input pattern such as $\mathbf{x}_i$ in the ith pattern, the following expression will be produced:

$$w = \sum_{i=1}^{N} \alpha_i d_i \varphi(x_i) \tag{4.28}$$

Therefore, the inner-product kernel can be defined as:

$$K(x, x_i) = \varphi^T(x)\varphi(x_i) = \sum_{j=0}^{m_1} \varphi_j(x)\varphi_j(x_i) \tag{4.29}$$

The Mercer's theorem states that given $K(x, x')$ is a continuous symmetric kernel defined in the closed interval $a \leq x \leq b$. The same is true for the $\mathbf{x}'$, therefore, the kernel $\mathbf{K(x,x')}$ can be expanded as:

$$K(x, x') = \sum_{j=0}^{\infty} \lambda_i \varphi_i(x)\varphi_i(x'), \tag{4.30}$$

where λ_i is a positive coefficient for all i. The function $\varphi_i(\mathbf{x})$ is called eigenfunction and the constant values λ_i are called eigenvalues. Haykin in his book [32] indicates two major observations using the Mercer's theorem:

- For $\lambda_i \neq 1$, the ith image $\sqrt{\lambda_j}\varphi_j(x)$ induced in the feature space by input vector $\mathbf{x}$ is an eigenfunction of the expansion.
- In theory the dimensionality of the feature space (i.e. the number of the eigenvalues/eigenfunctions) can be indefinitely large.

Therefore, the objective function with constraint optimization can be derived to be:

$$Q(\alpha) = \sum_{i=1}^{N} \alpha_i - \frac{1}{2} \sum_{i=1}^{N} \sum_{j=1}^{N} \alpha_i \alpha_j d_i d_j K(x_i, x_j); \qquad \alpha_i \geq 0 \tag{4.31}$$

Given the following constraints:

$$\sum_{i=1}^{N} \alpha_i d_i = 0$$
$$0 \leq \alpha_i \leq C \quad for \ i = 1, 2, \ldots, N \qquad (4.32)$$

C is a positive user specific parameter. Hence the optimum weight vector can be presented as:

$$w_O = \sum_{i=1}^{N} \alpha_{o,\,i} d_i \varphi(x_i) \qquad (4.33)$$

4.5.1 Support Vector Machine in Anomaly Detection

In [56], Mukkamala et al. have applied kernel classifiers and classifier design methods to network anomaly detection problems. They evaluate the impact of kernel type and parameter values on the accuracy with which a support vector machine (SVM) performs intrusion classification. It was showed that classification accuracy varies with the kernel type and the parameter values; thus, with appropriately chosen parameter values, intrusions can be detected by SVMs with higher accuracy and lower rates of false alarms. Detection results with the KDD Cup 99 data set reported in [56] show that more than 99% attacks are detected by SVM using 6 most important features. However, the authors don't give detailed description about their experiments in their paper. Whether they use full KDD 1999 Cup data or not has not been addressed yet. Hwang et al. applied SVM classifier in their three-tier architecture of intrusion detection [36]. A multi-class SVM classifier is used in last layer and it classifies instances into four categories: PROBE, DoS, R2L and U2R. The whole system is evaluated with the KDD'99 benchmark data set and it was claimed in the paper that detection rate for Pobe, DoS, U2R and R2L attacks is 99.16%, 97.65%, 76.32% and 46.53%, respectively. Although their detection rate is better than the winner of KDD Cup 99 competition, the corresponding false positive rate is not analyzed and reported in the paper.

4.6 Evolutionary Computation

There are two major evolutionary computation algorithms: genetic algorithm (GA) and genetic programming (GP) both of which can be applied for network anomaly detection. Genetic Programming is an extension of Genetic Algorithm [42] which is a general search method that uses analogies from natural selection and evolution. The main difference between these two approaches lies in the solution encoding method. GA encodes potential solutions for a specific problem as a simple population of fixed-length binary strings named chromosomes and then applies reproduction and recombination operators to these chromosomes to create new chromosomes. In contrast to GA, GP encodes multi potential solutions for specific problems as a population of programs or functions. The programs can be represented as parse trees which are usually composed of internal nodes and leaf nodes. Internal nodes are called primitive functions and leaf nodes are called terminals. The terminals can be viewed as the inputs to the specific problem. They might include the independent variables and the set of constants. The primitive functions are combined with the terminals or simpler function calls to form more complex function calls. For instance, GP can be used to evolve new rules from general ones. The rules are represented as *if condition 1 and condition 2 and condition N, then consequence*. In this case, the primitive function corresponds to AND operator and the terminals are the conditions (e.g. *condition1, condition2,, condition N*).

GP randomly generates an initial population of solutions. Then, the initial population is manipulated using various genetic operators to produce new populations. These operators include reproduction, crossover, mutation, dropping condition, etc. The whole process of evolving from one population to the next population is called a generation. A high-level description of GP algorithm can be divided into a number of sequential steps:

1. Create a random population of programs, or rules, using the symbolic expressions provided as the initial population.
2. Evaluate each program or rule by assigning a fitness value according to a pre-defined fitness function that can measure the capability of the rule or program to solve the problem.
3. Use reproduction operator to copy existing programs into the new generation.
4. Generate the new population with crossover, mutation or other operators from a randomly chosen set of parents.
5. Repeat steps 2 onwards for the new population until a pre-defined termination criterion has been satisfied or a fixed number of generations have been completed.

The solution to the problem is the genetic program with the best fitness within all the generations.

Genetic Algorithm as an Alternative Tool for Security Audit Trails Analysis (GASSATA) is one of the earliest attempts for using genetic algorithm (GA) for intrusion detection [55]. In GASSATA, Me defines a n-dimensional hypothesis vector H, where $H_i = 1$ if attack i is taking place according to the hypothesis, otherwise $H_i = 0$. As a result, the intrusion detection becomes the problem of finding the H vector that maximizes the product $W \times H$, subject to the constraint $(AE \times H)_i \leq O_i$, where W is a n-dimensional weight vector, AE is an attacks-events matrix, and O is the observed n-dimensional audit trail vector. Each individual in the population corresponds to a particular H vector. The fitness function is defined as follows:

$$Fitness = \sum_{i=1}^{n} W_i \times I_i, \qquad (4.34)$$

where I_i stands for an individual. The experimental evaluation shows that GA for intrusion detection has a low false alarm rate and the likelihood of detecting misuse

behaviors is 0.996. However, the major limitation of GASSATA is that it cannot
locate attacks precisely.

Another attempt using GA for intrusion detection is made by Chittur [13]. Chittur
uses a certainty formula C_i to classify whether a record is an intrusive behavior or a
normal behavior. C_i is defined as follows:

$$C_i(x) = \sum_{j=1}^{n} \Re_{ij} \times x_j, \tag{4.35}$$

where $\Re_{ij}$ is the Ephemeral Random Constant-based coefficient for attribute x_j and
n is the number of attributes. A threshold value for C_i is established and any certainty
value exceeding this threshold value is classified as a malicious attack. Besides, the
fitness function is defined as follows:

$$F(\delta_i) = \frac{\alpha}{A} - \frac{\beta}{B} \tag{4.36}$$

where δ_i refers to the individual; α means the number of correctly detected attacks,
and A stands for the number of total attacks; β refers to the number of false positives
and B is the total number of normal connections. The range of the fitness value is
from -1 to 1. A high detection rate $\frac{\alpha}{A}$ and a low false positive rate $\frac{\beta}{B}$ will yield a high
fitness value for an individual.

The experimental results show that GA successfully generates an accurate empirical behavior model from the training data. However, the major limitation of this
approach is that an improper threshold value might easily lead to a high false alarm
rate in detecting new attacks.

4.6.1 Evolutionary Computation in Anomaly Detection

Crosbie and Spafford propose a framework combining GP and agent technology for
detecting anomalous behaviors in a system [14]. Autonomous agents are used to
detect intrusions using log data of network connections. Each autonomous agent is
used to monitor a particular network parameter. Autonomous agents whose predication is correct are assigned a higher weight value to decide whether a session is
intrusive or not. There are a number of advantages to having many small agents,
instead of a single large one. However, large number of communications among so
many agents decreases the detection efficiency; moreover, an improper primitive for
each agent will make the training time long.

In a different approach, Lu and Traore proposed a rule evolution approach based
on Genetic Programming (GP) for detecting novel attacks on networks in [52]. In
their framework, four genetic operators, namely reproduction, mutation, crossover
and dropping condition operators, are used to evolve new rules. New rules are used
to detect novel or known network attacks. Experimental results show that rules generated by GP with part of KDD 1999 Cup data set has a low false positive rate

(FPR), a low false negative rate (FNR) and a high rate of detecting unknown attacks. However, an evaluation with full KDD training and testing data is missed in the paper.

More efforts using GA for intrusion detection are made in [25, 4, 10]. Gmez et al. propose a linear representation scheme for evolving fuzzy rules using the concept of complete binary tree structures. GA is used to generate genetic operators for producing useful and minimal structure modifications to the fuzzy expression tree represented by chromosomes. However, the training process in this approach is computationally very expensive and time consuming. Bridges and Vaughn employ GA to tune the fuzzy membership functions and select an appropriate set of features in their intelligent intrusion detection system. Balajinath and Raghavan use GA to learn individual user behaviors. Active user behaviors are predicted based on past observed user behaviors, which can be used for intrusion detection. The training process for both approaches is, however, time consuming.

4.7 Association Rules

Association rule learning is one of many data mining techniques that describe events that tend to occur together. The concept of association rules can be understood as follows: Given a database D of transactions where each transaction $T \in D$ denotes a set of items in the database, an association rule is an implication of the form $X \Longrightarrow Y$, where X is subset of D, Y is subset of D and $X \cap Y = \emptyset$.

The general form of the rule that relates objects to one another is shown below [30]:

$$X \Longrightarrow Y \qquad [Support, Confidence] \qquad (4.37)$$

The confidence value is a measure of our belief in the association rule and is presented in percentage. It represents the certainty, reliability or accuracy of the rule. The confidence value is also known as Certainty Factor (CF) as in the fuzzy logic or other rule based systems. Support and Confidence are two parameters for measuring the rule interestingness. Han [30] defines the support as "The **support** of an association pattern refers to the percentage of task-relevant data tuples(or transactions) for which the pattern is true". The **itemset** is considered as a set of items. The number of transactions contained in an itemset is called occurrence frequency, support count or the frequency of an itemset.

Both of the support and confidence values are compared against a threshold. A rule will look interesting if both its support and confidence values fall above minimum support and minimum confidence thresholds. These thresholds are set by users or experts in that domain of work. Formulas for the support and confidence value are listed in below:

$$support(A \Longrightarrow B) = P(A \cup B) \qquad (4.38)$$

$$confidence(A \implies B) = P(B|A) \qquad (4.39)$$

Han [30] introduces two steps for associate rule mining:

Find all frequent itemsets: By definition, each of these items will occur at least as frequently as a pre-determined minimum support count.

Generate strong association rules from the frequent itemsets: By definition, these rules must satisfy minimum support and minimum confidence.

4.7.1 The Apriori Algorithm

One of the influential algorithms in data mining is the Apriori algorithm. This algorithm is applied on the boolean association rules and is used for mining frequent itemsets. This approach is also known as the level-wise search. In this search k-itemsets are used to explore (k+1)-itemsets. In this process once the first set (L1) is found, it is used to find the second itemset (L2) that will produce the set of frequent 2-itemsets. This new itemset is used to find the next itemset (L3) and so on. To improve the efficiency of the algorithm Apriori property is defined. Han [30] says "By definition, if an itemset I does not satisfy the minimum support threshold, min_sup, then I is not frequent, that is, $P(I) < min\_sup$". Han describes this algorithm as a two step process of **join** and **prune** actions.

1. **The join step:** Let the itemsets to be sorted, then a set of k-candidate itemsets can be joined if the first k-1 of their items are identical. Let l_1 and l_2 be two itemsets. The members l_1 and l_2 of L_{k-1} are joined if
   $(l_1[1] = l_2[1]) \wedge (l_1[2] = l_2[2]) \wedge \cdots \wedge (l_1[k-1] < l_2[k-1])$
   Then the result of joining these two will be $l_1[1]l_1[2]\ldots l_1[k-1]l_2[k-1]$.
2. **The Prune step:** Han indicates that any k-1 itemset that is not frequent can not be a subset of frequent k-itemset. Then he follows: "Hence, if any (k-1)-subset of a candidate k-itemset is not in L_{k-1}, then the candidate cannot be frequent either so can be removed from C_k". Where C_k is a superset of L_k.

4.7.2 Association Rules in Anomaly Detection

Lee et al. [46] proposed an association rule based data mining approach for anomaly detection where raw data was converted into ASCII network packet information, which in turn was converted into connection-level information. These connection level records contained connection features like service, duration, etc. Association rules were then applied to this data to create models to detect intrusions.

In another paper, Barbara et al. [5] describe Audit Data Analysis and Mining (ADAM), a real-time anomaly detection system that uses a module to classify the suspicious events into false alarms or real attacks. ADAM was one out of seven systems tested in the 1999 DARPA evaluation. It uses data mining to build a customizable profile of rules of normal behavior and then classifies attacks (by name) or declares false alarms. To discover attacks in TCPdump audit trail, ADAM uses a combination of association rules, mining and classification.

During the training phase, ADAM builds a database of "normal" frequent item sets using attack free data. Then it runs a sliding window online algorithm that finds frequent item sets in the last D connections and compares them with those stored in the normal item set repository. With the remaining item sets that have deemed suspicious, ADAM uses a classifier which has previously been trained to classify the suspicious connections as a known attack, unknown attack, or a false alarm. Association rules are used to gather necessary knowledge about the nature of the audit data. If the item set's support surpasses a threshold, then that item set is reported as suspicious. The system annotates suspicious item sets with a vector of parameters. Since the system knows where the attacks are in the training set, the corresponding suspicious item set along with their feature vectors are used to train a classifier. The trained classifier will be able to, given a suspicious item set and a vector of features, classify the item set as a known attack (and label it with the name of attack), an unknown attack, or a false alarm.

4.8 Clustering

The core method used to implement unsupervised learning algorithms is clustering. The principle goal of clustering is to group objects into clusters so that intra-cluster similarity, i.e. the similarity between objects assigned to the same cluster is maximized and inter-cluster similarity, i.e. the similarity between objects assigned to different clusters is minimized. However, given a corresponding metric used to measure the similarity between objects finding an optimal solution to this problem is NP-hard. Hence, a variety of algorithms to find accurate solutions for clustering problems have been developed using the following assumptions:

1. Samples are from a known number of classes.
2. The priori probability $P(\omega_j)$ of each class is known.
3. Class-conditional probability densities $p(x|\omega_j, \theta)$ are available.
4. The values for the parameter vectors $\theta_1, \ldots, \theta_c$ are not available.
5. There is no information about the labels for the categories.

Duda in his book [20] defines the mixture density in the following form:

$$p(x|\theta) = p(x|\omega_j, \theta_j)P(\omega_j), \tag{4.40}$$

where $\theta = (\theta_1, \ldots, \theta_c)^t$. In addition, the $p(x|\omega_j, \theta_j)$ are called component densities and the $P(\omega_j)$ are called mixing parameters. He also proves that in order to be able to uniquely identify two densities it would be necessary to have $P(\omega_1) \neq P(\omega_2)$. For binary classes x the following formula will be true:

$$p(x|\theta) = \frac{1}{2}\theta_1^x(1-\theta_1)^{1-x} + \frac{1}{2}\theta_2^x(1-\theta_2)^{1-x} \tag{4.41}$$

However, as for a more common problem such as mixtures of normal densities the formula will become:

$$p(x|\theta) = \frac{P(\omega_1)}{\sqrt{2\pi}}\exp[-\frac{1}{2}(x-\theta_1)^2] + \frac{P(\omega_2)}{\sqrt{2\pi}}\exp[-\frac{1}{2}(x-\theta_2)^2] \tag{4.42}$$

4.8.1 Taxonomy of Clustering Algorithms

Generally, clustering algorithms can be divided according to several criteria. The first important criterion for distinguishing clustering approaches concerns the basic procedure of the algorithm:

1) Hierarchical clustering groups data objects with a sequence of partitions, either from singleton clusters to a cluster including all individuals or vice versa. It usually creates a tree of clusters. Each node in the tree is linked to one or several children clusters while sibling clusters share a common parent node. According to the method used for trees building, hierarchical clustering approaches are divided into two categories, agglomerative and divisive. Agglomerative methods recursively merge central points of different clusters while divisive methods start from a cluster including all data and then gradually split them into smaller clusters. The most widely used hierarchical clustering approach currently is agglomerative due to a lower complexity than divisive. Based on the different similarity measures, agglomerative hierarchical algorithms mainly include single linkage hierarchical, complete linkage hierarchical and average linkage hierarchical clustering. We summarize these agglomerative hierarchical algorithms as follows:

1. Start by assigning each data object to a cluster, so that you have N clusters, each containing just one item.
2. Find the closest (most similar) pair of clusters and merge them into a single cluster, so that now you have one cluster less.
3. Compute distances (similarities) between the new cluster and each of the old clusters.
4. Repeat steps 2 and 3 until all items are clustered into a single cluster of size N.

The algorithm is single linkage-based if the similarity measurement S between two clusters C_m and C_n is calculated with the following formula:

$$S = min\{d(x,y) : x \in C_m, y \in C_n\} \tag{4.43}$$

where x and y are data points in C_m and C_n respectively and $d(x,y)$ is the distance between x and y.

The algorithm is complete linkage-based if the corresponding similarity measurement is as follows:

$$S = max \{d(x,y) : x \in C_m, y \in C_n\} \tag{4.44}$$

The algorithm is average linkage-based if the similarity measurement is computed by the following formula:

$$S = \frac{1}{|C_m| \cdot |C_n|} \sum_{x \in C_m} \sum_{y \in C_n} d(x,y) \tag{4.45}$$

2) Non-hierarchical clustering assigns all objects to final clusters without generating a hierarchy of clusters.

3) Model based clustering assigns objects by using an explicit (usually, parametric) statistical model of individual clusters and the entire sample distribution is represented as a statistical mixture of the component clusters. Bayesian techniques or maximum likelihood techniques can be used for estimating both the number of clusters and their parameters.

Another criterion used to classify clustering approaches concerns the representation of the individual clusters:

1) Similarity based clustering groups objects together according to a pairwise determination of the objects similarity. Here, the clusters are typically simply represented by the list of belonging objects.

2) Centroid based clustering applies a certain model (i.e. its centroid) to represent the corresponding individual cluster. Here, the assignment of an object to a certain cluster is usually based on an evaluation of the correspondence between the object and the cluster model. Centroid based clustering algorithms are commonly more efficient than similarity based approaches since they avoid a pairwise comparison of all N objects to be clustered.

While similarity based algorithms usually have a complexity of at least $O(N^2)$ (due to the pairwise similarity computations), centroid based approaches are more scalable and achieve a complexity of $O(NKM)$, where K is the number of clusters and M is the number of iterations [74]. Because network intrusion detection systems have to deal with huge amount of network traffic audit data, the application of similarity based approaches is limited due to their complexity. At least for online learning only centroid based algorithms may be applicable.

4.8.2 K-Means Clustering

One of the most popular and most widely used clustering algorithms is K-Means [54], which is a non-hierarchical centroid-based approach. The popularity of this algorithm can be explained by its simplicity, low time complexity, and fast convergence.

In this method, the Euclidean distance is the distance between the sample and the center of the cluster. The value of the mean $\hat{\mu}_m$ is used to determine if the sample belongs to that cluster or not (approximate $\hat{P}(\omega_i|x_k, \hat{\theta})$).

$$\hat{P}(\omega_i|x_k, \hat{\theta}) \simeq \begin{cases} 1 & if \; i = m \\ 0 & otherwise \end{cases} \tag{4.46}$$

The training method for this algorithm is:

1. Initialize the number of samples n and number of clusters $c = k$.
2. Classify n samples with respect to the nearest μ_i.
3. Compute the new value for the μ_i.
4. Repeat from step 2 until there is no change in the μ_i value.
5. Return μ_i, $i = 1, \ldots, c$

4.8.3 Y-Means Clustering

As mentioned in the previous section, K-Means has two shortcomings in clustering large data sets: number of clusters dependency and degeneracy. Number of clusters dependency is that the value of k is very critical to the clustering result. Obtaining the optimal k for a given data set is an NP-hard problem. Degeneracy means that the clustering may end with some empty clusters. This is not what we expect since the classes of the empty clusters are meaningless for the classification.

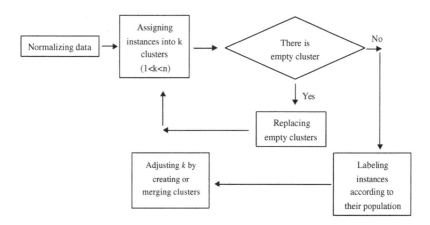

Fig. 4.7 Y-means algorithm

These shortcomings are addressed by Y-Means clustering [28]. As illustrated in Figure 4.7, similar to K-Means, Y-means partitions the normalized data into k clusters. The number of clusters , k, can be a given integer between 1 and n exclusively, where n is the total number of instances. The next step is to find whether there are any empty clusters. If there are, new clusters will be created to replace these empty clusters; and then instances will be re-assigned to existing centers. This iteration will continue until there is no empty cluster. Subsequently, the outliers of clusters will be removed to form new clusters, in which instances are more similar to each other; and overlapped adjacent clusters will merge into a new cluster. In this way, the value of k will be determined automatically by splitting or merging clusters. The last step is to label the clusters according to their populations; that is, if the population ratio of one cluster is above a given threshold, all the instances in the cluster will be classified as normal; otherwise, they are labeled intrusive.

4.8.4 Maximum-Likelihood Estimates

Let the given set $\mathscr{D} = \{x_1, \ldots, x_n\}$ have the mixture density as it is defined in Section 4.8. Then the likelihood of the observed samples will be:

$$p(\mathscr{D}|\theta) = \prod_{k=1}^{n} p(x_k|\theta) \tag{4.47}$$

The value θ which maximizes the $p(\mathscr{D}|\theta)$ will be the value for the maximum likelihood estimate $\hat{\theta}$. l is the logarithm of the likelihood

$$l = \sum_{k=1}^{n} \ln p(x_k|\theta) \tag{4.48}$$

Given $\hat{P}(\omega_i)$ as a maximum likelihood of the $P(\omega_i)$ and the same for θ_i and $\hat{\theta}_i$, also considering $\hat{P}(\omega_i) \neq 0$ to make the maximum likelihood function differentiable. Then $\hat{P}(\omega_i)$ and $\hat{\theta}_i$ must satisfy the following equations:

$$\hat{P}(\omega_i) = \frac{1}{n} \sum_{k=1}^{n} \hat{P}(\omega_i|x_k, \hat{\theta}) \tag{4.49}$$

$$\sum_{k=1}^{n} \hat{P}(\omega_i|x_k, \hat{\theta}) \nabla_{\theta_i} \ln p(x_k|\omega_i, \hat{\theta}_i) = 0 \tag{4.50}$$

$$\hat{P}(\omega_i|x_k, \hat{\theta}) = \frac{p(x_k|\omega_i, \hat{\theta}_i)\hat{P}(\omega_i)}{\sum_{k=1}^{n} p(x_k|\omega_j, \hat{\theta}_j)\hat{P}(\omega_j)} \tag{4.51}$$

There are three scenarios considered for these type of problems:

1. Case 1: μ_i is unknown but the Σ_i, $P(\omega_i)$ and c (number of classes) are known.
2. Case 2: μ_i, Σ_i and $P(\omega_i)$ are unknown but c (number of classes) is known.
3. Case 3: None of the μ_i, Σ_i, $P(\omega_i)$ or c are known.

Unfortunately case 3 is the only case among others that Maximum-Likelihood method is not suitable for it. Therefore, in this text only cases 1 & 2 will be discussed. In the following, the first case will be studied where the mean vectors μ_i are unknown. Here θ_i will consist of μ_i as its components. The estimated mean vector $\hat{\mu}_i$ can be calculated using the following equations.
Likelihood is:

$$p(x|\omega_i, \mu_i) = -\ln[(2\pi)^{d/2}|\Sigma_i|^{1/2}] - \frac{1}{2}(x - \mu_i)^t \Sigma_i^{-1}(x - \mu_i) \qquad (4.52)$$

The estimated value for the $\hat{\mu}_i$ will be:

$$\hat{\mu}_i = \frac{\sum_{k=1}^{n} P(\omega_i|x_k, \hat{\mu})x_k}{\sum_{k=1}^{n} P(\omega_i|x_k, \hat{\mu})} \qquad (4.53)$$

The above equation shows that the maximum likelihood estimate for μ_i is simply the weighted average of the samples. In here the weight of the $k_t h$ sample will tell us about the likeliness of having that sample belong to the $i_t h$ class. Consequently, the following equation can be derived:

$$\hat{\mu}_i(j+1) = \frac{\sum_{k=1}^{n} P(\omega_i|x_k, \hat{\mu}(j))x_k}{\sum_{k=1}^{n} P(\omega_i|x_k, \hat{\mu}(j))} \qquad (4.54)$$

In this way the next average will be calculated recursively. It will also help with the hill-climbing procedure to maximize the log-likelihood function. This approach is something similar to the gradient ascendent. Recalling the aforementioned equation:

$$p(x|\theta) = \frac{P(\omega_1)}{\sqrt{2\pi}} \exp[-\frac{1}{2}(x - \theta_1)^2] + \frac{P(\omega_2)}{\sqrt{2\pi}} \exp[-\frac{1}{2}(x - \theta_2)^2] \qquad (4.55)$$

and substituting μ instead of θ will lead to a new equation such as:

$$p(x|\mu_1, \mu_2) = \underbrace{\frac{P(\omega_1)}{3\sqrt{2\pi}} \exp[-\frac{1}{2}(x - \mu_1)^2]}_{\omega_1} + \underbrace{\frac{P(\omega_2)}{3\sqrt{2\pi}} \exp[-\frac{1}{2}(x - \mu_2)^2]}_{\omega_2} \qquad (4.56)$$

where the log-likelihood function will be:

$$l(\mu_1, \mu_2) = \sum_{k=1}^{n} \ln p(x_k|\mu_1, \mu_2) \qquad (4.57)$$

and the intension is to maximize this function.
After the case 1, the text will proceed to case 2 where μ_i, Σ_i and $P(\omega_i)$ are unknown. In here singular solutions are of no interest. This is because once the σ approaches zero, the likelihood of it will become so large that it will lead to the failure of the maximum likelihood principle. However, Duda in his book [20] suggests that

"Meaningful solution can still be obtained if we restrict our attention to the largest of the finite local maxima of the likelihood function". Thereby the local-maximum-likelihood estimates $\hat{\mu}_i, \hat{\Sigma}_i$ and $\hat{P}_i(\omega)$ can be calculated using the following formulas:

$$\hat{P}(\omega_i) = \frac{1}{n} \sum_{k=1}^{n} \hat{P}(\omega_i | x_k, \hat{\theta}) \tag{4.58}$$

$$\hat{\mu}_i = \frac{\sum_{k=1}^{n} \hat{P}(\omega_i | x_k, \hat{\theta}) x_k}{\sum_{k=1}^{n} \hat{P}(\omega_i | x_k, \hat{\theta})} \tag{4.59}$$

$$\hat{\Sigma}_i = \frac{\sum_{k=1}^{n} \hat{P}(\omega_i | x_k, \hat{\theta})(x_k - \hat{\mu}_i)(x_k - \hat{\mu}_i)^t}{\sum_{k=1}^{n} \hat{P}(\omega_i | x_k, \hat{\theta})} \tag{4.60}$$

$$\hat{P}(\omega_i | x_k, \hat{\theta}) = \frac{p(x_k | \omega_i, \hat{\theta}_i) \hat{P}(\omega_i)}{\sum_{j=1}^{c} p(x_k | \omega_j, \hat{\theta}_j) \hat{P}(\omega_j)}$$
$$= \frac{|\hat{\Sigma}_i|^{-1/2} \exp[-\frac{1}{2}(x_k - \hat{\mu}_i)^t \hat{\Sigma}_i^{-1}(x_k - \hat{\mu}_i)] \hat{P}(\omega_i)}{\sum_{j=1}^{c} |\hat{\Sigma}_j|^{-1/2} \exp[-\frac{1}{2}(x_k - \hat{\mu}_j)^t \hat{\Sigma}_j^{-1}(x_k - \hat{\mu}_j)] \hat{P}(\omega_j)} \tag{4.61}$$

4.8.5 Unsupervised Learning of Gaussian Data

A one dimensional two component combination of samples where μ, $P(\omega_1)$ and $P(\omega_2)$ are known can be related with:

$$p(x|\theta) = \underbrace{\frac{P(\omega_1)}{\sqrt{2\pi}} \exp[-\frac{1}{2}(x - \mu)^2]}_{\omega_1} + \underbrace{\frac{P(\omega_2)}{\sqrt{2\pi}} \exp[-\frac{1}{2}(x - \theta)^2]}_{\omega_2} \tag{4.62}$$

The goal is to find the mean θ of the second component. After the first observation $(x = x_1)$ the following equation will be derived:

$$p(\theta|x_1) = \alpha p(x_1|\theta) p(\theta) = \begin{cases} \alpha'\{P(\omega_1)\exp[-\frac{1}{2}(x_1 - \mu)^2] \\ +P(\omega_2)\exp[-\frac{1}{2}(x_1 - \theta)^2]\} & if \ a \leq \theta \leq b \\ 0 & otherwise \end{cases} \tag{4.63}$$

where α and α' are independent of θ. These two are normalizing constants. Once the second sample x_2, $P(\theta|x_1)$ is included, in a kind of a recursive process the formula will change into the following form:

$$p(\theta|x_1, x_2) = \beta p(x_2|\theta)p(\theta|x_1) = \begin{cases} \beta'\{P(\omega_1)P(\omega_1)\exp[-\frac{1}{2}(x_1 - \mu)^2 - \frac{1}{2}(x_2 - \mu)^2] \\ +P(\omega_1)P(\omega_2)\exp[-\frac{1}{2}(x_1 - \mu)^2 - \frac{1}{2}(x_2 - \theta)^2] \\ +P(\omega_2)P(\omega_1)\exp[-\frac{1}{2}(x_2 - \theta)^2 - \frac{1}{2}(x_1 - \mu)^2] \\ +P(\omega_2)P(\omega_2)\exp[-\frac{1}{2}(x_2 - \theta)^2 - \frac{1}{2}(x_1 - \theta)^2]\} \\ \qquad\qquad if\ a \leq \theta \leq b \\ \\ \qquad\qquad 0 \\ \qquad\qquad otherwise \end{cases}$$

(4.64)

As is clear from the recursive approach point of view, the process will require computation power and there is no easy way to simplify the process. One of the major differences between the maximum-likelihood and the Bayesian solutions is that once number of samples becomes large the priori knowledge $p(\theta)$ losses its importance.

4.8.6 Clustering Based on Density Distribution Functions

Han in his book [30] introduces an interesting clustering method: "DENsity-Based CLUstEring (DENCLUE) is a clustering method based on a set of density distribution functions. The foundation of this method consists of three main ideas:

1. Influence of each data point on its neighbors can be modeled by a function called *Influence Function*.
2. The overall influence can be modeled as the sum of the influences of all the data points.
3. The data set can be clustered by identifying the density attractors whom are the local maxima of the overall density function.

In other words, the density function is a measure of the distance between the two data points within a certain neighborhood. Han [30] also emphasizes that "the distance function should be reflexive and symmetric, such as Euclidean distance function". This distance function is implemented in *square wave influence* function:

$$f_{Square}(x,y) = \begin{cases} 0\ if\ d(x,y) > \sigma \\ 1\quad otherwise \end{cases}$$

(4.65)

A Gaussian influence function will be:

$$f_{Gauss}(x,y) = \exp(-\frac{d(x,y)^2}{2\sigma^2})$$

(4.66)

Let data set $D = \{x_1,\ldots,x_n\} \subset F^d$ to have a population of n data objects. The density function of $x \in F^d$ is defined to be the sum of influence functions of all data points within the data set.

$$f_B^D(x) = \sum_{i=1}^{n} f_B^{x_i}(x) \tag{4.67}$$

From the density function the *gradient* of the function (in simple words, direction of the change) can be determined. The density attractor can be used to calculate the local maxima of the overall density function. Han [30] says "A point x is said to be density attracted to a density attractor x^* if there exits a set of points $x_0, x_1, ..., x_k$ such that $x_0 = x$, $s_k = x^*$". However, it is clear that the term s_k is a mistake in the print and the correct term is x_k. The density attractor x^* is the center of the cluster. Han indicates "For a continuous and differentiable influence function, a hill climbing algorithm guided by the gradient can be used to determine the density attractor of a set of data points". Han has also presented a number of sample drawings for the density functions for 2D data set in his book [30], that are very interesting.

4.8.7 Clustering in Anomaly Detection

As mentioned in Section 4.1, unsupervised techniques do not require training data. Instead, this approach is based on two basic assumptions [48]. First, it assumes that the majority of the network connections represent normal traffic and that only a very small percentage of the traffic is malicious [60]. Second, it is expected that malicious traffic is statistically different from normal traffic [38]. Based on these two assumptions, data instances that build groups of similar instances and appear very frequently are supposed to represent normal traffic, while instances that appear infrequently and are significantly different from the majority of the instances are considered to be suspicious.

As one of the most popular clustering algorithms, K-Means has been widly evaluated in the area of anomaly detection. For example, Zhong et al. have compared its performance against three other centroid-based clustering algorithms using the KDD Cup 99 data set [74]. Their results show that the algorithm is very fast and that it scales linearly with the number of clusters k. Concerning the quality of the constructed clusters the authors report achieved attack detection rates of about 72% in combination with false alarm rates of about 4.5%. However, their results show also a general problem of the K-Means algorithm namely its dependence the predefined number of clusters k. While for some values of k the algorithm is able to construct accurate clusters resulting with a high detection rate, for other values of k the achieved detection rates are not very satisfying. Similar results have been reported by Zanero and Savaresi [73]. In addition they observed problems with the random initialization of the cluster centroids making the quality of the final results unpredictable since the algorithm seem to converge rapidly to a local minimum in the distribution of the centroids.

In particular the requirement or the K-Means algorithm to predefine the number of clusters k makes it less suitable for the anomaly detection scenario. Here, the number of clusters is usually not known in advance and it would require additional network security domain knowledge in order to be able to determine a meaning-ful value for k. Another drawback of K-Means is the possible generation of empty clusters containing no data vectors at all.

A variant of the k-means algorithm, the Y-means algorithm, has been proposed by Guan et al. [28]. Y-Means performs additional steps in order to ensure that no empty clusters are generated and that the number of generated clusters is appropri-ate with respect to the intrusion detection task, namely the identification of normal and intrusive data. The authors showed experimentally that Y-Means was able to de-termine a meaningful number of clusters leading to better detection rates compared with a slightly modified version of K-Means (called H-Means$^+$) that only avoids the generation of empty clusters. They report an average detection rate of 86.63% in combination with a false alarm rate of 1.53% on the KDD Cup 99 data set.

Besides the more popular general-purpose clustering algorithms, many researchers have focused on specifically designed approaches for network anomaly detection. Some clustering techniques employ the popular Expectation Maximization (EM) algorithm. An example of such an algorithm called Mixture-Of-Spherical Gaussian (MOSG) has been evaluated against other clustering algorithms in [74]. In both rel-evant properties, time complexity and quality of clustering results, the algorithm achieved only average results. It was faster than Neural-Gas but significantly slower than K-Means and SOM. Moreover it was the only algorithm that scaled super-linearly in the number of clusters.

Leung and Leckie have proposed a density-based and grid-based clustering al-gorithm [48] called fpMAFIA. The algorithm has in particular been designed with respect to low time complexity in order to ensure its applicability for network in-trusion detection. Therefore, the authors also present a detailed complexity analysis of the algorithm showing that it scales linearly with the number of data instances. However, concerning the achieved detection rates when applying the algorithm to network intrusion detecting using the KDD Cup 99 data set, the algorithm shows relatively poor results. The achieved detection rates measured as integrals over the resulting ROC curves are approximately 3-12% worse than other tested algorithms.

An approach for applying Unsupervised Niche Clustering (UNC) in combination with fuzzy sets theory to network intrusion detection is described in [47]. UNC is a robust and unsupervised clustering algorithm that uses an evolutionary algorithm with a niching strategy. The major advantage of the algorithm is its ability to handle noise and to determine the number of clusters automatically. The reported detection rates of about 94-99% in combination with 2-8% false alarm rates seem to demon-strate the strength of the algorithm. Unfortunately, the authors do not report any numbers concerning the time complexity of the algorithm. Because it is known that evolutionary algorithms do not belong to the fastest algorithms we have doubts that the approach is applicable for network intrusion detection in practical scenarios.

Another approach that uses a Fuzzy approach for unsupervised clustering is pre-sented in [68]. The authors employ the Fuzzy c-Medoids (FCMdd) [43] in order indexFCMdd to cluster streams of system call, low level Kernel data (e.g. mem-ory usage) and network data. However, because the experimental evaluation was performed using a specific web server scenario, the reported results are difficult to interpret. Moreover, the results vary extremely under different parameter settings. Due to reported false positive rates of 4% up to over 50% the approach seems not to be applicable in its current form.

4.9 Signal Processing Techniques Based Models

Although machine learning techniques have achieved good results at detecting network anomalies so far, they are still faced with some major challenges, such as 1) security of machine learning techniques [53]; 2) behavioral non-similarity in the training and testing data will totally fail leaning algorithms on anomaly detection [65]; and 3) limited capability for detecting previously unknown attacks due to large number of false alerts [59]. Considered as an alternative to the traditional network anomaly detection approaches or a data preprocessing for conventional detection approaches, recently signal processing techniques have been successfully applied to the network anomaly detection due to their ability in point change detection and data transforming (e.g. using CUSUM algorithm for DDoS detection [29]).

As one the most significant signal processing techniques, The wavelet analysis technique has been widely used for network intrusion detection recently due to its inherent time-frequency property that allows splitting signals into different components at several frequencies. Some examples of typical works include literatures [8, 37, 11, 40, 64, 61, 49, 1].

In the work of Barford et al. [8], wavelet transform is applied for analyzing and characterizing the flow based traffic behaviors, in which NetFlow signals are split into different components at three ranges of frequencies. In particular, low frequency components correspond to patterns over a long period, like several days; mid frequency components capture daily variations in the flow data; high frequency components consist of short term variations. The three components are obtained through grouping corresponding wavelet coefficients into three intervals and signals are subsequently synthesizing from them. Based on different frequency components, a deviation algorithm is presented to identify anomalies by setting a threshold for the signal composed from the wavelet coefficients at different frequency levels. The evaluation results show that some forms of DoS attacks and port scans are detected within mid-band and high-band components due to their inherent anomalous alterations generated in patterns of activity. Nevertheless, low-frequency scans and other forms of DoS attacks do not generate such patterns even their behaviors are obviously anomalous.

To address some limitations of wavelet analysis based anomaly detection, such as scale sensitive during anomaly detection, high computation complexity of wavelet transformation. Chang et al. proposed a new network anomaly detection method based on wavelet packet transform, which can adjust the decomposition process adaptively, and thus improving the detection capability on the middle and high frequency anomalies that cannot otherwise be detected by multi-resolution analysis

[37]. The evaluation results with simulated attacks show that the proposed method detects the network traffic anomaly efficiently and quickly.

Some anomaly detection system prototypes based on wavelet analysis techniques have also been developed and implemented recently, such as Waveman by Huang et al. [11] and NetViewer by Kim et al. [40]. The evaluation results for Waveman with part of the 1999 DARPA intrusion detection data set and real network traffic data show that the Coiflet and Paul wavelets perform better than other wavelets in detecting most anomalies under same benchmark environment. The NetViewer is based on the idea that "by observing the traffic and correlating it to the previous normal states of traffic, it may be possible to see whether the current traffic is behaving in an anomalous manner" [40]. In their previous work [64], Kim et al. proposed a technique for traffic anomaly detection through analyzing correlation of destination IP addresses in outgoing traffic at an egress router. They hypothesize that the destination IP addresses will have a high correlation degree for a number of reasons and the changes in the correlation of outgoing addresses can be used to identify network traffic anomalies. Based on this, they apply discrete wavelet transform on the address and port number correlation data over several time scales. Any deviation from historical regular norms will alter the network administrator of the potential anomalies in the traffic.

Focusing on specific types of network attacks, wavelet analysis is used to detect DoS or DDoS attacks in [61, 49, 1]. In [61], Ramanathan presented an approach named WADeS (Wavelet based Attack Detection Signatures) for detecting DDoS attacks. Wavelet transform is applied on traffic signals and the variance of corresponding wavelet coefficients is used to estimate the attack points. In [49], Li and Lee found that aggregated traffic has strong bursty across a wide range of time scales and based on this they applied wavelet analysis to capture complex temporal correlation across multiple time scales with very low computational complexity. The energy distribution based on wavelet analysis is then used to find DDoS attack traffic since the energy distribution variance changes always cause a spike when traffic behaviors affected by DDoS attacks while normal traffic exhibits a remarkably stationary energy distribution. In [1], Dainotti et al. presented an automated system to detect volume-based anomalies in network traffic caused by DoS attacks. The system combines the traditional approaches, such as adaptive threshold and cumulative sum, with a novel approach based on the continuous wavelet transform.

Some recent works on applying network signal modeling techniques for detecting anomalies on networks are illustrated in [51, 70, 57]. Combining the wavelet approximation and system identification theory, Lu and Ghorbani propose a new network signal modeling technique for detecting network anomalies, consisting of three components, namely feature analysis, normal daily traffic modeling based on wavelet approximation and ARX, and intrusion decision.

The major goal of feature analysis is to select and extract robust network features that have the potential to discriminate anomalous behaviors from normal network activities. The following five basic metrics are used to measure the entire networks behavior: FlowCount, AverageFlowPacketCount, AverageFlowByteCount, AveragePacketSize and FlowBehavior. Based on the above five metrics, Lu and Ghorbani define a set of features to describe the traffic information for the entire network. For this purpose, they use a 15-dimensional feature vector. Table 4.1 shows the list of features.

Notation of Features	Description
f1	Number of TCP Flows per Minute
f2	Number of UDP Flows per Minute
f3	Number of ICMP Flows per Minute
f4	Average Number of TCP Packets per Flow over 1 Minute
f5	Average Number of UDP Packets per Flow over 1 Minute
f6	Average Number of ICMP Packets per Flow over 1 Minute
f7	Average Number of Bytes per TCP Flow over 1 Minute
f8	Average Number of Bytes per UDP Flow over 1 Minute
f9	Average Number of Bytes per ICMP Flow over 1 Minute
f10	Average Number of Bytes per TCP Packet over 1 Minute
f11	Average Number of Bytes per UDP Packet over 1 Minute
f12	Average Number of Bytes per ICMP Packet over 1 Minute
f13	Ratio of Number of flows to Bytes per Packet (TCP) over 1 Minute
f14	Ratio of Number of flows to Bytes per Packet (UDP) over 1 Minute
f15	Ratio of Number of flows to Bytes per Packet (ICMP) over 1 Minute

Table 4.1 List of features

The Fourier transform is well suited only to the study of stationary signals in which all frequencies are assumed to exist at all times and it is not sufficient to detect compact patterns. In order to address this issue, the Short Term Fourier Transform (STFT) was proposed, in which the Fourier analysis has been localized by taking into account a sliding window. The major limitation of STFT is that it can either give a good frequency resolution or a good time resolution (depending upon the window width). In order to have a coherence time proportional to the period, Wavelet transform has been proposed that can achieve good frequency resolution at low frequencies and good time resolution at high frequencies.

In [51], Lu and Ghorbani use the Discrete Wavelet Transform (DWT) since the network signals we consider have a cut-off frequency. DWT is a multi-stage algorithm that uses two basis functions called wavelet function $\psi(t)$ and scaling function $\phi(t)$ to dilate and shift signals. The two functions are then applied to transform input signals into a set of approximation coefficients and detail coefficients by which the input signal X can be reconstructed.

System identification deals with the problem of identifying mathematical models of dynamical systems by using observed data from the system. In a dynamical system, its output depends both on its input as well as on its previous outputs. As well known, ARX model is widely used for system identification. Let $x(t)$ represent the regressor or predictor input and $y(t)$ denote the output generated by the system we are trying to model. Then ARX [p,q,r] can be represented by a linear difference equation 4.68:

$$y(t) = \sum_{i=1}^{p} a_i y(t-i) + \sum_{i=r}^{q} b_i x(t-i) + e(t), \qquad (4.68)$$

where a_i and b_i are the model parameters. Given an ARX model with parameters θ, we have the equation 4.69: to predict the value of next output:

$$y(t|\theta) = \sum_{i=1}^{p} a_i y(t-i) + \sum_{i=r}^{q} b_i x(t-i), \qquad (4.69)$$

and the prediction error is given by:

$$\xi(t) = y(t) - y(t|\theta), \qquad (4.70)$$

The purpose for deciding a particular set of values of parameters from given parametric space is to minimize the prediction error. The least-square estimate technique is usually used to obtain the optimal value of parameters θ.

Modeling the normal network traffic consists of two phases, namely wavelet decomposition/reconstruction and generation of auto regressive model. Generally, the implementation of wavelet transform is based on filter bank or pyramidal algorithm. In practical implementation, signals are passed through a low pass filter (H) and a high pass filter (G) at each stage. After the low level details have been filtered out, the rest of coefficients represent a high level summary of signal behaviors. During the wavelet decomposition/reconstruction process, the original signals are transformed into a set of wavelet approximation coefficients that represent an approximate summary of the signal, since details have been removed during filtering.

Next, in order to estimate ARX parameters and generate ARX prediction model, Lu and Ghorbani use the wavelet coefficients from one part of training data as inputs and wavelet coefficients from the other part of training data as the model fitting data. The ARX fitting process is used to estimate the optimal parameters based on least square errors. After the prediction model for the normal network traffic is obtained, it can be used to identify anomalous signals from normal ones. When the input to the model includes only normal traffic, its output, called residuals, will be close to 0, which means the predicted value generated by the model is close to the actual input normal behaviors. Otherwise, when the input to the model includes normal traffic and anomalous traffic, the residuals will include a lot of peaks where anomalies occur. In this case, residuals are considered as a sort of mathematical transformation which tries to zeroize normal network data and amplify the anomalous data. The whole procedure for modeling the normal network traffic is illustrated in Figure 4.8.

The higher the value of residuals, the more anomalous the flow is. As a result, in order to identify the peaks (or outliers) of residuals, an outlier detection algorithm based on Gaussian Mixture Model (GMM) is implemented and intrusion decisions are made based on the results of the outlier detection algorithm. In pattern recognition, it was established that Gaussian mixture distribution could approximate any distribution up to arbitrary accuracy, as long as a sufficient number of components are used, and thus the unknown probability density function can be expressed as a

Fig. 4.8 Procedure for modeling normal network traffic

weighted finite sum of Gaussian with different parameters and mixing proportions. Given a random variable x, its probability density function p(x) can be represented as a weighted sum of components:

$$p(x) = \sum_{i=1}^{k} a_i f_i(x, \mu_i, v_i), \tag{4.71}$$

where k is the number of mixture components; a_i ($1 \leq i \leq k$) stand for the mixing proportions, whose sum is always equal to 1. $f_i(x, \mu_i, v_i)$ refers to the component density function, in which μ_i stands for the mean of variable x and v_i is the variance of x. The density function can be a multivariate Gaussian or a univariate Gaussian.

Expectation-Maximization (EM) algorithm has been suggested as an effective algorithm to estimate the parameters of GMM. The outlier detection algorithm is based on the posterior probability generated by EM algorithm. The posterior probability describes the likelihood that the data pattern approximates to a specified Gaussian component. The greater the posterior probability for a data pattern belonging to a specified Gaussian component, the higher the approximation is. As a result, data are assigned to the corresponding Gaussian components according to their posterior probabilities. However, in some cases there are some data patterns whose posterior probability of belonging to any component of GMM is very low or close to zero. These data are naturally seen as the outliers or noisy data. The detailed outlier detection algorithm is illustrated in Table 4.2.

Function: GMM Outlier Detection (data set and k) **returns** outlier data
Inputs: *data set, such as the residuals and the estimated number of components k*
Initialization: $j = 0$; *initial parameters aij, uij, vij, $1 \leq i \leq k$, are randomly generated;*
calculate the initial log-likelihood L_j;
Repeat:
If *(aij outlierthres)* **then** emph*compute posterior probability $pj(i|x_n)$* else $pj(i|xn) = 0$; $j = j + 1$;
re-estimate aij, uij, vij by using $p_j - 1(i|x_n)$;
calculate the current log-likelihood L_j;
Until: $|L_j - L_j - 1| < th1$ *or* $j > th2$
If $(p_j - 1(i|x_n) = 0)$, $1 \leq i \leq k$ and $1 \leq n \leq N$ **then** x_n is outlier
Return x_n;

Table 4.2 The proposed outlier detection algorithm

Thresholds *th1* and *th2* correspond to the termination conditions associated with the outlier detection algorithm: *th1* measures of the absolute precision required by the algorithm and *th2* is the maximum number of iterations of our algorithm. Threshold $outlier_t hres$ refers to the minimum mixing proportion. Once the mixing proportion corresponding to one specified Gaussian component is below $outlier_t hres$, the posterior probability of the data pattern belonging to this Gaussian component will be set to 0.

The intrusion decision strategy is based on the outcome of outlier detection: if no outlier data are detected, the network flows are normal; otherwise, the network flows represented by this outlier is reported as the intrusion.

Evaluation results with the 1999 DARPA intrusion detection data set show that the proposed signal processing based anomaly detection approach achieves high detection rates in terms of both attack instances and attack types. Moreover, a full day's evaluation in a real large-scale WiFi ISP network shows that five attack types are successfully detected from over 30 millions flows.

4.10 Comparative Study of Anomaly Detection Techniques

With the growing interest in intrusion detection systems among the researchers during the past decade, the evaluation of these systems has received a great attention. However, evaluating intrusion detection systems is a difficult task due to several reasons [45]. First, capturing high-quality network data for performing the evaluation is problematic due to the privacy issues. Second, even if real life data were available, labeling network connections as normal or intrusive requires enormous amount of time for many human experts. Third, the constant change of the network traffic can not only introduces new types of intrusions but can also change the aspects of the normal behavior, thus making construction of useful benchmarks even more difficult.

Although many of the existing evaluations are not able to completely cope with the mentioned problems and provide an accurate comparison, they are still helpful to make a rough estimation about the performance of existing intrusion detection approaches.

In [22] Eskin etal. compare three outlier detection schemes including a fix-width clustering technique, K-nearest neighbor and unsupervised SVM on the KDD CUP 99 data set. Lazarevic et al. [45] report the comparative results of several distance-based (NN, KNN and Mahalanobis distance) and density-based (Local Outlier Function) outlier detection schemes as well as unsupervised SVM. In this work, the authors construct a data set from DARPA'98 for training and test, which contains their own proposed features. Zhong et al. [74] use KDD data set to compare the performance of some clustering techniques (including k-means, Mixture-of-Spherical Gaussian, Self-organizing Map and Neural-Gas) using their proposed labeling heuristic. In [24], the authors have compared four supervised learning techniques namely Naive Bayes, Gaussian Classifer, Decision Tree and Random Forest. Their experimental results show that probabilistic techniques (Naive Bayes and Gaussian Classifer) are more robust than predictive techniques (Decision Tree and

Random Forest) when trained using different training data sets. It has also been observed that probabilistic techniques show better detection rate for R2L, U2R and Probe attacks which have less training samples, while for DoS that has more samples available, the predictive techniques outperform the probabilistic techniques.

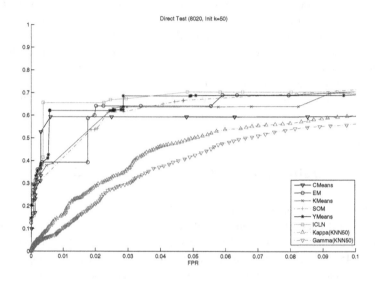

Fig. 4.9 Comparison of unsupervised intrusion detection techniques

One of the most comprehensive evaluations of the existing unsupervised intrusion detection techniques is done in [67] , in which the authors have compared 7 detection technique namely C-Means, EM, K-Means, SOM, Y-Means, SVM and Improved Competitive Learning Network (ICLN). Their observations show that: 1) all techniques perform poorly in detecting R2L attacks; 2) SVM and Y-means are clearly superior over the other techniques in detecting U2R attacks. Moreover, C-means delivers the worst results in almost all the experiments. It seems that fuzzy clustering is not suitable for distinguishing normal and abnormal data in intrusion detection. Figure 4.9 illustrates the ROC curve of the compared methods using a test set containing 80% normal traffic and 20% intrusive traffic.

References

1. A. Pescape A. Dainotti and G. Viorgio, *Wavelet-based detection of dos attacks*, Proceedings of IEEE Global Telecommunications Conference, 2006.
2. S.I. Amari, *Mathematical foundations of neurocomputing*, Proceedings of the IEEE **78** (1990), no. 9, 1443–1463.

3. M. Amini and R. Jalili, *Network-Based Intrusion Detection Using Unsupervised Adaptive Resonance Theory (ART)*, Proceedings of the 4th Conference on Engineering of Intelligent Systems (EIS), 2004.
4. B. Balajinath and SV Raghavan, *Intrusion detection through learning behavior model*, Computer Communications **24** (2001), no. 12, 1202–1212.
5. D. Barbará, J. Couto, S. Jajodia, and N. Wu, *ADAM: A testbed for exploring the use of data mining in intrusion detection*, ACM SIGMOD Record **30** (2001), no. 4, 15–24.
6. D. Barbara, S. Jajodia, N. Wu, and B. Speegle, *The ADAM project*.
7. Daniel Barbara, N. Wu, and S. Jajodia, *Detecting novel network intrusions using bayes estimators*, Proceedings of the First SIAM International Conference on Data Mining (SDM 2001) (Chicago, USA), April 2001.
8. Paul Barford, Jeffery Kline, David Plonka, and Amos Ron, *A signal analysis of network traffic anomalies*, Proceedings of the second ACM SIGCOMM Workshop on Internet measurment (Marseille, France), SIGCOMM: ACM Special Interest Group on Data Communication, ACM Press New York, NY, USA, 2002, pp. 71–82.
9. A. Bivens, C. Palagiri, R. Smith, B. Szymanski, and M. Embrechts, *Network-based intrusion detection using neural networks*, Rensselear Politechnic Institute, New York (2002).
10. Susan M. Bridges and M. Vaughn Rayford, *Fuzzy data mining and genetic algorithms applied to intrusion detection*, Proceedings of the Twenty-third National Information Systems Security Conference, National Institute of Standards and Technology, October 2000.
11. Y.-J. Shin C.-T. Huang, S. Thareja, *Wavelet-based real time detection of network traffic anomalies*, Proceedings of Workshop on Enterprise Network Security (WENS 2006), 2006.
12. G. A. Carpenter and S. Grossberg, *The ART of Adaptive Pattern Recognition by a Self-Organizing Neural Network*, Computer **21** (1988), no. 3, 77–88.
13. A. Chittur, *Model generation for an intrusion detection system using genetic algorithms*, High School Honors Thesis, Ossining High School in cooperation with Columbia University (2001).
14. M. Crosbie and E. H. Spafford, *Applying genetic programming to intrusion detection*, Proceedings of the 1995 AAAI Fall Symposium on Genetic Programming, November 1995.
15. D. Dasgupta and N.S. Majumdar, *Anomaly detection in multidimensional data using negative selection algorithm*, Proceedings of the IEEE Conference on Evolutionary Computation, 2002, pp. 1039–1044.
16. D. Dasgupta and F. Nino, *A comparison of negative and positive selection algorithms in novelpattern detection*, 2000 IEEE International Conference on Systems, Man, and Cybernetics, vol. 1, 2000, pp. 125–130.
17. J. Denker, D. Schwartz, B. Wittner, S. Solla, R. Howard, L. Jackel, and J. Hopfield, *Large automatic learning, rule extraction, and generalization*, Complex systems **1** (1987), no. 5, 877–922.
18. John E. Dickerson and Julie A. Dickerson, *Fuzzy network profiling for intrusion detection*, Proceedings of NAFIPS 19th International Conference of the North American Fuzzy Information Processing Society (Atlanta, USA), July 2000, pp. 301–306.
19. D. Dubois and H. Prade, *Fuzzy sets and probability: misunderstandings, bridges and gaps*, Second IEEE International Conference on Fuzzy Systems, 1993, pp. 1059–1068.
20. Richard O. Duda, *Pattern classifcation*, 2 ed., John Wiley and Sons, 2001.
21. John Durkin, *Expert system design & development*, Prentice Hall, 1994.
22. E. Eskin, A. Arnold, M. Prerau, L. Portnoy, and S. Stolfo, *A geometric framework for unsupervised anomaly detection*, Applications of Data Mining in Computer Security (2002), 77–101.
23. K.L. Fox, R.R. Henning, J.H. Reed, and R. Simonian, *A neural network approach towards intrusion detection*, Proceedings of the 13th National Computer Security Conference, vol. 10, 1990.
24. F. Gharibian and A.A. Ghorbani, *Comparative Study of Supervised Machine Learning Techniques for Intrusion Detection*, Fifth Annual Conference on Communication Networks and Services Research (CNSR), 2007, pp. 350–358.

25. J. Gómez, D. Dasgupta, O. Nasraoui, and F. Gonzalez, *Complete expression trees for evolving fuzzy classifier systems with genetic algorithms*, Proceedings of the North American Fuzzy Information Processing Society Conference (NAFIPS-FLINTS), 2002, pp. 469–474.
26. F. Gonzalez and D. Dasgupta, *Neuro-immune and self-organizing map approaches to anomaly detection: A comparison*, First International Conference on Artificial Immune Systems, 2002.
27. F.A. González and D. Dasgupta, *Anomaly detection using real-valued negative selection*, Genetic Programming and Evolvable Machines **4** (2003), no. 4, 383–403.
28. Y. Guan, A. Ghorbani, and N. Belacel, *Y-means: A clustering method for intrusion detection*, Proceedings of Canadian Conference on Electrical and Computer Engineering, 2003.
29. D. Zhang H. Wang and K. G. Shin, *Detecting syn flooding attacks*, Proceedings of IEEE INFOCOM 2002, 2002.
30. Jiawei Han and Micheline Kamber, *Data mining concepts and techniques*, Academic Press, San Diego, California, 2001.
31. Trevor Hastie, *The elements of statistical learning data mining inference and prediction*, Springer Series in Statistics, Springer-Verlag, Heidelberg ; New York, 2001.
32. Simon Haykin, *Neural networks a comprehensive foundation*, 2 ed., Prentice Hall, 1999.
33. R. Hecht-Nielsen, *Theory of the backpropagation neural networks*, Proceedings of the international joint conference on neural networks, 1989, pp. 593–605.
34. K. Hornik, M. Stinchcombe, and H. White, *Multilayer feedforward networks are universal approximators*, Neural networks **2** (1989), no. 5, 359–366.
35. H.H. Hosmer, *Security is fuzzy!: applying the fuzzy logic paradigm to the multipolicy paradigm*, Proceedings of the 1992-1993 workshop on New security paradigms, ACM New York, NY, USA, 1993, pp. 175–184.
36. T.S. Hwang, T.J. Lee, and Y.J. Lee, *A three-tier IDS via data mining approach*, Proceedings of the 3rd annual ACM workshop on Mining network data, ACM New York, NY, USA, 2007, pp. 1–6.
37. X. Yao J. Gao, G. Hu and Rocky K. C. Chang, *Anomaly detection of network traffic based on wavelet packet*, Proceedings of Asia-Pacific Conference on Communication, 2006.
38. H. S. Javitz and A. Vadles, *The nides statistical component: Description and justification*, Tech. Report A010, SRI International, 1993.
39. J. Kim and P.J. Bentley, *An evaluation of negative selection in an artificial immune system for network intrusion detection*, Proceedings of GECCO, 2001, pp. 1330–1337.
40. S. S. Kim and A. L. N. Reddy, *Image-Based Anomaly Detection Technique: Algorithm, Implementation and Effectiveness*, IEEE Journal on Selected Areas in Communications **24** (2006), 1942–1954.
41. Teuvo Kohonen, *Self-organizing maps*, 3 ed., Springer, 2001.
42. J.R. Koza, *Genetic programming: on the programming of computers by means of natural selection*, MIT press, 1992.
43. R. Krishnapuram, A. Joshi, O. Nasraoui, and L. Yi, *Low-complexity fuzzy relational clustering algorithms for web mining*, IEEE transactions on Fuzzy Systems **9** (2001), no. 4, 595–607.
44. K. Labib and R. Vemuri, *NSOM: A real-time network-based intrusion detection system using self-organizing maps*, Networks and Security (2002).
45. A. Lazarevic, L. Ertoz, A. Ozgur, J. Srivastava, and V. Kumar, *A comparative study of anomaly detection schemes in network intrusion detection*, Proceedings of Third SIAM Conference on Data Mining (San Francisco), May 2003.
46. Wenke Lee, Salvatore J Stolfo, and Kui W Mok, *Adaptive intrusion detection: A data mining framework*, Artificial Inteligence Review **14** (2000), no. 6, 533–567.
47. E. Leon, O. Nasraoui, and J. Gomez, *Anomaly detection based on unsupervised niche clustering with application to network intrusion detection*, Proceedings of the IEEE Conference on Evolutionary Computation (CEC), vol. 1, 2004.
48. K. Leung and C. Leckie, *Unsupervised anomaly detection in network intrusion detection using clusters*, Proceedings of the Twenty-eighth Australasian conference on Computer Science-Volume 38, 2005, pp. 333–342.
49. L. Li and G. Lee, *Ddos attack detection and wavelets*, Proceedings of 12th International Conference on Computer Communications and Networks, 2003.

50. P. Lichodzijewski, A.N. Zincir-Heywood, and M.I. Heywood, *Host-based intrusion detection using self-organizing maps*, IEEE International Joint Conference on Neural Networks, 2002, pp. 1714–1719.
51. W. Lu and A.A. Ghorbani, *Network anomaly detection based on wavelet analysis*, EURASIP Journal on Advances in Signal Processing **2009** (2009).
52. W. Lu and I. Traore, *Detecting new forms of network intrusion using genetic programming*, Computational Intelligence **20** (2004), no. 3, 475–494.
53. R. Sears-A. D. Joseph M. Barreno, B. Nelson and J. D. Tygarcan, *Can machine learning be secure?*, Proceedings of the 2006 ACM Symposium on Information, Computer and Communications Security, 2006.
54. J.B. MacQueen, *Some methods for classification and analysis of multivariate observations*, Proceedings of Fifth Berkeley Symposium on Mathematical Statistics and Probability, 1966.
55. Ludovic Me, *Gassata, a genetic algorithm as an alternative tool for security audit trails analysis*, Proceedings of the 1st International Symposium on Recent Advances in Intrusion Detection (RAID'98) (Louvain-la-Neuve, Belgium), September 1998.
56. S. Mukkamala, A. Sung, and B. Ribeiro, *Model Selection for Kernel Based Intrusion Detection Systems*, Proceedings of International Conference on Adaptive and Natural Computing Algorithms, 2005, pp. 458–461.
57. H. Nayyar and A.A. Ghorbani, *Approximate autoregressive modeling for network attack detection*, Journal of Computer Security **16** (2008), 165– 197.
58. B.V. Nguyen, *Self organizing map (som) for anomaly detection*, Tech. Report CS680, School of Electrical Engineering and Computer Science, Ohio University, 2002.
59. A. Patcha and J. M. Park, *An Overview of Anomaly Detection Techniques: Existing Solutions and Latest Technologies Trends*, Computer Networks: The International Journal of Computer and Telecommunications Networking **51** (2007), 3448–3470.
60. L. Portnoy, E. Eskin, and S.J. Stolfo, *Intrusion detection with unlabeled data using clustering*, Proceedings of ACM CSS Workshop on Data Mining Applied to Security (DMSA'01), Philadelphia, PA, 2001, pp. 76–105.
61. A. Ramanarran, *Wades: A tool for distributed denial of service attack detection*, TAMU-ECE-2002, 2002.
62. B.C. Rhodes, J.A. Mahaffey, and J.D. Cannady, *Multiple self-organizing maps for intrusion detection*, Proceedings of the 23rd national information systems security conference, 2000.
63. I. Rish, *An empirical study of the naive Bayes classifier*, IJCAI 2001 Workshop on Empirical Methods in Artificial Intelligence, 2001, pp. 41–46.
64. A. L. N. Reddy S. S. Kim and M. Vannucci, *Detecting traffic anomalies through aggregate analysis of packet header data*, Proceedings of Networking 2004, 2004.
65. M. Sabhnani and G. Serpen, *Analysis of a Computer Security Dataset: Why Machine Learning Algorithms Fail on KDD Dataset for Misuse Detection*, Intelligent Data Analysis **8** (2004), 403–415.
66. M. Sabhnani and G. Serpen, *Application of machine learning algorithms to kdd 1999 cup intrusion detection dataset within misuse detection context*, International Conference on Machine Learning, Models, Technologies and Applications Proceedings, 2004, pp. 209–215.
67. R. Sadoddin and A.A. Ghorbani, *A comparative study of unsupervised machine learning and data mining techniques for intrusion detection*, LECTURE NOTES IN COMPUTER SCIENCE **4571** (2007), 404.
68. H. Shah, J. Undercoffer, and A. Joshi, *Fuzzy clustering for intrusion detection*, Proceedings of the 12th IEEE International Conference on Fuzzy Systems, vol. 2, 2003.
69. G.M. Shepard, *The synaptic organization of the brain*, 5 ed., Oxford University Press, USA, 2003.
70. M. Tavallaee W. Lu and A.A. Ghorbani, *Detecting network anomalies using different wavelet basis functions*, Proceedings of Sixth Annual Conference on Communication Networks and Services Research, 2008.
71. P.J. Werbos, *Beyond regression: New tools for prediction and analysis in the behavioral sciences*, Ph.D. thesis, Harvard University, 1974.

72. L.A. Zadeh, *Fuzzy sets*, Information and Control **8** (1965), 338–353.
73. Zonghua Zhang and Hong Shen, *Online training of svms for real-time intrusion detection*, Proceedings of the 18th International Conference on Advanced Information Networking and Applications (AINA), vol. 1, March 2004, pp. 568–573.
74. S. Zhong, T.M. Khoshgoftaar, and N. Seliya, *Evaluating clustering techniques for network intrusion detection*, Proceedings of 10th ISSAT International Conference on Reliability and Quality Design, 2004, pp. 149–155.

Chapter 5
Architecture and Implementation

Based on the place where data source are collected and analyzed, the IDS can be classified into centralized, distributed and agent based. In this Chapter, we discuss each category in terms of its architecture and implementation.

5.1 Centralized

The first generation of IDSs is generally implemented inside the mainframe computer systems that they monitor and protect. These host-based IDSs run on the target system in order to monitor and analyze the operating system and host activities and to detect malicious activities. Due to the overhead caused by IDSs on the target system, the next generation of IDSs is proposed in which the intrusion monitoring, analysis and detection are moved from the target system to a separate system. Most of current IDSs are centralized systems. With a centralized architecture, all of the monitoring, detection, and response activities are controlled directly by a central console. Figure 5.1 illustrates a generic centralized IDS architecture.

5.2 Distributed

Different with the centralized IDS architecture , the partially distributed (i.e. hierarchical) architecture is proposed so that data collection is implemented locally in each subnet and is then reported to one or more central locations. Figure 5.2 illustrates a typical hierarchical IDS architecture, in which a subnet IDS console collects reports from local sensors and then sends reports to the higher level IDS console (e.g., enterprise-level IDS console). This higher level IDS consol might send all reported information to another higher level IDS console that manages the detection and response among a set of cooperating networks. Recent literatures have proposed some prototypes and frameworks for hierarchical IDSs, and the major techniques applied

A.A. Ghorbani et al., *Network Intrusion Detection and Prevention: Concepts and Techniques*,   115
Advances in Information Security 47, DOI 10.1007/978-0-387-88771-5_5,
© Springer Science + Business Media, LLC 2010

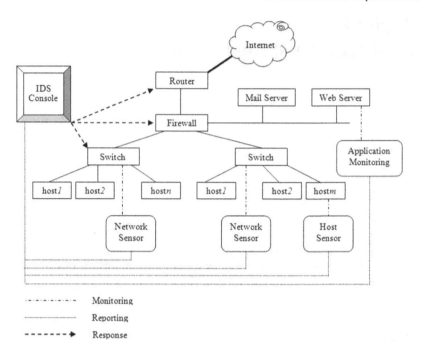

Fig. 5.1 Centralized IDS Architecture

are based on the agent technology. Agent based approach is used for hierarchical IDSs, they are also utilized for implementing fully distributed IDSs where data is collected and analyzed at a number of locations which is directly proportional to the number of monitored components [1]. Figure 5.3 shows a fully-distributed architecture.

5.2.1 Intelligent Agents

Traditional approaches to intrusion detection are centralized and have two major limitations [13], (1) existing commercial solutions to network intrusions cannot cover all possible attacks on the network accurately (i.e., they drop packets, but generate a huge number of false alarms) and (2) existing approaches are unable to respond to attacks in a timely manner. As a result, a distributed intelligent agent-based system is proposed to overcome these shortcomings of conventional systems.

Instead of applying an individual IDS to defend the network, agents offer a new approach for the implementation of IDSs in which several independent and intelligent processes cooperate in securing the network. Such an agent-based IDS framework has many advantages, consisting of the distribution of the computation cost, the reduction in the amount of information sent over the network, the platform inde-

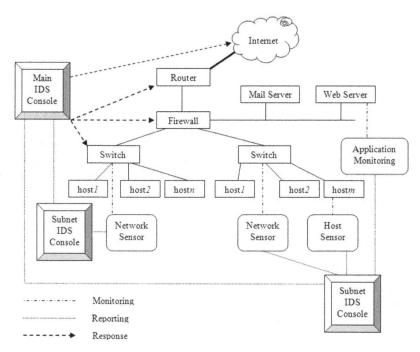

Fig. 5.2 Hierarchical IDS Architecture

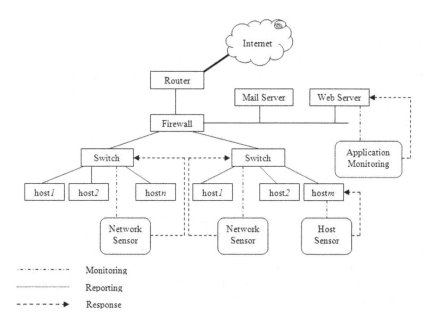

Fig. 5.3 Distributed IDS Architecture

pendence, the asynchronous operation, and the ease of updating [6]. Some other benefits using the agent-based approach are also mentioned in [18] and include efficiency, fault tolerance, extensibility, scalability, and resilience to degradation. Furthermore, the application of intelligent agents allows the complex IDS to be implemented in a highly modular manner and provides a possibility for the IDS to do an active defense instead of reporting intrusions passively.

In an agent-based system, the individual agents are designed to manage a particular task and work together to fulfill the requirements of the whole system. The main drawbacks of agent systems include the overhead of a large number of processes and the lack of viable research in understanding and addressing agents' potential security problems. In this section, we discuss some typical examples regarding the agent-based intrusion detection.

5.2.1.1 Autonomous Agents for Intrusion Detection (AAFID)

AAFID is a distributed IDS developed by the Center for Education and Research in Information Assurance and Security (CERIAS) at the Purdue University [17]. The agents in AAFID are organized in a hierarchical fashion for data collection and analysis, and there are four components included in the system architecture, namely *agents*, *filters*, *transceivers*, and *monitors*.

Filters provide a subscription-based service to agents with two main functions, namely data selection and data abstraction. Each data source has only one filter that can be subscribed by multiple agents. When an agent starts a subscription request to a filter, it specifies which records it wants based on some criteria and then the filter replies the request with records satisfying the criteria to the agent (i.e. function of data selection). On the other hand, filters implement all the system-dependent mechanisms to obtain the data requested by the agents (i.e. function of data abstraction). As a result, the same agent can be operated under different architectures by simply connecting to the appropriate filter.

A transceiver in AAFID receives findings reported by agents. Agents do not communicate directly with each other in the AAFID architecture and their operations are monitored by the transceivers on host entities. The transceiver has the ability to start, stop or send configuration commands to agents and can also perform data reduction on the data received from different agents.

The transceivers report their results to one or more monitors. Since monitors have access to network-wide data, they are able to perform higher-level intrusion detection and correlation that involves several hosts. Monitors can also be organized in a hierarchical fashion so that one monitor may in turn report to the other higher-level monitor. In case a monitor is down or fails to do operations, the transceiver can send its report to more than one monitor, thus providing the redundancy and resistance to the failure of one of the monitors.

The proposed AAFID system can be distributed over any number of hosts in a network. Each host contains a large number of agents that monitor important events occurring in the host. The monitor agent can be a very simple program to monitor a specific event, e.g. counting the number of telnet connections within last five minutes, or a complex software system, e.g. an instance of IDIOT [3] looking for a set of local intrusion patterns.

5.2.1.2 Multi-agents System-based Network Security Management Architecture

Boudaoud et al. apply Belief- Desire-Intention (BDI) agents for intrusion detection and propose an architecture called MANSMA (Multi-Agents system-based Network Security Management Architecture) consisting of two layers, namely the *Manager Layer* and the *Local Layer*. The Manager Layer is used to manage the global security of a large network; and the Local Layer is to manage the security of a domain. There are three types of agents identified in the Manager Layer, namely *Security Policy Manager Agent* (SPMA), *Extranet Manager Agent* (EMA), and *Intranet Manager Agent* (IMA). The SPMA maintains the global security policy that is determined by a human administrator. The EMA takes the control of IMAs and manages the distributed Extranet. Each IMA manages the security of a local network and is able to control specified agents. The security of a domain is managed in the Local Layer, where three types of *Local Agents* (LAs) are defined including *Extranet LA*, *Intranet LA*, and *Internet LA*. The main functions of LAs contain monitoring specified activities and sending report to the Manager Agents.

In [2], Boudaoud et al. also define three functions for each agent, namely Event Filtering, Interaction and *Deliberation. Event filtering* function filters detected security events according to the event class specified in the detection goal of the agent. The detection goal for each agent determines a set of event classes to be observed. *Interaction function* allows agents to communicate and exchange their analysis and knowledge. *Deliberation function* determines the agent's capability to built knowledge and experience and to reason according to its mental attitudes. According to Boudaoud et al., agents on each layer communicate and exchange knowledge and analysis results for detecting intrusive activities. It is still unclear on the proposed architecture regarding the protocol applied for supporting the analysis, communication, and cooperation among different agents. Even though it was claimed by the authors that the BDI solution can be used to model a security management system and corresponding agents have the deliberation function to built knowledge and experience in a rational way and to reason and extrapolate according to their mental attitudes, more details about the system's design is missed in the paper. Moreover, the description about the implementation is very brief and the illustrated case study is more like an adhoc detection instead of a systematic approach.

5.2.1.3 Hummingbird

In [4], Frincke et al. described a distributed IDS , called *Hummingbird*, in which a set of *Hummer* agents are deployed on a single host or a set of hosts for detecting intrusions. Hummers in the system communicate with each other through a manager, a subordinate, and peer relationships. During the communication, managers transmit commands to subordinates. Such commands include gather/stop for data gathering or forward/stop for data forwarding. Peers send requests to other peers for gathering, forwarding or receiving data, and other peers then decide whether to accept or reject such requests.

The Hummingbird system allows a system administrator to monitor security threats on multiple computers from one central console. The main objective of Hummingbird is to gather data about possible security problems and then re-organize them into a standard format. Different with most security tools, Hummingbird compiles data collected from multiple workstations on different networks through running a local hummer on each workstation. As a result, system administrators can react more quickly to security threats.

The biggest advantage of Hummingbird system is that it can share data with other sites and at the same time does not compromise the security and confidentiality of the system. Moreover, individual hummer agents in the Hummingbird system can be used to generate and distribute misuse reports, thus maximizing the system's modularity.

The architecture of Hummingbird system mainly consists of three parts, namely *Message Distribution Unit* (MDU), *Data Distribution Unit* (DDU) and *Data Collection Unit* (DCU). MDU communicates with other hummers; DDU decides which data should be sent to other hummers; and DCU uses data collection modules to collect data. The three components communicate with each other through a local hummer network that is implemented based on sockets. Frincke et al. deployed the system as a testbed for investigating and studying issues regarding data sharing among different sites, such as the reliability of intrusion alerts and misuse data, the safety of data sharing and the data collection associated with a quantifiable contribution to intruder identification.

5.2.1.4 Multi-agent-based IDS

In [5], Hegazy et al. propose a multi-agent IDS where they classify agents into four categories: (1) *Simple Reflex Agents*, connecting with networks and being able to collect packets moving around, (2) *Analysis Agents*, requesting the buffer (i.e., logs) from the Simple Reflex Agents (i.e. sniffing agents) and building a list of suspicious packets, (3) *Goal-based Agents*, requesting the list of suspicious packets from their complementary analysis agents for making an intrusion decision and taking necessary actions, and (4) *Utility-based Agents*, mapping the percept states into a set of numbers that measure how closely the goals are achieved. The simulation results show that the system can detect the X-mass tree attack. Although Hegazy et al. present a lot of advantages of multi-agent technology over traditional object-oriented programming, some important advantages of multi-agent systems, e.g. co-operation in a distributed domain and their intelligent and flexible behavior, have not been discussed in the paper. Moreover, the utility-based agents are missed to be described in the paper.

5.2.1.5 Adaptive Hierarchical Agent-based Intrusion Detection System

An Adaptive Hierarchical Agent-based Intrusion Detection System , called AHA! IDS, is proposed by Ragsdale et al. in [14], which is based on a fully distributed, multi-agent framework, consisting of 4 major components: (1) *Director Agents*, being responsible for detecting intrusive behavior, (2) *Surrogate Agents*, taking and covering the responsibilities of Director Agent when it fails in some cases, (3) *Manager Agents*, being responsible for detecting intrusive activities on a subset of systems for which a Director is responsible, and (4) *Tool Agents*, employed by a Manager agent to detect intrusive activity. Three types of detection adaption are provided by the AHA!IDS framework, namely adjusting the amount of system resources devoted to intrusion detection according to perceived degree of threat; invoking dynamically new combinations of low-level detection agents in response to changing circumstances; and, adjusting the confidence metric associated to the low-level Tool agents.

5.2.1.6 Fuzzy Adaptive Survivability Tools (FAST)

In [15, 16], Shajari and Ghorbani proposed an intelligent multi-agent based intrusion detection system, called Fuzzy Adaptive Survivability Tools (FAST) , in order to protect a network against the large-scale intrusions. The FAST system is based on an automated detection model and a response approach for survivability, in which different intelligent agents are used to identify normal and abnormal patterns automatically and adaptively. The anomalous network variables are identified and then are used for detecting the threat degree of known attacks and events of interest. Moreover, the FAST system is able to make decisions about events that meet the predefined criteria and site-specific policies. In FAST, fuzzy logic is used to identify the degree of suspicion of each attack and to deal with the uncertainties of response.

There are four different types of agents implemented in the FAST, namely *HCI*, *Monitor*, *Detection*, and *Decision* agents. The HCI agent provides an appropriate user interface for the control of a human operator. The Monitor agent identifies and detects anomalous network activities represented by different variables. The Detection agent inspects each flow in order to find the attack sign appeared on the network. The Decision agent, upon receiving an attack alert will initiate a task that involves selecting and executing a predefined plan that is both relevant and applicable to the event in the current context.

A general implementation architecture for the FAST system is illustrated in Figure 5.4. There are three basic components of the system, namely Sensor (S-box), Manager (MS-box) and Console Software. MS-box consists of a management box (M-box) along with its dedicated sensor.

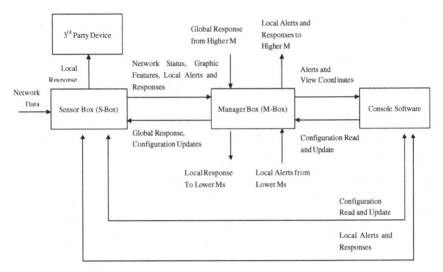

Fig. 5.4 Overall Design of the FAST System

A sensor operates at the lowest level of the system hierarchy. The sensor is responsible for monitoring network traffic, detecting malicious activities and providing appropriate local responses. Each sensor has two interfaces to the local network. The first interface connects to the mirror port of the local switch and is used for collecting network data in promiscuous mode. The second interface connects to a regular network port and is used for communication with a higher level MS-box, console, and third party devices.

The management module is responsible for managing S-boxes and MS-boxes at a lower level of hierarchy in the network. This module includes an S-box module within itself. Therefore, MS-box is capable of performing jobs related to the S-box as well as high level management of the sensors at lower level.

The management tasks of this box include correlation of the data received from the sensors as well as planning a global response according to the current condition of the network. Each MS-box will communicate with other MS-boxes at a higher hierarchical level of the network. The management modules at the higher level will control and respond to their corresponding lower level management modules in addition to the sensors that are connected to them. Management modules monitor the network and they apply a global response to their lower level sensors/managers considering the correlated information received from them and the global response received from the higher level management.

The console is the user interface for the FAST. The console software will run on a separate computer and is designed to communicate with all management and sensor modules in the network. Using the console software, the system administrator can update the configuration of S- and MS-boxes. The console software also displays different graphical and text information regarding the attacks and current status of the network.

5.2.2 Mobile Agents

Mobile agents have been commonly used to design and implement distributed applications in a dynamic environment. Recent reports show that they can be applied for the purpose of intrusion detection. Typical examples include [9] and [10]. In reality, it is not an easy task to achieve an effective detection for network intrusions when applying mobile agents. In [19], Vigna discusses the reasons why mobile agents have not been well received by the current intrusion detection research community. It was claimed in the paper that mobile agents are: (1) expensive, (2) difficult to develop, test and debug, (3) difficult to authenticate and control, and (4) vulnerable to a number of attacks coming from malicious executing environments. Moreover, they do not have a ubiquitous infrastructure and a shared language/ontology, and might be easily exploited by worm attacks. In this section, we introduce two typical mobile-agent based IDSs.

5.2.2.1 Intrusion Detection Agent system (IDA)

In [11], Asaka et al. propose and implement an intrusion detection prototype system based on mobile agents, called Intrusion Detection Agent system (IDA) . The agents in IDA collect the information related to the intrusion along the intrusion-route and then apply them to make decisions about whether an intrusion has occurred. The IDA system provides a set of functions that enable efficient information retrieval and also make it possible to detect compromised intermediate hosts.

Instead of detecting precisely all intrusions, the IDA system focuses on detecting intrusions efficiently. Therefore, the IDA monitors and inspects events that are only related to intrusions and these suspicious events are called Marks Left by Suspected Intruder (MLSI). When an MLSI gets detected, the IDA will collect and analyze corresponding information, and then make an intrusion decision. One advantage to use mobile agents in IDA is that they can autonomously migrate to target systems to collect information related to intrusions, thus eliminating the need to transfer system logs to the server. In practice, the IDA system is composed of 6 components, namely *manager*, *sensors*, *bulletin boards*, *message boards*, *tracing agents*, and *information-gathering agents*. The IDA manager resides on each network segment. The sensors are deployed on each target system and are used to monitor system logs for inspecting MLSIs. Once a MLSI is found by a sensor, it will be reported to the manager agent. The intrusion-route tracing agent traces the path of an intrusion and identifies the original point of a real attacker. During the intrusion route tracing period any intermediate node that is compromised can be detected.

In the IDA system, the manager, sensors, and tracing agents cooperate in an effective way. In particular, the sensor detects an MLSI and reports it to the manager and then the manager launches a tracing agent to the target system. The tracing agent migrates autonomously from machine to machine and traces the intrusion independently without the involvement of the manager. Although a tracing agent can migrate to any system in which IDA is installed, it cannot make any judgment about intrusions.

The mobile information-gathering agent in IDA collects information related to MLSIs from a target system. Each time a tracing agent is launched into a target system, it activates an information-gathering agent deployed in the system. Next, the information gathering agent collects information according to the MLSI type and then reports the results to the manager. Same with the tracing agent, the information gathering agent is not able to decide whether an intrusion has occurred.

The bulletin board and the message board are built for the purpose of information exchange between the tracing agents and information-gathering agents. The message board is deployed on each target system and is used by tracing agents for exchanging information. The bulletin board is installed on the manager's computer and is used not only for recording information collected by information-gathering agents on target systems, but also for integrating the information gathered about tracing routes. In IDA, the final intrusion decision is made by the manager through analyzing information gathered by the information-gathering agents. The manager agent has an interface between administrators and the system, in which it manages the mobile agents and bulletin boards, and accumulates and weighs the information entered by the mobile agents on the bulletin board. In case the weights exceed a predefined threshold, an intrusion alert will be reported.

5.2.2.2 Mobile Agents for Intrusion Detection (MAIDS)

In [7], Helmer et al. propose and implement an intrusion detection system based on distributed intelligent mobile agents. They called the system MAIDS in which data mining techniques are performed to provide global and temporal views for the entire network system. The so-called lightweight agents in MAIDS can complete their essential tasks with minimal code (cost) and can be updated or upgraded dynamically due to their smaller size. In MAIDS, data gathering agents parse system logs and activity data into a common format. The low level agents classify recent activities and then send data and current classification states to other peers or higher level agents. The higher level agents implement data mining based on the entire knowledge base and data sources on the system. Distributed data cleaning agents process data collected from log files, networks, and system activities. The mobile agents are above this layer. They focus on system calls, TCP connections, and logins. These lower-level agents form a rough opinion of intrusions and can travel to each of their associated data cleaning agents, gather recent information, and classify the data to determine whether suspicious activity is occurring. Above the layer of mobile agents is a mediation component that is connected to database and data mining and data fusion agents. Intelligent agents on this level maintain the data warehouse by combining knowledge and data from the lower layer of agents and then applying data mining algorithms to them. As a result, they offer a potential to discover associations among suspicious events that occur together with some frequency and attack patterns as well. An interface agent is located on top of the whole structure and is an analysis console in which system status reported from the low level agents are shown.

5.3 Cooperative Intrusion Detection

Distributed IDSs rely on information exchange and sharing among different sites where there is not a common administrator. As a result, an effective cooperation is required in order to detect and respond to security incidents. In [12], McConnell et al. propose some basic principles of information sharing among networks without any central administration. Such an information sharing is very helpful to identify and counter large-scale Internet attacks. Below are brief descriptions about these basic principles:

1. Local control over policy decisions by each cooperating network is important since most likely the sites do not trust each other.
2. The local network collects the information to be used in identifying the policy violations and decides whether to provide the information to other parties or not.
3. The data authenticity and integrity on different domains must be proved since the source can be compromised and may submit misleading data.
4. Hosts and networks that identify some policy violations are not responsible for the policy enforcement. Instead, the policy enforcement remains a local decision.
5. An authentication mechanism is necessary among cooperating networks.
6. A hierarchical architecture of cooperative entities is necessary. The high level manager has higher authority than low level subordinates. Information sharing on the hierarchy can be vertical (i.e. a manager in high level and its subordinate in low level) or horizontal (i.e. between two subordinates).
7. Data collection should be redundant so that the system can keep operating when one data collector is compromised or becomes unavailable.
8. Data reduction is necessary when collecting data in order to avoid high volume data exchange among cooperating partners.
9. Data sanitization is required to avoid possible security risks to the transmitting network caused by the sharing of critical host and network specific attributes.
10. In a cooperating framework with a large number of cooperating networks, the data volume is huge and as a result, the data visualization tools are required for the human system/network administrator to analyze the data in a timely manner.

In [8], Huang et al. address the problem of large-scale distributed intrusion detection and propose a cooperative IDS based on the goal-tree representation of attack strategies. A high level information exchange and work coordination mechanism is implemented among different IDSs. The basic idea behind the system is that the cooperation of remote IDSs is driven by a common goal for identifying an intruder's attack strategies and intentions. Intrusion intentions are seen as high-level platform-independent attack strategies and the IDSs can recognize attacks at the strategic level through the intention analysis. In the paper, the goal-tree is presented to formalize intrusion intentions, in which the root node represents the final target of an intrusion and the lower level nodes represent ordered sub-goals. Such as augmented goal-tree includes three basic constructs namely OR, AND, and ordered AND. Global agent performs intention analysis and local IDSs search for more evidences that match the sub-goals of the intention and trends predicated by a global agent. Although the idea in the paper is interesting the authors do not provide any formalization, architecture, implementation or evaluation to validate their proposal. Moreover, some important issues such as the trust relationship among remote IDSs and the architecture and location of the global IDS agent, are missed in the paper.

The cooperative strategy for intrusion detection is also used to discover the connection chain of an intrusion [20]. In practice, network based attackers seldom attack directly from their own computers. Instead, they prefer to start the attacks through a set of intermediate stepping stones to hide their identity and origin. Therefore, in order to identify real attackers behind stepping stones, IDSs must be able to trace through the stepping stones and reconstruct the correct intrusion connection chain [20].

In the cooperative IDS, the secure communication protocol between agents is very important since the whole IDS might be simply broken down by a compromised agent. In [21], Xue et al. propose a multi-agent system for distributed intrusion detection in which different types of agents communicate with each other through a public-key encryption algorithm used to encrypt all the communication and passwords in the system.

References

1. S. Axelsson, *Intrusion detection systems: A survey and taxonomy*, Tech. Report 99-15, Chalmers University of Technology, Department of Computer Engineering, 2000.
2. Karima Boudaoud and Zahia Guessoum, *A multi-agents system for network security management*, Telecommunication Network Intelligence, IFIP TC6 WG6.7 Sixth International Conference on Intelligence in Networks (SMARTNET 2000) (Vienna, Austria) (Harmen R. van As, ed.), IFIP Conference Proceedings, vol. 178, Kluwer, September 2000, pp. 172–189.
3. M. Crosbie, B. Dole, T. Ellis, I. Krsul, and E. Spafford, *Idiot - users guide, technical report*, Tech. Report TR-96-050, Purdue University, COAST Laboratory, September 1996.
4. D. Frincke, D. Tobin, J. McConnell, J. Marconi, and D. Polla, *A framework for cooperative intrusion detection*, Proceedings of the 21st National Information Systems Security Conference (Arlington, VA), October 1998, pp. 361–373.
5. I.M. Hegazy, T. Al-Arif, Z.T. Fayed, and H.M. Faheem, *A multi-agent based system for intrusion detection*, IEEE Potentials **22** (2003), no. 4, 28–31.
6. G. Helmer, *Intelligent multi-agent system for intrusion detection and countermeasures*, Ph.D. thesis, Iowa State University, Computer Science Department, Ames, IA, 2000.
7. G. Helmer, J.S.K. Wong, V. Honavar, L. Miller, and Y. Wang, *Lightweight agents for intrusion detection*, The Journal of Systems & Software **67** (2003), no. 2, 109–122.
8. M.Y. Huang, R.J. Jasper, and T.M. Wicks, *Large scale distributed intrusion detection framework based on attack strategy analysis*, COMPUT. NETWORKS **31** (1999), no. 23, 2465–2475.

9. W. Jansen, P. Mell, T. Karygiannis, and D. Marks, *Applying mobile agents to intrusion detection and response*, Tech. Report NIST Interim Report (IR) 6416, National Institute of Standards and Technology, Computer Security Division, October 1999.

10. _____, *Mobile agents in intrusion detection and response*, 12th Annual Canadian Information Technology Security Symposium (Ottowa, Canada), 2000.

11. A. Taguchi M. Asaka, S. Okazawa and S. Goto, *A method of tracing intruders by use of mobile agent*, Proceedings of the 9th Annual Internetworking Conference (INET) (San Jose, California), 1999.

12. J. McConnell, D. Frincke, D. Tobin, J. Marconi, and D.Polla, *A framework for cooperative intrusion detection*, Proceedings of the 21st National Information Systems Security Conference (NISSC), October 1998, pp. 361–373.

13. X. Qin, W. Lee, L. Lewis, and JBD Cabrera, *Integrating intrusion detection and network management*, IEEE/IFIP Network Operations and Management Symposium (NOMS), 2002, pp. 329–344.

14. D.J. Ragsdale, C.A. Jr. Carver, J.W. Humphries, and U.W. Pooch, *Adaptation techniques for intrusion detection and intrusion response systems*, Proceedings of the 2000 IEEE International Conference on Systems, Man, and Cybernetics (Nashville, TN USA), vol. 4, 2000, pp. 2344–2349.

15. M. Shajari and A. Ghorbani, *Using fuzzy logic to manage false alarms in intrusion detection*, Proceedings of the 18th International Conference on Information Security (SEC), 2003, pp. 241–252.

16. M. Shajari and A. A. Ghorbani, *Application of Belief-Desire-Intention agents in intrusion detection and response*, Proceedings of Privacy, Security, Trust(PST04) Conference, 2004.

17. Eugene H. Spafford and Diego Zamboni, *Intrusion detection using autonomous agents*, Computer Networks **34** (2000), no. 4, 547–570.

18. A. Sundaram, *An introduction to intrusion detection*, Crossroads **2** (1996), no. 4, 3–7.

19. G. Vigna, *Mobile agents: Ten reasons for failure*, 2004 IEEE International Conference on Mobile Data Management, 2004. Proceedings, 2004, pp. 298–299.

20. X. Wang, *The loop fallacy and serialization in tracing intrusion connections through stepping stones*, Proceedings of ACM Symposium on Applied Computing (SAC), March 2004.

21. Q. Xue, J. Sun, and Z. Wei, *TJIDS: an intrusion detection architecture for distributed network*, IEEE CCECE Canadian Conference on Electrical and Computer Engineering, vol. 2, 2003.

Chapter 6
Alert Management and Correlation

Alert management includes functions to cluster, merge and correlate alerts. The clustering and merging functions recognize alerts that correspond to the same occurrence of an attack and create a new alert that merges data contained in these various alerts. The correlation function can relate different alerts to build a big picture of the attack. The correlated alerts can also be used for cooperative intrusion detection and tracing an attack to its source.

6.1 Data Fusion

Data Fusion is the process of collecting information from multiple and possibly heterogeneous sources and combining them in order to get a more descriptive, intuitive and meaningful result[40]. According to Bass [2], the output of fusion-based IDSs are estimates of current security situation including the identity of a threat source, the malicious activity, attack rate and an assessment of the potential severity of the projected target.

Siaterlis et al. [40] propose the use of Dempster-Shafer's Theory of Evidence (D-S theory for short) as the underlying data fusion model for creating a DDoS detection engine. The engine takes into account knowledge gathered from totally heterogeneous information sources. The prototype reported in this paper consists of two sensors: a Snort preprocessor-plug in and a SNMP data collector. The D-S inference engine fuses the knowledge collected from the reports of various sensors, in order to infer the state of the monitored network. Sensors try to leverage on what network operators empirically know as signs of flooding attacks. The implementation is evaluated against a UDP flooding attack in an academic research network.

D-S theory can be considered as extension of Bayesian inference [40], but it differs from the Bayesian inference in that it allows the explicit representation of ignorance and combination of evidence. Therefore, D-S theory is more suitable for complex systems whose states are hard to be modeled. In addition to the DDOS detection engine proposed by Siaterlis et al.[40], the "intrusion early warning model"

A.A. Ghorbani et al., *Network Intrusion Detection and Prevention: Concepts and Techniques*,   129
Advances in Information Security 47, DOI 10.1007/978-0-387-88771-5_6,
© Springer Science + Business Media, LLC 2010

proposed by Zhai et al. [22], and the distributed intrusion detection system proposed by Wang et al.[53] are other two examples in which the D-S theory has been used for data fusion in intrusion detection. The mathematical framework of D-S theory is as follows:=

- **Frame of discernment (FOD)** is a set Θ that consists of all possible, mutually exclusive system states $\theta_1, \theta_2, \ldots \theta_n \in \Theta$. A hypothesis H_i is a subset of Θ, denoted by 2^{Θ}.
- **Basic Probability Assignment (bpa)** is a mass function m which computes belief in hypothesis,

$$m : 2^{\Theta} \longrightarrow [0,1]$$

$$m(\emptyset) = 0, m(H) \geq 0, \sum_{H \subseteq \Theta} m(H) = 1$$

- **Belief Function** is defined as function $Bel : 2^{\Theta} \to [0,1]$, which describes the belief in a hypothesis H:

$$Bel(H) = \sum_{B \subseteq H} m(B)$$

- **Plausibility** represents the degree of reliability of a hypothesis, accordingly, the plausibility function is defined as:

$$Pl : 2^{\Theta} \to [0,1]$$

$$Pl(H) = \sum_{B \cap H \neq \emptyset} m(B)$$

The relationship between Bel and Pl can be expressed as follows:

$$Pl(H) = 1 - Bel(\overline{H})$$

Where $\overline{H}$ is the complement of H. $Bel(\overline{H})$ indicates the degree of doubt for hypothesis H.

- **Rule of Combination** in D-S theory defines a rule to combine independent evidences in order to obtain a new belief in a hypothesis.

$$m_{12}(H) = \frac{\sum_{B \cap C = H} m_1(B) m_2(C)}{\sum_{B \cap C \neq \emptyset} m_1(B) m_2(C)}$$

Defining FOD is the first important step when using D-S theory for intrusion detection, it is actually classifying the attacks [53, 22]. For example, {*Probe, DDOS, Worm, R2L,unknown*} and {*Normal, SYN-flood, UDP-flood, ICMP-flood*} [40] are two different attack classifications for FOD. The assignments of basic probabilities depend on the evidences that are available. The evidences are results of our observations for information provide by INFOSEC devices such as IDSs and SNMP collectors[22, 40]. Consequently, the final states of the system are then estimated based on the evidences to support the decision making.

Fuzzy Cognitive Map (FCM) is another technique that can be applied to the data fusion. Siraj et al. [41] describe a decision engine for the Intelligent Intrusion Detection System (IIDS) that uses multi-sensor data fusion using fuzzy rule-bases and FCMs. The system is host-based and uses a rule-based detection mechanism for misuse detection. The output of misuse detection module could be fuzzy (e.g., *number of failed login*) or crisp (e.g., *SYNflooding attack*). The next step of misuse inference in IIDS is dedicated to computing the level of alert for each host by combining the individual suspicious alerts. A FCM (designed based on expert knowledge) is used to combine evidences of malicious activities to generate user and host alerts.

6.2 Alert Correlation

Since the Intrusion Detection Systems (IDS) increasingly deployed in the network, they could generate overwhelming number of alerts with true alerts mixed with false ones. Most of these alerts are raised independently [33], hence, it is very hard for network administrator or intrusion response system to understand the real security situation of the protected network. It would be even harder for them to respond to the intrusions. Consequently, alert correlation has become a critical process in intrusion detection and response.

Alert correlation is defined as a process that contains multiple components with the purpose of analyzing alert and providing high-level insight view on the security state of the network under surveillance. The components involved in an alert correlation process are different for various correlation approaches. The following table gives three related works that use different components for alert correlation.

Table 6.1 Alert Correlation Process

[28]	[8]	[37]
Data Aggregation	Alert-based Management	Alert aggregation
Data Reduction	Alert Clustering	Alert Clustering
Data Correlation	Alert Merging	Alert prioritization
Data Induction	Alert Correlation	Alert time Series Formulation
	Intention Recognition	Alert Correlation
		Scenario Construction

A recent work by Valeur et al.[48] provides a more comprehensive model for alert correlation. It consist of 10 components, namely *Normalization, Pre-Processing, Alert Fusion, Alert Verification, Thread Reconstruction, Attack Session Reconstruction, Focus Recognition, Multi-step Correlation, Impact Analysis, Prioritization.* Different approaches have varied number of components, but their processes are similar to each other. For the sake of generalization, the process can be broken into three stages based on the general data process procedure. These three stages include *Preprocess, Process (Alert Correlation Techniques)* and *PostProcess*. In the following subsections the research efforts with respect to each stage are summarized. Firstly, *Preprocess* section explains techniques that are used to normalize the alert data, eliminate redundancy and tackle the false positive problem. Then different *Alert Correlation Techniques* for attack scenario reconstruction are discussed. The high level analysis of correlated alert including prioritization and intension recognition is presented in the *postprocess* section.

6.2.1 Preprocess

The primary goal of the preprocess is to convert the alerts to a generic format and reduce the number of alerts to be correlated. False alerts also need to be handled at an early stage as they will have negative impact on the correlation result.

6.2.1.1 Date Normalization

The alerts generated by different IDSs (possibly heterogenous IDSs) are normally represented in different format. In order for other components to understand these alerts, they have to be translated into a standard format. The Intrusion Detection Message Exchange Format (IDMEF)[20] drafted by the IETF Intrusion Detection Working Group (IDWG) is a standard format for intrusion alerts. By its definition, IDMEF "defines data formats and exchange procedures for sharing information of interest to intrusion detection and response systems, and to the management systems which may need to interact with them" [20]. It has been used in many research works[37, 28, 6, 4] that are related to alert correlation. Figure 6.1 shows a simplified version of IDMEF model.

There are two types of IDMEF messages, namely, *Heartbeat* and *Alert*. A *Heartbeat* message is sent by an analyzer in a regular period indicating that it is up and running. An *Alert* message is composed of nine aggregate classes, these aggregate classes are briefly described in the following:

- **Analyzer:** Identification information for the analyzer that generated the alert.
- **CreateTime:** The time when the alert was generated.
- **DetectTime:** The time when the event(s) leading up to the alert was detected. This could be different from the CreateTime in some circumstances.
- **AnalyzerTime:** Current time on the analyzer.
- **Source:** The source that triggers the alert. It is also composed of four aggregate classes, namely, Node, User, Process and Service.
- **Target:** The target of the alert. It has same aggregate classes as *Source* has with one additional class named FileList.
- **Classification:** Information that describes the alert.
- **Assessment:** Information about the impact of the event, actions in response to it, and confidence in valuation; and
- **AdditionalData:** Additional information that does not fit into the data model.

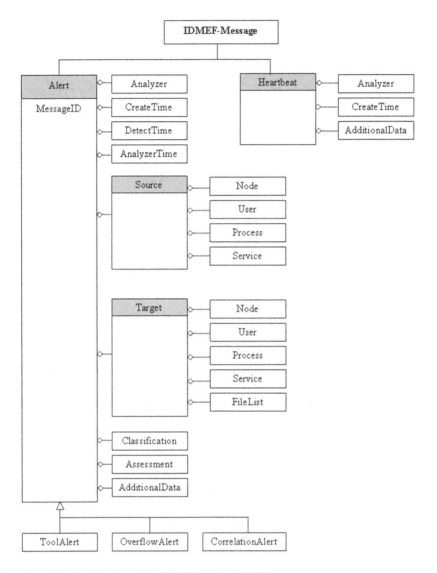

Fig. 6.1 A Simplfied Version of the IDMEF Model v1.2 [20]

The alert class has one attributes named *MessageId*, which is used to uniquely identify itself. There are three subclass of *Alert* class, and each one is used for specific purpose. *ToolAlert* class specifies the attacking tool used by the attacker. *Over-
flowAlert* class contains the information about buffer overflow attacks such as the
size of the contents in the buffer and the content itself. Finally, *CorrelationAlert*
class provides a means to group alerts together.

An IDMEF messages represented in the XML DTD [20] is as follows:

```
<!ENTITY % attlist.idmef                      ''
   version              CDATA        #FIXED    '1.0'
  ''>
<!ELEMENT IDMEF-Message                       (
   (Alert | Heartbeat)*
  )>
<!ATTLIST IDMEF-Message
   %attlist.idmef;
  >
```

and an IDMEF *Alert* is represented as:

```
<!ELEMENT Alert                       (
    Analyzer, CreateTime, DetectTime?, AnalyzerTime?,
  Source*, Target*, Classification, Assessment?, (ToolAlert
    | OverflowAlert | CorrelationAlert)?, AdditionalData*
   )>
<!ATTLIST Alert
   messageid            CDATA                 '0'
  >
```

In a distributed environment with heterogenous IDSs, specifying a common alert format is fundamental for providing interpretability among IDSs, moreover, high level analysis such as alert correlation also requires that the alerts that are processed to be in a generic format.

6.2.1.2 Data Reduction

One of the issues with deploying multiple IDSs is that they might generate large number of alerts, which many of them are redundant alerts and false positives. Therefore, data reduction is a critical process to reduce the number of alerts without losing important information.

Alert Aggregation

With multiple IDSs deployed in the network, not only one single attack might trigger multiple alerts from different IDSs, but also a single IDS can generate lots of duplicate alerts (e.g., port scans). So the purpose of using alert aggregation is to reduce the redundancy of alerts by grouping duplicate alerts and making them a single one. Alerts are considered to be aggregated in terms of their attributes. These attributes include *timestamp, source IP, target IP, port(s), user name, process name, attack class* and *sensor ID*, which are defined in IDMEF. Normally the alerts raised by different sensors with same attributes (e.g., timestamp, source IP, target IP, port(s), and attack class) can be fused together [37, 35]. *Timestamps* can be slightly different but should be close enough to fall into a predefined time windows. A similar method used by Debar and Wespi in their Aggregation and Correlation Component(ACC) [11] is called duplicate relationship. The duplicate relationship between alerts are defined in a duplicate definition file. Based on the definitions in duplicate definition file, the attributes of new alerts are compared with those of previous alerts for aggregation.

In a fairly different approach Sadoddin et al. [39, 38] have considered three general patterns to model every single-step attack:

- **Many-to-One** single-step pattern is the abstraction of a set of alerts with the same type, the same destination IP, and multiple source IPs. This general pattern is referred to as Many-to-One Hyper Alert and is represented by $A^{*>}$.
- **One-to-Many** single-step pattern, represented by $A^{*<}$, is defined similarly for a set of alerts with the same type, same source IP, and multiple destination IPs.
- **Multi-One-to-One** single-step pattern, represented by $A^{*=}$, is the abstraction of a set of alerts with the same type, the same source IP, and the same destination IP.

These general patterns have the advantage of reducing a huge number of alerts into a reasonable number of high-level patterns which are more readable by human beings. In addition, these patterns take a smaller amount of memory compared to the raw alerts.

In addition to the aggregation, alert compression [44] is another simple technique for dealing with duplicate alerts. This techniques use a Run Length Encoding (RLE) to represent a particular type of repeated alerts, that is, recurring sequence of alerts is simply replaced by RLE with a single alert and a run count.

In most cases, identifying redundant or duplicate alerts is not a difficult task, but for more complex cases, some predefined criteria are required. For example, an attacker is scanning different range of the IP addresses in a network, this will trigger multiple alerts with different ranges of target IPs, but still they should be aggregated into one alert.

Alert Filtering

Alert filtering involves filtering out low-interest alerts classes and some known false alerts. These alerts are normally predefined by administrators. To give an example, consider the alerts raised by Snort flagging that a critical file has been changed. If this is caused by *Syslog* doing garbage collecting, the corresponding alerts should be filtered out [5]. Besides, knowledge about the topology of the network is also important for identifying the low interest alerts. If the target of IIS attacks is an Apache web server [28] or the target does not even exist, the corresponding alert can be safely ignored. However, this kind of static filtering is only efficient when dealing with the known situation, and moreover, it is time-consuming. It is also impossible to identify all the low-interest alerts and set the corresponding filters. As the result, some adaptive alert filtering techniques have been proposed in order to address these problems.

The adaptive filtering technique for Syslog proposed by Chyssler et al. [5] uses learning algorithm to update Syslog filters. The idea is to train a Naive Bayesian text classifier to classify messages by checking the words that appear in alert messages. Some examples labeled as interesting or not interesting are presented to the classifier in the training process. Later on, a knowledge base is built up and becomes on-line. The alert messages will have different "score" after being classified, and only the top "scoring" messages are selected while others are filtered out. As a result, the number of alerts need to be further processed decreases. To be adaptive the filter is launched on a periodic basis or on demand, and the feedback from human experts is used to optimize the classifier.

Token Bucker Filter [45] is another type of adaptive filter that can be used to tackle the alert flood problem [44]. Unlike above-mentioned filters, token bucket filter targets alert flood attack against IDSs. A token bucket filter has two parameters, namely buffer size and token rate. Token rate is the rate at which tokens are generated, and bucket is the buffer that stores tokens. If the bucket becomes full, all extra tokens are discarded since each alert has to have a token in order to pass through the filter. The alerts without tokens are discarded as well. This normally happens when alert rate is higher than the token rate, which indicates an alert flood attack. The token bucket filter could be applied per signature, per attack type, or in more complex hierarchies to significantly reduce the number of alerts in the case of an alert flood attack. However, without further analysis on alerts themselves, token bucker filter can also produce high false negative rate.

Reducing False Alerts

In context of intrusion detection, a false positive is the result of an IDS raising alerts for legitimate activities. According to some reported works [24, 1, 17], IDSs can easily trigger thousands of alerts per day, and up to 99% of them are false positives. Therefore, identifying those false positives and dealing with them properly (e.g., filtering them out or using them for further analysis) can significantly reduce the number of alerts that need to be further processed.

False positive rate has become one of the most important evaluation criterion for intrusion detection systems. However, it is hard to significantly reduce false positives by only improving intrusion detection techniques. Therefore, some alert analysis techniques are introduced to address the problem at a higher level.

Pietraszek propose an Adaptive Learner for Alert Classification (ALAC) [34] framework to classify the alerts into true positive and false positive in real-time. One of the key features of ALAC is that it incorporates some background knowledge in its real-time machine learning techniques. The background knowledge includes:

- **Network Topology**: The structure of network, assigned IP addresses, and so on.
- **Alert Context**: Other alerts that are related to a given one.
- **Alert Semantics and Installed Software**: Alert semantics means the interpretation of an alert. Installed software normally refers to the operating system and other applications that are installed in the target system.

The alerts are represented using attribute-value format with background knowledge represented as additional attributes. The RIPPER learner is used to incrementally train the classifier with labeled examples. ALAC can operate in two modes, namely *Recommender* mode and *Agent* mode. In both modes, ALAC needs feedback from human analyst in order to update the classifier. The difference between these two modes is that, in *Agent* mode the system discards false alerts classified with high confidence and forwards random number of alerts to analyst, while in *Recommender* mode, all the alerts are forwarded to analyst for correction of misclassification.

Julisch [25] proposes a different method to address the false positive issue. Instead of identifying false alerts the author uses clustering technique to identify the root causes of the false alerts. The author shows that most of the alerts triggered by IDSs can be attributed to a small number of root causes. He also argues that we can significantly reduce by identifying the benign root causes and remove them. The root cause by its definition is the reason for which a alert is triggered. It can also be viewed as a problem that causes a component to trigger alerts. For example, a failure in the implementation of a TCP/IP stack may result in fragmentation of all outbound IP traffic and therefore triggers "fragmented IP" alerts, which are false positives. Root cause analysis is the task of identifying such root causes and the corresponding components that they affect. Continuing with the above example, if the root cause of "fragmented IP" alerts can be identified by observing these alerts, then the problem can be fixed so that it will no longer trigger false alerts. Consequently, overall number of alerts will be reduced.

Julisch proposes an alarm clustering framework to target the benign root causes [25]. The author believes that most of the false alerts are triggered by these benign root causes, so primary purpose of alarm clustering is to find large alarm clusters that are adequately modeled by so-called generalized alarms (see below for definition). This is based on the hypothesis that root causes frequently manifest themselves in these large alarm clusters. The hypothesis is plausible because of the fact that the benign root causes account for the majority of alarms and moreover, they are systematic and repetitive.

To explain the proposed alarms clustering technique, the author introduces formal definitions of some terms including *Alarm, Generalized Attribute Value, Generalized Alarm* and *Generalization Hierarchies*:

Alarms: In the proposed framework for alarm clustering, the alarms are modeled as tuples over the Cartesian product $dom(A_1) \times \cdots \times dom(A_n)$, where $A_1, \cdots, A_n$ is the set of alarm attributes such as the source IP address, destination IP address, alarm type and so on; and $dom(A_i)$ is the domain of attribute A_i that contains the possible values of attribute A_i. Alarms are stored in an alarm log and ordered by their timestamp.

Generalized Attribute Value: A subset of an attribute domain $dom(A_i), i \in 1, 2, ..., n$. For example, the generalized attribute value *Web-Server* might represent the subset of IP addresses that host Web servers. Accordingly, the extended domain $Dom(A_i)$ of attribute A_i is defined as the union of $dom(A_i)$ and the set of generalized attribute value defined for A_i).

Generalized Alarm: A generalized alarm g is a tuple in
$$[Dom(A_1) \times \cdots \times Dom(A_n)] \setminus [dom(A_1) \times \cdots \times dom(A_n)]$$
that models a set of ungeneralized alarm a:
$$\{a | \forall A_i : (a[A_i] = g[A_i] \vee a[A_i] \in g[A_i])\}$$

Generalized Hierarchies: A generalized hierarchy $,g_i$, of attribute A_i is a single root directed acyclic graph (DAG) on the elements of the extended domain $Dom(A_i)$.

Figure 6.2 gives an example showing how generalization hierarchies are defined for attributes IP address. More specifically, Figure6.2(a) shows the topology of example network. The domain of attribute IP can the represented as:

$$dom(IP) = \{p.q.r.s | p,q,r,s \in \{0,...,255\}\} \,,$$

and the extended domain of IP $Dom(IP)$ is the union of $dom(IP)$ and generalized IP addresses. The domain and extended domain of port number can be defined in a equivalent way. Figure 6.2(b) gives the corresponding generalization hierarchies of IP. It expresses the relationship between two different levels, where higher level is more general than lower one.

As mentioned above, the purpose of alarm clustering is to find large alarm clusters that are adequately modeled by generalized alarms. The adequacy is measured by a dissimilarity function $d(\cdot,\cdot)$. If the value of dissimilarity function over two alarms a_1 and a_2 returns a small value, then these two alarms are adequately similar and can be modeled by a generalization alarm. Before the dissimilarity of two alarms can be calculated the dissimilarity of the attributes which are defined for those two alarms needs to be measured. For each of these attributes $A_i, 1 = 1,...,n$, there is a corresponding generalization hierarchy G_i, and the dissimilarity $d(x_1,x_2)$ between two attribute values $x_1,x_2 \in Dom(A_i)$ is defined as the length of shortest path in G_i that connects x_1 and x_2 via a common parent p_i:

$$d(x_1,x_2) = min\{\delta(x_1,p) + \delta(x_2,p) | p \in G_i, x_1 \trianglelefteq p, x_2 \trianglelefteq p\},$$

where $\delta(\cdot,\cdot)$ is the length of shortest path between two node in G_i. For the example given in Figure6.2, $d(ip1,ip1) = 0$ and $d(ip1,ip3) = 3$ represent the dissimilarity of the corresponding two pairs of IP address, respectively. To this end, the dissimilarity of the two alarms a_1 and a_2 is defined to be the sum of the corresponding attribute dissimilarities:

$$d(a_1,a_2) = \sum_{i=1}^{n} d(a_1[A_i], a_2[A_i])$$

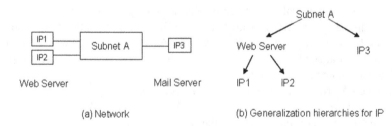

(a) Network   (b) Generalization hierarchies for IP

Fig. 6.2 Example of network and generalization hierarchies

In order to find the alarm cluster C with group of alarms that potentially share a common root cause, the heterogeneity $H(C)$ and average dissimilarity, $\overline{d}(g,C)$, are defined as follow:

$$\overline{d}(g,C) := 1/|C| \times \sum_{a \in C} d(g,a)$$

$$H(C) := min\{\overline{d}(g,C)|g \in X_{i=1}^{n}Dom(A_i), \forall a \in C : a \ll g\}$$

Let Ł be the alarm log, $min\_size \in N$ and $G_i, i = 1...n$, is the generalization hierarchy for attribute A_i. Eventually, the goal of alarm clustering is to find a set $C \subseteq$ Ł that minimizes the heterogeneity $H(C)$, subject to the constraint $|C| \geq min\_size$ holds. However, this problem is proved to be NP-complete, so a heuristic alarm-clustering method need to be developed. Julisch proposes an algorithm [25] for this problem. The output of the algorithm are generalized alarms with size greater or equal to min_size. Each of these generalized alarms represents an alarm cluster. By analyzing these alarms, root causes that account for large number of false alarms can be identified and removed. If the root causes are too expensive to remove, corresponding filters can be defined to discard false alarms.

A similar method based on *triggering events* and *common resources* can be found in [12], but this approach focuses on the alert correlation to recognize the attack scenario instead of dealing with the false positives.

6.2.2 Correlation Techniques

Generally, alerts are raised independently by IDSs but they may have some logical connections with each other. These interrelated alerts might represent attack that contains multiple stages starting form probing to compromising and escalating, or a large scale of cooperative attack. The correlation reconstructs attack scenarios from alerts reported by intrusion detection systems. Important research on alert correlation techniques are classified and described in this section.

6.2.2.1 Alert Correlation Based on Feature Similarity

This type of alert correlation approach correlates alerts based on the similarities of some selected features, such as source IP addresses, destination IP addresses, and port numbers. Alerts with higher degree of overall feature similarity will be correlated.

A good example of this technique is the probabilistic alert correlation by Alfonso Valdes and Keith Skinner [47]. Their correlation algorithm considers some matchable features as reported in a standard alert template proposed by IETF/IDWG [14]. For each of these features, a similarity function is defined. The new alert is then compared with a list of existing meta alerts based on the similarity functions. In order to determine which meta alert should be correlated with the new one, the overall weighted similarity will be calculated. If the overall similarity between new alert and the most similar meta alert is higher than a predefined minimum threshold, these two alerts will be correlated. Otherwise, the new alert becomes a new meta alert in the list.

Measuring the feature similarities is the central part of this approach. In order to obtain the overall similarity between two alerts, four metrics are considered: feature overlap, feature similarity, expectation of similarity and minimum similarity. They are briefly described as follows:

Feature Overlap: Some common features are shared by two alerts (typically new alert and meta alert). Such features include source address, target address, flag, class of attack and time information. Only the common features of two alerts will be considered to measure the similarity.

Feature Similarity: Each of the common features has a different similarity function that calculates the similarity of the particular feature. For example, the similarity between two source address can be calculated in terms of the higher bit of the IP addresses (network address), while the similarity between attack classes is obtained by consulting a incident class similarity matrix which encodes prior knowledge about this feature.

Expectation of similarity: It is used as the normalization similarity of overall similarity. it "expresses our prior expectations that the feature should match if the two alerts are related, considering the specific of each". For example, in the case of probing attack, an attacker is trying to connect to different hosts in the network, therefore, the expectation of matching target IP address is low.

Minimum Similarity: The minimum degree of similarity that must be met for certain features. It expresses the necessary but not sufficient conditions for correlation. If the similarity value of any feature is lower than the corresponding minimum similarity, the match is rejected regardless of the overall similarity.

Finally, the overall similarity of two alerts are computed using the following formula:

$$Sim(X^i, Y) = \frac{\sum_j E_j Sim(X_j^i, Y_j)}{\sum_j E_j}$$

where

- X^i: Candidate meta alert i for matching
- Y: New alert
- j: Index over the alert features
- E_j: Expectation of similarity for feature j
- X_j, Y_j: Value for feature j in alerts X and Y, respectively

The goal is to find an i such that $Sim(X^i, Y)$ is maximum. if $Sim(X^i, Y)$ is greater or equal to minimum similarity, X^i and Y will be correlated, otherwise, Y will become a new meta alert.

Other similar approaches based on the feature similarities include the work by Cuppen [6] and the work by Julisch [24]. One of the common weakness of these approaches is that they cannot fully discover the causal relationships between related alerts [31].

6.2.2.2 Alert Correlation Based on Known Scenarios

This approach correlates alerts based on the known attack scenarios. An attack scenario is either specified by an attack language such as STATL [13] or LAMDBA [9], or learned from training data sets using data mining approach [10].

STATL, proposed by Eckmann et al., is a state-transition-based attack language used by analyst to describe sequence of actions that an attacker performs to compromise the system. As an attack detection language, STATL has its own syntax and semantics, these include *Lexical Elements, Data Type, Scenario, Front Matter, State, Transition, EventSpec, NamedSigAction, CodeBlock, Timers, Assertsions* and *Annotations. State* and *Transition* are two fundamental ones. In a multistage attack scenario, a state represents the status of the attack in a particular stage. Each State has a name, and other optional elements such as annotations, assertion, and code block. A transition is a connection between two states, a transition may have annotations and code block, but must specify a type and event type to match. The event type of a transition can be specified either directly by the *EventSpec*, which define what events to match and under what condition or by the *NamedSigAction*, which is a reference to a named EventSpec. STATL uses these syntax and semantics to specify the attack scenarios, and to correlate alerts that match these predefined scenarios. Consider the example of ftp-write attack, in which an attacker creates a bogus *.rhost* file in any user's home directory using the ftp service. Having the file created, the attacker is able to open a remote session using *rlogin* service. This scenario can be described using STATL specification as follows [13].

```
use ustat; scenario ftp_write {
    int user;
    int pid;
    int inode;

    initial state s0 { }

    transition create_file (s0 -> s1)
        nonconsuming
    {
        [WRITE w] : (w.euid != 0) && (w.owner != w.ruid)
        { inode = w.inode; }
    }

    state s1 { }
    transition login (s1 -> s2)
        nonconsuming
    { [EXEC e] :
        match_name(e.objname, "login")
        {
            user = e.ruid;
            pid = e.pid;
        }
    }

    state s2 { }
    transition read_rhosts (s2-> s3)
        consuming
        {
            [READ r] : (r.pid == pid) && (r.inode == inode)
        }
```

```
state s3
{
    {
        string username;
        userid2name(user, username);
        log("remote user %s \gained local access", username);
    }
}
}
```

A corresponding transition diagram of *ftp-write* attack can be used to visualize the scenario. The objective of alert correlation with STATL language is to find a sequence of alerts that match the pre-specified scenarios.

In addition to STATL, LAMDBA [9] and CAML [4] are two other attack languages that can be used to specify attack scenarios. Instead of specifying attack scenario using states and transitions, these two languages construct the scenarios based on the precondition and post condition relationship between two alerts.

Standard data mining and machine learning techniques can also be applied to correlate alerts based on the knowledge learned from tracing examples. The work done by Dain et al.[10] is a good example of this approach. The data mining techniques they used include radial basis function (RBF), multi-layer perceptrons (MLP) and decision tree. The authors did not explain in detail about these techniques, instead, they focus on the feature selection. According to their approach, the following features were selected:

- The bucket membership of the new alert. Bucket membership refers to the category of an attack.
- The bucket membership of three most recent alerts in the scenario.
- The time between new alert and the most recent alert in the scenario.
- The maximum number of consecutive bits that are identical between the IP addresses of new alert and the most recent alert. This is used to measure the similarity of two IP address.
- A feature indicating if the most recent alert in the scenario is the exact same type as the new alert.
- A feature indicating if the target of the new alert was the target of any alert in the scenario.
- Maximum similarity of IP addresses when the new alert is compared to each alert in the scenario.
- Maximum similarity of IP addresses when the source IP of new alert is compared to source IP of each alert in the scenario.
- Maximum similarity of IP addresses when the source IP of new alert is compared to target IP of each alert in the scenario. This is used to indicate if a compromised machine is being used for further attacks.

Dain et al. used RealSecure as the IDS in their experiments. However, several problems related to RealSecure were revealed. Firstly, the source IP and destination IP of the alerts reported by RealSecure were reversed sometimes. Secondly, the alert might be sent twice with source IP and destination IP of two alerts exactly switched, which is called "echo effect". Therefore, in addition to the features described above, two other features which indicate these two situations are included.

The next step is to apply the data mining techniques to training data using these features. The data set is separated into training, validation and test data set. Data for training was manually labeled by the authors, it contained 16,250 alerts and these alerts were mapped into 89 scenarios. The decision making process of this method is similar to the above-mentioned feature-similarity correlation in a sense that it considers a new alert against each of the existing scenarios and determines if it should join one of these scenarios or not. However, the difference is that these two method use different ways to assign probabilities: the feature-similarity correlation assigns the probabilities by measuring the similarities between two alerts in terms of some similarity functions, while data mining approach assigns the probabilities using some standard data ming techniques.

A common weakness of the correlation techniques discussed in the section is that they are all restricted to known situation. In other words, the scenarios have to be pre-specified by a human expert or learned from labeled training examples. Besides, similar to those feature-similarity correlation approaches, the data mining approaches cannot explicitly show the causal relationship between the alerts.

6.2.2.3 Alert Correlation Based on Prerequisite and Consequence Relationship

This approach is based on the assumption that most alerts are not isolated, but related to different stages of attacks, with the early stages preparing for the later ones. By taking advantage of this observation, several works (e.g., [30], [43], [8]) propose to correlate alerts using prerequisites and consequences of corresponding attacks. This kind of approach requires specific knowledge about the attacks in order to identify their prerequisites and consequences. Based on this information, alerts are considered to be correlated by matching the consequences of some previous alerts and the prerequisites of later ones. For example, if *sadmind ping* attack is found to be followed by a buffer overflow attack against the corresponding sadmind service, then two alerts can be correlated as part of the same attack scenario.

Ning et al. [29] provide a good example of this approach. The basic constructs of their correlation model are the predicates that represent the prerequisites and consequences of attacks. For example, the predicate *UDPVulnerableToBOF(VictimIP, VictimPort)* is used to represent the attacker's discovery that a host with the IP address *VictimIP* is running a UDP service on *VictimPort*, and this service is vulnerable to buffer overflow attack. Logical operators can also be applied to the predicates to represent some complex conditions.

Based on the basic constructs, Ning et al. introduce the notion of *hyper-alert type*, which is used to represent the prerequisite and consequence of each type of alerts. By their definition, a hyper-alert type T is a triple with three dimensions, namely *fact, prerequisite and consequence. fact* is the set of attribute names; *prerequisite* and *consequence* are the logical combinations of predicates whose free variables are all in *fact*. For example, consider the buffer overflow attack against the sadmind remote administration tool, this can be represented using following hyper-alert type named *SadmindBufferOverflow*:

```
SadmindBufferOverflow =({VictimIP, VictimPort},
                         {ExistHost(VictimIP) & VulnerableSadmind(VictimIP)},
                         {GainRootAccess(VictimIP)})
```

where *VictimIP*, *VictimPort* is the fact contains two attributes; *ExistHost(VictimIP)* and *VulnerableSadmind(VictimIP)* are the prerequisites that must be satisfied in order to have a successful attack, and *GainRootAccess(VictimIP)* is the possible consequence if the attack proceeds successfully.

For a given hyper-alert type $T = \{fact, prerequisite, consequence\}$, a instance hyper-alert h of type T is defined as a finite set of tuples on $fact$, where each tuple is associated with an interval-based timestamp $\{begin\_time, end\_time\}$. The instantiated hyper-alerts have no free variables in prerequisites and consequences as they are replaced by specific values. Consider the previous example, an instance of hyper-alert type *SadmindBufferOverflow*, namely $h_{SadmindBOF}$ can be represented as follows:

- *fact*: $\{(VictimIP = 152.10.19.5, VictimPort = 1235), (VictimIP = 152.10.19.7, VictimPort = 1235)\}$;
- prerequisites $P(h_{SadmindBOF})$: $\{(ExistHost (152.10.19.5) \land VulnerableSadmind (152.10.19.5)), (ExistHost (152.10.19.7) \land VulnerableSadmind (152.10.19.7))\}$
- consequence $C(h_{SadmindBOF})$: $\{GainRootAccess (152.10.19.5), GainRootAccess (152.10.19.7)\}$

where $P(h_{SadmindBOF})$ and $C(h_{SadmindBOF})$ denote the sets of all predicates that appear in prerequisite and consequence of a hyper-alert $h_{SadmindBOF}$, respectively. Hence, hyper-alert h_2 can be correlated with a previous hyper-alert h_1, if there exist $p \in P(h_2)$ and $C \subseteq C(h_1)$ such that for all $c \in C, c.end\_time < p.begin\_time$ and the conjunction of all the predicates in C implies p. Hyper-alert h_1 is said to prepare for hyper-alert h_2. This idea can be explained by using the following example from Ning's work [29]:

Sadmind Ping is a probing attack which discovers possibly vulnerable sadmind services in a target system. A corresponding hyper-alert type named SadmindPing can be defined for this attack, where *SadmindPing=(VictimIP,VictimPort,ExistHost (VictimIP), VulnerableSadmind (VictimIP))*. Suppose that a hyper-alert instance $h_{SadmindPing}$ of type *SadmindPing* has following tuples:

- *fact*:$\{VictimIP = 152.10.19.5, VictimPort = 1235, VictimIP = 152.10.19.7, VictimPort = 1235\}$;
- prerequisites $P(h_{SadmindPing})$:$\{ExistHost (152.10.19.5) ExistHost(152.10.19.7)\}$
- consequence $C(h_{SadmindPing})$: $\{VulnerableSadmind (152.10.19.5), Vulnerable-Sadmind (152.10.19.7)\}$

The relationship between $h_{SadmindPing}$ and the hyper-alert $h_{SadmindBOF}$ can be evaluated by comparing the contents of $C(h_{SadmindPing})$ and $P(h_{SadmindBOF})$. Since predicate $VulnerableSadmind(152.10.19.5)$ appears in both $C(h_{SadmindPing})$ and $P(h_{SadmindBOF})$, $h_{SadmindPing}$ is said to prepare for $h_{SadmindBOF}$, and therefore it can be correlated with $h_{SadmindBOF}$.

The outcome of this alert correlation method is a set of hyper-alert correlation graphs. A hyper-alert correlation graph $HG = (N, E)$ is a connected directed acyclic graph (DAG), the nodes in the graph represent a set of hyper-alerts. The edge from node n_1 to node n_2 $(n_1, n_2 \in N)$ represents that n_1 prepares for n_2.

When intensive attacks trigger a large amount of alerts, The size of hyper-alert correlation graph that is generated by using this method can be very large. Therefore, Ning et al. propose three utilities reduce the size of the graph after the correlation. These three utilities include:

- *Adjustable graph reduction.* Reduce the number of nodes and edges while keeping the important sequence of attacks.
- *Focused analysis.* Only focus on the hyper-alerts of interest. The size of graph may be much smaller if using focus analysis.
- *Graph decomposition.* Cluster the hyper-alert correlation graphs, and decompose them into smaller graphs according to the clusters.

Some high level analysis such as strategy and intention recognition can be carried out based on the hyper-alert correlation graphs, which will be described in the section entitled Intention Recognition.

As mentioned above, LAMDBA also use precondition and postcondition paradigm, which is similar to Ning et al.'s approach, but they only used the language to specify the entire attack scenarios, which are restricted to known situation. On the contrary, JIGSAW[30] and the MIRADOR[43] are more close to the approach proposed by Ning et al., and therefore are classified into the same category. These approaches target recognition of multistage attacks and have the potential of discovering unknown attacks patterns. However, this class of approaches have one major limitation, that is, they cannot correlated unknown attacks (not attack patterns) since its prerequisites and consequences are not defined. Even for known attacks, it is difficult to define all prerequisites and all of their possible consequences.

6.2.3 Postprocess

6.2.3.1 Alert Prioritization

Intrusion detection systems often produce numerous alerts each day. Many of these alerts are related to failed attacks and false alarms caused by normal network traffic. Only a very small number of the alerts are caused by successful attacks. Even for those real alerts, not all of them are equally important in terms of their severity and criticality of the target being attacked. Therefore, it is essential to separate the few important alerts from the rest.

Porras et al. [35]proposes a comprehensive mechanism for alert prioritization and incident ranking in their "Mission-Impact" correlation model named M-Correlator [35]. In order to provide more meaningful alert representation for incident ranking, the M-Correlator includes a *Incident Handling Fact Base* to interpret alert content against the mission specification and the dependencies of an accident to the configuration of target machine. The *Incident Handling Fact Base* accordingly defines entries such as Incident Code, Incident Class, COST Codes, Description, Vulnerable OS and Hardware and Bound Ports and Applications. It provides necessary information for incident ranking calculation.

In M-Correlator model, incident ranking represents the final assessment of a security incident. It is calculated based on three factors: alert outcome, relevance and security incident priority.

Alert outcome: The possibility that the security incident has indeed happened, in other words, alert outcome represents the confidence that an INFOSEC device has correctly reported an accident. Where possible, this information is provided by corresponding INFOSEC devices when they report the incident.

Relevance: Relevance is the other important factor for assessing the likelihood of successful intrusion. M-Correlator calculates the relevant score for an alert by comparing its attributes that are defined in incident handling fact base, against the known topology of the target host, which includes following attributes:

- The type and version of the operating system.
- The type of the hardware of target host.
- The service suit that is installed on target host.
- The network services that are enabled on target host.
- The applications that are installed on target host.

The result relevance score is a value between 0 and 255. 0 indicates that the vulnerabilities required for the successful intrusion were not matched to the known topology of target host, which in turn might reduce the overall score of incident ranking. Score closer to 255 indicates the opposite situation.

Security incident priority: The security incident priority is formally defined as follows: let *Stream* be a set of incident events $\{e_1, e_2, ..., e_n\}$, the objective of prioritization is to find a set of events $HighImpact = e_{h_1}, e_{h_2}, ..., e_{h_n} \subseteq Stream$ such that $\forall Threat\_Rank(e_j, Mission) > T_{acceptable}$ with $e_j \in HighImpact$. The *Mission*, which is expressed thought mission specification, is the underlying objective for which the network assets are brought together and used. The mission specification contains two parts: the first part is the list of the most critical assets and services of the protected network, which includes critical computing assets, critical network service, sensitive data assets and important user accounts. The second part is the types of incidents that are of greatest concern to the analyst, example incident types can be PRIVILEGE_VIOLATION, PROBE, DENIAL_OF_SERVICE and so on. For a particular incident type, analyst can specify low, medium -low, medium-high, and high interest.

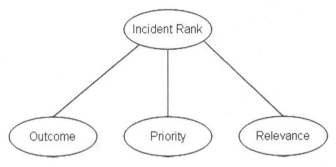

Fig. 6.3 Incident Ranking Calculation using M-Correlator [35]

The incident ranking is defined as an assessment and ranking of events $\{e_1, e_2, ..., e_n\}$ with respect to $MissionProfile = \{CR_{assets}, CR_{resources}, CR_{users}, Incident_{weight}\}$ and the *probabilityofsucess*, which is determined by alert outcome and relevance. The calculation of incident ranking is based on an adaptation of the Bayes framework for belief propagation in tree, which is described in [46]. In this framework, each node has a conditional probability table (CPT), that encodes the prior knowledge between the child node and its parent node. The likelihood for each node is propagated to the parents. Finally, the belief in hypotheses at root node is calculated in terms of the propagated belief in hypotheses and CPTs at other nodes. Consider the complete incident rank tree shown in Figure 6.3, the incident rank is calculated in terms of *Outcome, Priority* and *Relevance*. Let H_i denote the *ith* hypothesis state of the root node (normally high and low of incident rank), and $S_i, i = 1, 2, 3$ denote the hypothesis state of its *ith* child nodes. Then the incident rank $P(H_i|S_1, S_2, S_3)$ is given by:

$$P(H_i|S_1, S_2, S_3) = \frac{P(H_i)\Pi_{k=1}^{3}P(S_k|H_i)}{P(S_1, S_2, S_3)}$$

The belief in hypotheses at each of the nodes *Outcome, Priority* and *Relevance*, can be calculated in a equivalent way.

The alert priority computation model proposed by Qin et al. [37] is also based on Bayesian networks, which is similar to M-Correlator, but they used alert prioritization for scenario analysis instead of incident ranking. Another related work by Lippmann et al. [26] focuses particularly on using vulnerability information to prioritize alerts. Note that all these alert prioritization methods involve incorporating additional information about the protected network. Without using this information, alert prioritization would not be able to produce meaningful result that can be used for proper response.

6.2.3.2 Intention Recognition

Intention or plan Recognition is the process of inferring the goals of an intruder by observing his actions [18]. It is of great importance in terms of providing early warning and preventing intrusion from escalating. However, it is also a difficult task since the behavior of intruders is unpredictable, they tend to change or cover their behavior so that they can not to be identified. Knowing the strategies or plans of an intruder is essential to intention recognition. Using alert correlation, the intruders' relevant behavior can be grouped into attack scenarios, and later on, their attack strategy or plan can be extracted.

The attack scenario that contains multiple stages can be modeled as a planning process [7], meaning that the intruder must perform several actions in order to achieve his or her final goal. Alert correlation provides a means to reconstruct a typical attack scenario. The next step is to extract strategies or plans of the intruder by analyzing the correlated alerts. This requires the constraints intrinsic to attack strategy to be extracted from correlated alerts in such way that they can be applied to all instance of the same strategy [33].

Ning et al. proposed a strategy learning technique based on their alert correlation model [30]. In the proposed approach, an attack strategy is represented as a directed acyclic graph (DAG) called attack strategy graph, similar to the hyper-alert correlation graph which is constructed using correlation technique. Nodes in the attack strategy graph also represent attacks, but edges represent the temporal order of attacks with certain constraints. The graph construction based on the correlated alerts includes two steps:

- Firstly, alerts that belong to the same step of a multistep attack are aggregated into one hyper-alert. This provides more compact representation of an attack strategy.
- Secondly, constraints between the two steps are extracted and used to construct to attack strategy graph.

The constrains are conditions that must be met by the related attacks. For example, Consider the following hyper-alert types:

- *SadmindPing = ({VictimIP, VictimPort}, ExistsHost(VictimIP), {VulnerableSadmind (VictimIP)}).*
- *SadmindBufferOverflow =({VictimIP, VictimPort}, {ExistHost (VictimIP) ∧ VulnerableSadmind(VictimIP)}, {GainRootAccess (VictimIP)}).*

two corresponding attacks are related to each other as two different step in a attack scenario only if the consequences of first one satisfies the prerequisites of the second one, the equality constraint can hereby be extracted:

$$VictimIP_{SadmindPing} = VictimIP_{SadmindBufferOverflow}$$

To deal with variation of attacks, the authors use generalization techniques to hide the extrinsic difference in attack strategies. The goal is to build a generalization mapping with specific alerts mapped to corresponding alerts that are more general.

A simple example of generalization can be: Apache2, Back and Crashiis can be generalized into one WebServiceDOS because they are all Denial of Service attack against the web service. The generalization mapping can be specified manually, but it is time-consuming and error-prone [30]. To address this problem, the authors proposed an automatic generalization technique based on the similarity measurement between prerequisites and consequences of hyper-alert types. Note that the prerequisites and consequences are both represented as sets of predicates. The Jaccard similarity coefficient is used to compute the similarity of two sets of predicates:

$$Sim(S_1, S_2) = \frac{a}{a+b+c}$$

where a is the number of predicates in both S_1 and S_2, b is the number of predicates only in S_1, and c is the number of predicates only in S_2. Accordingly, the similarity between two hyper-alerts T_1 and T_2 is calculated as follows:

$$Sim(T_1, T_2) = Sim(P_1, P_2) \times w_p + Sim(C_1, C_2) \times w_c$$

where $P1$, C_1 and P_2, C_2 are prerequisites and consequences of T_1 and T_2, respectively, and w_p and w_c are weights for prerequisites and consequents, respectively. Finally, a threshold t is set, and hyper-alert types with similarity measure greater or equal to t are grouped together and are represented by a general hyper-alert type. As mentioned by the authors, this generalization technique hides unnecessary difference between different attack types. However, it may also cause the loss of important information, which will lead to an incomplete attack strategy. Therefore, properly controlling the degree of generalization is important in terms of dealing with variation of attacks while keeping the important information.

Cuppens et al. proposes a correlation model based on their previous work [8]. An extension to their previous work was made by introducing a intrusion objective model to target the recognition of malicious intention of intruders. The intrusion objective model contains two fields: objective name and set of conditions called *State_Condition*. The *State_Condition* represents the conditions that must be met in order for the intruders to achieve their attack goal. Basically, the whole process is still correlation. However, in addition to correlating alerts, the method by Cuppens et al also correlate the alerts with the objectives. Their approach is very similar to the one proposed by Ning et al. in a sense that they both use prerequisite and consequence (or, precondition and post-condition) to reconstruct the attack scenarios and treat the objectives of intruders as part of the scenarios. But Ning et. al provide more details in high level analysis such as dealing with variation of an attack, measuring the similarity of the attack strategies and so on.

Geib and Goodman also emphasize the importance of plan recognition in intrusion detection systems in their work [16]. One of the main contribution of their work is a set of requirements they place on their plan recognition system. According to the requirements, Geib and Goodman define a efficient plan recognition system as a system that is able to handle the following situation:

- **Unobserved action:** It is always possible to have attacks go unnoticed, they could be important steps in a multistage attack scenario, a successful plan recognition system must be able to infer the occurrence of actions that are not reported by IDSs.

- **Observation of state changes:** The state change that happens in a protected system provides a sign that there might be a malicious action. Plan recognition system should be able to infer that what the action was by combining information from different sources such as host-based IDSs and network-based IDSs.

- **Partially ordered plans:** The order of plan steps which an attacker follows in order to achieve the goal is rather flexible. This requires that the plan recognition system be able to recognize the different instantiation orderings created by these plans.

- **Multiple concurrent goals:** Attacks might have multiple goals after gaining certain level of privileges. Therefore, being able to identify the possible goals of an attack is crucial for a plan recognition system, especially to correctly identify the potential victims.

- **Actions used for multiple effects:** A single action of an attacker can have multiple effects. For example, the information gathered by the attacker using a scanning, can be use for multiple goals such as DOS attack, and R2L attack, it is a critical requirement for plan recognition system to be able to handle these kinds of situations.

- **Failure to observe:** When a malicious activity is identified, another malicious activity is normally expected to follow the previous one, the failure to observe that activity result in the change of our belief that the previous activity is part of ongoing attack. The plan recognition system is responsible for managing the belief and distinguishing the isolated activities and those that are part of a complex attack plan.

- **Impact of world state on adopted plans:** Attacks normally target important resource of the network, the knowledge about topology of a protected network can help attackers to make their plans. On the other hand, this knowledge can also be used by plan recognition system to recognize the attackers' plans. Taking this into consideration is an important requirement for effective plan recognition system.

- **Consideration of multiple possible hypotheses:** As mentioned above, plans carried out by the attackers can be very flexible. They can have multiple goals, a single action can have multiple effect, however, the likelihood of each of possibilities are not always the same. the ability of a plan recognition system to compute and rank the possibilities is of great importance especially for intrusion response.

6.2.4 Alert Correlation Architectures

The correlation architectures are generally agent-based. They can be further divided into two groups in terms of the locations where the alerts are correlated. One is centralized correlation, in which all the alerts are sent to one correlation center for processing, the correlation center analyzes the alerts, and presents the output to higher level response components. The other one is hierarchical correlation, where the alerts are correlated locally by correlators and sent to central correlator for global correlation.

6.2.4.1 Centralized Correlation

Carey et al. proposes a prototype for IDS interoperability [28], the alert correlation framework of their prototype contains three major compenents:

- **Alert Agent**: The each alert agent is attached to a corresponding IDS, it is responsible for translating the alert message into IDMEF format, and passing these message to a component called Control Unit.
- **Control Unit**: The Control Unit takes the IDMEF messages, preprocess them and stores them in a database.
- **Administrative Console**: This is where the correlation actually happens, here, the alerts stored in a database are centrally processed in an offline manner.

The Adaptive Agent-based Intrusion Response System (AAIRS) proposed by Carver [3] contains a similar correlation architecture. The AAIRS uses an *Interface* component for each IDS, which has a similar functionality as the Alert Agent in the framework proposed by Carry et al. above. The alert classification and correlation is done by the Master Analysis component.

6.2.4.2 Hierarchical Correlation

Qin et al. [36] propose another agent-based architecture for an IDS. The proposed architecture is designed hierarchically and divides the protection and analysis scope to *Local-analysis*, *Regional-Analysis* and *Global-Analysis*. The ID agents are deployed locally to detect intrusive behavior on the network components. An *ID Correlator* manages some local ID agents and combines the security alarms sent by local ID agents. The ID Correlator is responsible for a region and reports its findings to the *ID Manager*, which is responsible for the whole network (e.g., campus network).

The following are the main components of an ID agent:

- *Detection Module*, which uses three different engines, namely *Signature Engine*, *Profile Engine* and *MIB Engine*. Signature engine is responsible for detecting known signatures, whereas, profile engine is responsible for anomaly detection based on the normal profile of the users or the network. MIB Engine, checks the related values of the MIB objects and compares them to MIB profiles to detect the intrusions.
- *Knowledge-base*, which stores attack signatures or user/network/MIB profiles.
- *Response Module*, which launches countermeasures.

- *Control Module*, which adjusts Knowledge-base and Detection Engines based on the information it receives from the ID Correlator.
- *Alarm Engine*, which sends alarms to the ID correlator.
- *SNMP Interface*, which uses the SNMP packets to exchange information between ID agents and ID Correlator.

ID Correlator is designed to correlate alarms from the ID agents and to send them to ID Manager for global correlation. It also may take appropriate actions in response to intrusions. The main components of ID Correlator are:

- *Alarm Correlation Module*, which receives events from ID agents.
- *Security Correlation Engine*, which correlates alarms sent by the ID agents to predict and identify the intrusion purposes and trends.
- *Knowledge Database*, which stores knowledge about the network (e.g., topology) and information that is needed by the correlation algorithm.
- *Intrusion Response Module*, which launches intrusion response countermeasures based on the security policy defined for the domain.
- *Knowledge Controller*, which manages the Knowledge Database.

6.2.5 Validation of Alert Correlation Systems

Haines et al. [21] present the first experimental validation of correlation systems. They define three primary dimensions of high level reasoning that enable correlators to recognize attack and identify the target. These three dimensions represent the measurable capabilities provided by correlators, they are briefly described as follows:

Prioritization   : The ability of a correlator to weight alerts, assign priority based on the likelihood that an attack is detected, the severity of the attack and criticality of target.

Multistep Correlation   : The ability of a correlator to reconstruct a multistep attack scenario by correlating several individual attack steps. This is crucially important in terms of inferring the attack's intention and formulating effective response.

Multisensor Correlation   : The ability of a correlator to combine information from two or more sensors and to obtain an overall picture of the security status of the system.

The experimental result showed that most of the studied alert correlation models can produce satisfactory alert volume reduction as well as high level reasoning result such as multistage attack recognition. Several problems were revealed as well. The major one is the target recognition, which is crucially important when it comes to intrusion response. In addition, some correlator can not work in an online manner, all correlators produce output with different format.

As a conclusion, the authors suggested that, a hybrid type correlator with complementary correlation methods should be developed to provide more accurate and comprehensive correlation.

6.3 Cooperative Intrusion Detection

Distributed intrusion detection systems often rely upon data sharing between sites which do not have a common administrator and therefore cooperation will be required in order to detect and respond to security incidents [15].

6.3.1 Basic Principles of Information Sharing

The paper by McConnell et al. [27] discusses the principles of information sharing among networks without any central administration. Such information sharing is necessary to identify and counter large-scale Internet attacks. For example, a compromised network can be part of a multi-network attacking other systems. Several principles have been identified by the authors to be important in the development of a framework for cooperation among domains. The followings are the basic principles:

- Local control over policy decisions by each cooperating network is important, because sites are very unlikely to trust each other.
- Although networks may collect information that is necessary by the other networks to to be used in identifying the policy violations, the local network has the autonomy to decide on collecting and providing this data to other parties.
- The authenticity and the integrity of the data shared among different domains needs to be proved, because the source may be compromised and unknowingly submit misleading data.
- Hosts and networks who identify some policy violation related to other networks are not responsible for policy enforcement. The policy enforcement remains a local decision.
- An authentication mechanism is required among cooperating networks.
- There is a need for hierarchical arrangement of cooperative entities in which managers have higher authority than lower level subordinates. Information sharing would be both vertical (i.e., a manager and its subordinate) or horizontal (i.e., between two subordinates).
- Redundancy is necessary among data collectors, so that a system can continue in case one data collector is compromised or become unavailable.
- Data reduction is another important duty of a data collector, to avoid exchange of voluminous data among cooperating partners.
- Data sanitization is required to avoid sharing critical host and network specific attributes that might cause a security risk to the transmitting network.

- In a cooperating framework with a large number of cooperating networks, the volume of audit data collected is so huge that a human system/network administrator is unable to analyze them in a timely manner without the help from visualization tools.

McConnell et al. also briefly explains the HMMR protocol from Hummingbird system that is designed to address above-mentioned requirements.

6.3.2 Cooperation Based on Goal-tree Representation of Attack Strategies

Haung et al. [23], researchers at Boeing Company, address the problem of large-scale distributed intrusion detection and propose equivalence of strategic decision making and military command and control for intrusion detection. They propose a high-level information exchange, work division and coordination among Intrusion Detection Systems (IDSs). They also advocate a higher degree of autonomy for local IDS agents and cooperative global problem-solving.

Haung et al. believe that identifying an intruder's attack strategy or intention is the theme that drives remote IDSs to work together. According to the authors, intrusion intentions are high-level platform-independent attack strategies. In fact, IDSs can recognize attacks at the strategic level by intention analysis. The authors use the goal-tree to represent intrusion intention, in which the root node represents the ultimate goal of an intrusion and lower-level nodes represent ordered sub-goals. Three basic constructs, which are necessary for such an augmented goal-tree are OR, AND, and ordered AND. Global agent performs intention analysis. Similar to a battleground situation, local IDSs must search for more evidences that confirms the sub-goals of the intention and trends predicated by a global agent, upon request. For example, when a goal-tree for an intrusion is defined using an ordered AND, the intrusion is detected if sub-goals are confirmed in the temporal order that they have been defined.

A communication protocol, similar to military communication, is also proposed. Although the vision expressed in the paper is sound, the authors do not provide any formalization, architecture, implementation or evaluation to validate their proposal. Moreover, several important issues, such as the trust relationship among remote IDSs and the architecture and location of the global IDS agent, are ignored.

6.3.3 Cooperative Discovery of Intrusion Chain

Wang [49] discovers the connection chain of an intrusion in a cooperative manner. Network based intruders seldom attack directly from their own hosts, but rather stage their attacks through intermediate *stepping stones* to conceal their identity and origin. To identify attackers behind stepping stones, it is necessary to be able to trace through the stepping stones and construct the correct intrusion connection chain [49].

6.3.4 Abstraction-Based Intrusion Detection

Abstraction is important for intrusion detection in heterogeneous and distributed environments. Ning et al. [32] propose an abstraction-based intrusion detection system. They believe that abstraction not only hides the difference between heterogeneous systems, but also allows generic intrusion-detection models.

AAFID [42] also uses abstraction to hide differences in system architectures in a heterogenous environment. As we mentioned before, AAFID Filters provide a subscription-based service to agents and have two functions: data selection and data abstraction. There is only one filter per data source and multiple agents can subscribe to it. When an agent subscribes to a filter, it specifies which records it needs (using some criteria). The filter sends to the agent records that match the given criteria (data selection). Filters also implement all the system-dependent mechanisms to obtain the data that the agents need (data abstraction). Therefore, the same agent can run under different architectures simply by connecting to the appropriate filter.

6.3.5 Interest-Based Communication and Cooperation

Gopalakrishna and Spafford [19] propose an *interest-based* cooperation architecture for distributed autonomous agents that cooperate to build an intrusion detection system. In the interest-based cooperation and communication model, agents request and receive information solely on the basis of their interest. They can specify new interests as the result of a new event or alert, which avoids unnecessary data flow among the agents. The major advantage of interest-based model is that the entire system is not compromised if an agent fails. Instead of total failure, there is graceful degradation of system performance.

An *interest* is defined by the authors as a specification of data that an agent is interested, but is not available to the agent because of the locality of data collection or because the agent was not primarily intended to observe those data. Two important applications are:

- When more than one agent need the same data, interest-based communication will avoid duplication of effort that may result in higher overhead.
- An agent may need data from other agents because it does not have access to the source of data. This is specially important for detecting coordinated and distributed attacks, where an agent may need data from agents reside in multiple hosts in the network.

While an agent may know what data it want, it may or may not know if there are agents (from among thousands of agents) collecting that data. This represent the need for propagation of interests in the network. The authors define two types of interests:

- *directed interest*: agent knows another agent that collects the data it needs.
- *propagated interests*: when the agent doesn't know any specific host or domain that can provide the data that it needs, the interest should be propagated across the whole enterprise.

Gopalakrishna and Spafford then propose a hierarchical propagation of interests. This hierarchy is divided into 3 levels: *local, domain* and *enterprise*. Local level interest is defined as the interest to get data from local host. Domain level interest is defined as the interest to get data from local domain. Enterprise level interest is defined as the interest to get data from anywhere in the enterpise.

The paper also categorize interest to *permanent*, when an interest is specified for the whole lifetime of the agent, and *temporal*, when an interest is specified by an agent for a certain period of time.

The following architectural components are proposed for the interest-based co-operation model: *agent registry, interest registry* and *propagators* in three levels: local, domain and enterprise. The authors also specify some issues with considerable significance for future research. This issues are: security of agents, clock synchronization and redundancy of propagators.

6.3.6 Agent-Based Cooperation

Zhang et al. [52] propose an agent-based hierarchical architecture for intrusion detection. They define Detection Agents (DAs) with intrusion detection and response capabilities and Coordination Agents (CAs) with the capability of collaborative detection. Detection agents consists of communication module, security verification module, detection module, response module and a knowledge-base. Communication module uses KQML for communication with other agents and security verification is used to verify the identity of the other agents. When there is a suspicious activity that a detection agent is unable to decide, it reports the suspicious event to a higher level Coordination Agent.

A Coordination Agent uses a knowledge-base and is capable of assigning tasks to the Detection Agents and Collaborative detection of intrusions. Using its knowledge-base, a Coordination Agent can decide about different reports that it receives from Detection Agents. It may request for more information from the Detection Agents or may report the events to another higher-level Coordination Agent, when is unable to judge with the current information. An intrusion event called Millennium worm is presented as an example.

The authors in the above-mentioned paper does not contribute any new idea more than what have been proposed in the several previous papers with regards to hierarchical agent-based frameworks and prototypes. Moreover, the authors do not explain many key question such as the attack detection methods used by the Detection Agents and the correlation mechanism of the Coordination Agents. It is not clear how attack information are presented in different levels of the hierarchy, what is the degree of autonomy of the Detection Agents, what types of information are collected by Detection Agents without a request from a Coordination Agent and what types require an initiation from a Coordination Agent.

The paper by Zhang et al. [51] presents another hierarchical multiagent-based intrusion detection architecture for a LAN environment. Four kinds of agents are defined: 1) *Basic Agents*; 2) *Coordination Agents*; 3) *Global Coordination Agents*; and 4) *Interface* Agent. Basic agents monitor a workstation, a server or a network subnet. Coordination agents coordinate Basic agents to execute complex detection and there are three different types of coordination agents: Workstation Coordination agent, Server Coordination agent and Subnet Coordination agent. Global Coordination agent has global knowledge and coordinates other Coordination agents to finish more complex detection.

The above-mentioned paper describes agents and multi-agent systems and their main features, such as perception, communication, and proactiveness. However, the authors do not elaborate on how they have included such features in the proposed multiagent-based intrusion detection system. The main contribution of the paper is a very high-level architecture for a multi-agent based intrusion detection system as we described, but authors do not indicate anything about the detection methods and coordination and communication algorithms. Most of the paper is dedicated to background knowledge and survey of intrusion detection systems. The contribution is very weak, since there are several other papers, which have described similar architectures with more details.

6.3.7 Secure Communication Using Public-key Encryption

AALCP is proposed as a protocol for agent communication by Xue et al. [50]. They propose a multi-agent system for distributed intrusion detection. The architecture consists of many different types of agents that communicate with each other. A public-key encryption algorithm is used to encrypt all the communication and passwords in the system.

References

1. Stefan Axelsson, *The base-rate fallacy and its implications for the difficulty of intrusion detection*, Proceedings of the 6th ACM conference on Computer and communication security (Kent Ridge Digital Labs, Singapore), ACM Press, November 1999, pp. 1–7.
2. Tim Bass, *Intrusion detection systems and multisensor data fusion*, Communications of the ACM **43** (2000), no. 4, 99–105.

3. Curtis A. Carver, *Adaptive agent-based intrusion response*, Ph.D. thesis, Texas A&M University, 2001.
4. S. Cheung and U. Lindqvist; M.W Fong, *Modeling multistep cyber attacks for scenario recognition*, DARPA Information Survivability Conference and Exposition, vol. 1, IEEE, April 2003, pp. 284 – 292.
5. T. Chyssler, S. Nadjm-Tehrani, S. Burschka, and K. Burbeck, *Alarm reduction and correlation in defence of ip networks*, the 13th International Workshops on Enabling Technologies: Infrastructures for Collaborative Enterprises (WETICE04), June 2004.
6. F. Cuppens, *Managing alerts in a multi-intrusion detection environment*, Proceedings of the 17th Annual Computer Security Applications Conference, 2001, p. 22.
7. F Cuppens, F Autrel, A Miege, and S Benferhat, *Recognizing malicious intention in an intrusion detection process*, Proceeding of Soft Computing Systems - Design, Management and Applications, HIS 2002 (Santiago) (A Abraham, J Ruiz del Solar, and M Koppen, eds.), Frontiers in Artificial Intelligence and Applications, vol. 87, IOS Press, December 1-4 2002, http://www.rennes.enst-bretagne.fr/ fcuppens/Publications.htm, pp. 806–817.
8. F. Cuppens and A. Miege, *Alert correlation in a cooperative intrusion detection framework*, Security and Privacy, 2002. Proceedings. 2002 IEEE Symposium on, IEEE, 2002, pp. 202–215.
9. Frdric Cuppens and Rodolphe Ortalo, *Lambda: A language to model a database for detection of attacks*, Proceedings of Recent Advances in Intrusion Detection, 3rd International Symposium, (RAID 2000) (Toulouse, France) (H. Debar, L. M, and S.F. Wu, eds.), Lecture Notes in Computer Science, Springer-Verlag Heidelberg, October 2000, pp. 197–216.
10. O.M. Dain and R. K Cunningham, *Fusing a heterogeneous alert stream into scenarios*, Proceedings of the 2001 ACM Workshop on Data Mining for Security Applications, 2001, pp. 1–13.
11. Herv Debar and Andreas Wespi, *Aggregation and correlation of intrusion-detection alerts*, Proceedings of Recent Advances in Intrusion Detection, 4th International Symposium, (RAID 2001) (Davis, CA, USA) (W, L. M Lee, and A. Wespi, eds.), Lecture Notes in Computer Science, Springer-Verlag Heidelberg, October 2001, pp. 85–103.
12. Peng Ning Dingbang Xu, *Alert correlation through triggering events and common resources*, To appear in Proceedings of 20th Annual Computer Security Applications Conference(ACSAC), December 2004.
13. S.T. Eckmann, G. Vigna, and R.A. Kemmerer, *Statl: An attack language for state-based intrusion detection*, Proceedings of the 1st ACM Workshop on Intrusion Detection Systems (Athens, Greece), November 2000.
14. M. Erlinger and S. Stanniford, *Intrusion detection interchange format*, 11 2004.
15. Deborah Frincke, *Balancing cooperation and risk in intrusion detection*, ACM Transactions on Information and System Security (TISSEC) **3** (2000), no. 1, 1–29.
16. C.W. Geib and B.A. Goodman, *Plan recognition in intrusion detection systems*, DARPA Information Survivability Conference & Exposition II, 2001. DISCEX Ó1. Proceedings, vol. 1, June 2001, pp. 46 – 55.
17. C. Clifton; G. Gengo, *Developing custom intrusion detection filters using data mining*, 21st Century Military Communications Conference Proceedings, vol. 1, IEEE, Oct 2000, pp. 440 – 443.
18. Robert P. Goldman, *A stochastic model for intrusions*, Proceedings of Recent Advances in Intrusion Detection, 5th International Symposium, (RAID 2002) (Zurich, Switzerland) (A. Wespi, G. Vigna, and L. Deri, eds.), Lecture Notes in Computer Science, Springer-Verlag Heidelberg, October 2002, pp. 199–218.
19. Rajeev Gopalakrishna and Eugene Spafford, *A framework for distributed intrusion detection using interest driven cooperating agents*, Proceedings of Recent Advances in Intrusion Detection, 4th International Symposium, (RAID 2001) (Davis, CA, USA) (W, L. M Lee, and A. Wespi, eds.), Lecture Notes in Computer Science, Springer-Verlag Heidelberg, October 2001, pp. 172–189.
20. IETF Intrusion Detection Working Group, *Intrusion detection message exchange format*, http://www.ietf.org/internet-drafts/draft-ietf-idwg-idmef-xml-12.txt, 2004.

21. J. Haines, D. Ryder, L. Tinnel, and S. Taylor, *Validation of sensor alert correlators*, IEEE Security and Privacy (2003).

22. Jian-Qiang Zhai; Jun-Feng Tian; Rui-Zhong Du; Jian-Cai Huang, *Network intrusion early warning model based on d-s evidence theory*, Machine Learning and Cybernetics, 2003 International Conference on, vol. 4, November 2003, pp. 1972 – 1977.

23. Ming-Yuh Huang, Robert J. Jasper, and Thomas M. Wicks, *A large scale distributed intrusion detection framework based on attack strategy analysis*, Computer Networks **31** (1999), no. 23-24, 2465–2475, http://www.sciencedirect.com/science/article/B6VRG-3Y6HFD7-3/2/f434e03c9140282df6c29ccd919d0181.

24. K. Julisch, *Mining alarm clusters to improve alarm handling efficiency*, Proceedings of the 17th Annual Computer Security Applications Conference, 2001, p. 12.

25. K Julisch, *Clustering intrusion detection alarms to support root cause analysis*, ACM Transactions on Information and System Security **6** (2003), no. 4, 443–471, http://www.zurich.ibm.com/ kju/.

26. Richard Lippmann, Seth Webster, and Douglas Stetson, *The effect of identifying vulnerabilities and patching software on the utility of network intrusion detection*, Proceedings of Recent Advances in Intrusion Detection, 5th International Symposium, (RAID 2002) (Zurich, Switzerland) (A. Wespi, G. Vigna, and L. Deri, eds.), Lecture Notes in Computer Science, Springer-Verlag Heidelberg, October 2002, pp. 307–326.

27. J. McConnell, D. Frincke, D. Tobin, J. Marconi, and D.Polla, *A framework for cooperative intrusion detection*, Proceedings of the 21st National Information Systems Security Conference (NISSC), October 1998, pp. 361–373.

28. George M. Mohay Nathan Carey, Andrew Clark, *Ids interoperability and correlation using idmef and commodity systems*, Proceedings of the 4th International Conference on Information and Communications Security, December 2002, pp. 252–264.

29. Peng Ning and Yun Cui, *An intrusion alert correlator based on prerequisites of intrusions*, Tech. Report TR-2002-01, 26 2002.

30. Peng Ning, Yun Cui, and Douglas S. Reeves, *Constructing attack scenarios through correlation of intrusion alerts*, Proceedings of the 9th ACM conference on Computer and communication security (Washington D.C., USA), ACM Press, November 2002, pp. 245–254.

31. Peng Ning, Yun Cui, Douglas S. Reeves, and Dingbang Xu, *Techniques and tools for analyzing intrusion alerts*, ACM Transactions on Information and System Security (TISSEC) **7** (2004), no. 2, 274–318.

32. Peng Ning, Sushil Jajodia, and Xiaoyang Sean Wang, *Abstraction-based intrusion detection in distributed environments*, ACM Transactions on Information and System Security (TISSEC) **4** (2001), no. 4, 407–452.

33. Peng Ning and Dingbang Xu, *Learning attack strategies from intrusion alerts*, Proceedings of the 10th ACM conference on Computer and communication security (Washington D.C., USA), ACM Press, October 2003, pp. 200–209.

34. Tadeusz Pietraszek, *Using adaptive alert classification to reduce false positives in intrusion detection*, 21st Century Military Communications Conference Proceedings, vol. 1, IEEE, Oct 2004, pp. 440 – 443.

35. Phillip Porras, Martin W. Fong, and Alfonso Valdes, *A mission-impact-based approach to infosec alarm correlation*, Proceedings of Recent Advances in Intrusion Detection, 5th International Symposium, (RAID 2002) (Zurich, Switzerland) (A. Wespi, G. Vigna, and L. Deri, eds.), Lecture Notes in Computer Science, Springer-Verlag Heidelberg, October 2002, pp. 95–114.

36. X. Qin, W. Lee, L. Lewis, and J. B. D. Cabrera, *Integrating intrusion detection and network management*, Proceedings of the 8th IEEE/IFIP Network Operations and Management Symposium (NMOS) (Florence, Italy), April 2002, pp. 329–344.

37. Xinzhou Qin and Wenke Lee, *Statistical causality analysis of infosec alert data*, Proceedings of Recent Advances in Intrusion Detection, 6th International Symposium, (RAID 2003) (Pittsburgh, PA, USA) (G. Vigna, E. Jonsson, and C. Kruegel, eds.), Lecture Notes in Computer Science, Springer-Verlag Heidelberg, September 2003, pp. 73–93.

38. Reza Sadoddin, *An incremental frequent structure mining framework for real-time alert correlation*, Master's thesis, Faculty of Computer Science, University of New Brunswick, Fredericton, NB, Canada, July 2007.
39. Reza Sadoddin and Ali A. Ghorbani, *Real-time alert correlation using stream data mining techniques*, Proceedings of the Twenty-Third AAAI Conference on Artificial Intelligence, 2008, pp. 1731–1737.
40. Christos Siaterlis and Basil Maglaris, *Towards multisensor data fusion for dos detection*, Proceedings of the 2004 ACM symposium on Applied computing (Nicosia, Cyprus), ACM Press, March 2004, pp. 439 – 446.
41. A. Siraj, R.B. Vaughn, and S.M. Bridges, *Intrusion sensor data fusion in an intelligent intrusion detection system architecture*, Proceedings of the 37th Annual Hawaii International Conference on System Sciences, January 2004, pp. 279–288.
42. Eugene   H.   Spafford   and   Diego   Zamboni,   *Intrusion   detection   using   autonomous   agents*,   Computer   Networks   **34**   (2000),   no.   4,   547–570,   http://www.sciencedirect.com/science/article/B6VRG-411FRK9-2/2/f818f61028e80aa2cd740fdc4a3cd696.
43. Karl Levitt Steven J. Templeton, *A requires/provides model for computer attacks*, Proceedings of the 2000 workshop on New security paradigms, February 2001.
44. G. Tedesco and U. Aickelin, *Adaptive alert throttling for intrusion detection systems*, submitted and under review (2003).
45. J. Turner, *New directions in communications (or which way to the information age?)*, Communications Magazine **24** (1986), 5–11.
46. Alfonso Valdes and Keith Skinner, *Adaptive, model-based monitoring for cyber attack detection*, Proceedings of Recent Advances in Intrusion Detection, 3rd International Symposium, (RAID 2000) (Toulouse, France) (H. Debar, L. M, and S.F. Wu, eds.), Lecture Notes in Computer Science, Springer-Verlag Heidelberg, October 2000, pp. 80–92.
47. _____, *Probabilistic alert correlation*, Proceedings of Recent Advances in Intrusion Detection, 4th International Symposium, (RAID 2001) (Davis, CA, USA) (W, L. M Lee, and A. Wespi, eds.), Lecture Notes in Computer Science, Springer-Verlag Heidelberg, October 2001, pp. 54–68.
48. Fredrik Valeur, Giovanni Vigna, Christopher Kruegel, and Richard A. Kemmerer, *A comprehensive approach to intrusion detection alert correlation*, Dependable and Secure Computing, IEEE Transactions on **1** (2004), no. 3, 146–169.
49. Xinyuan Wang, *The loop fallacy and serialization in tracing intrusion connections through stepping stones*, Proceedings of the 2004 ACM symposium on Applied computing (Nicosia, Cyprus), ACM Press, March 2004, pp. 404–411.
50. Q. Xue, J. Sun, and Z. Wei, *Tjids: an intrusion detection architecture for distributed network*, Proceedings of the Canadian Conference on Electrical and Computer Engineering, IEEE CCECE 2003, May 2003, pp. 709–712.
51. Ran Zhang, Depei Qian, Chongming Ba, Weiguo Wu, and Xiaobing Guo, *Multi-agent based intrusion detection architecture*, Proceedings of 2001 IEEE International Conference on Computer Networks and Mobile Computing, October 2001, pp. 494–501.
52. Ran Zhang, Depei Qian, Heng Chen, and Weiguo Wu, *Collaborative intrusion detection based on coordination agent*, Proceedings of the Fourth International Conference on Parallel and Distributed Computing, Applications and Technologies (PDCAT'2003), August 2003, pp. 175–179.
53. Yong Wang; Huihua Yang; Xingyu Wang; Ruixia Zhang, *Distributed intrusion detection system based on data fusion method*, Intelligent Control and Automation, 2004. WCICA 2004. Fifth World Congress on, vol. 5, IEEE, June 2004, pp. 4331– 4334.

Chapter 7
Evaluation Criteria

For years, the research in intrusion detection field has been primarily focused on anomaly and misuse detection techniques. The latter method is traditionally favored in commercial products due to its predictability and high accuracy. In academic research, however, anomaly detection approach is perceived as a more powerful due to its theoretically higher potential to address novel attacks in comparison to misuse based methods. While academic community proposed a wide spectrum of anomaly based intrusion techniques, adequate comparison of the strengths and limitations of these techniques that can lead to potential commercial application is challenging. In this chapter we introduce the most significant criteria which have been proposed to have a more realistic evaluation of anomaly detection systems.

7.1 Accuracy

Accuracy is a statement of how correct an IDS works, measuring the percentage of detection and failure as well as the number of false alarms that the system is producing [5, 4, 15]. A system that has 80% accuracy is a system that correctly classifies 80 instances out of 100 in their actual class.

While there is a big diversity of attacks in intrusion detection, the main focus remains if the system detects an attack or not. Thus, the number of target classes can be considered to be two (i.e. normal and abnormal/intrusion). From the real life experience, one can infer that the actual percentage of abnormal data is much smaller than the percentage of normal one [6, 7]. Consequently, the intrusions are harder to detect than the normal traffic, which results in having excessive false alarms as the biggest problem facing IDSs. Joshi et al. [7] refer to this issue as the detection of Rare Class problem, where the Rare Class represents all the detected and undetected intrusions that happen in a certain interval of time.

A.A. Ghorbani et al., *Network Intrusion Detection and Prevention: Concepts and Techniques*, 161
Advances in Information Security 47, DOI 10.1007/978-0-387-88771-5_7,
© Springer Science + Business Media, LLC 2010

7.1.1 False Positive and Negative

In intrusion detection a *positive* data is considered to be an attack data, while a *negative* data is considered to be a normal data. Furthermore, when an IDS tries to classify data, its decision can be either right or wrong. Assume that *true* and *false* stands for right and wrong, respectively. Therefore, due to the two-class nature of the detection we have four combinations of the previous defined variables as follows: *True Positive* (TP) , *True Negative* (TN) , *False Positive* (FP) , and *False Negative* (FN) .

A TP occurs when an IDS correctly classifies an intrusion, whereas a FP occurs when a legitimate action is misclassified as being an intrusion. Likewise, a TN is produced whenever a normal data is correctly classified as a legitimate action, while a FN occurs when an attack is not detected by the IDS [26, 6, 7].

	The class of actual data	The prediction of the IDS
True Positive (TP)	Attack	Attack
False Positive (FP)	Normal	Attack
True Negative (TN)	Normal	Normal
False Negative (FN)	Attack	Normal

Table 7.1 IDS classification

Consequently, the aim of an IDS is to produce as many TP and TN as possible, while trying to reduce the number of both FP and FN.

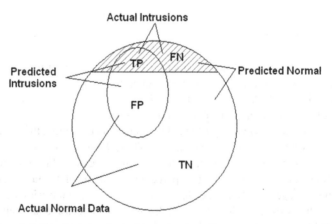

Fig. 7.1 The whole data space in a typical Intrusion Detection two-class scenario. (This figure is adapted from [7].)

Joshi et al. [7] propose a graphical method to visualize the relation between the four variables. Fig 7.1 depicts the normal case of an intrusion detection problem, as follows:

- the *big circle* defines the space of the whole data (i.e., normal and intrusive data)
- the *small ellipse* defines the space of all predicted intrusions by the classifier. Thus, it will be shared by both TP and FP.
- the ratio between the real normal data and the intrusions is graphically represented by the use of a *horizontal line*.

The previous four defined variables (i.e. TP, FP, TN, FN) encapsulate all the possible results of a two-class Intrusion Detection problem. Thus, the big majority of evaluation criteria metrics use these variables and the relations between them in order to model the accuracy of the IDSs.

7.1.2 Confusion Matrix

The Confusion Matrix is a ranking method applied to any kind of classification problem. The size of the matrix is determined by the number of distinct classes that are to be detected. The aim here is to compare the actual class labels against the predicted ones. Consequently, the diagonal will represent all the correct classifications.

		Predicted Class	
		Normal	Attack
Actual Class	Normal	TN	FP
	Attack	FN	TP

Fig. 7.2 The Confusion Matrix

A *Confusion Matrix* for intrusion detection is defined as a 2-by-2 matrix, since the number of classes (i.e., intrusion, and normal) is two [26, 6, 7]. Thus, the TN and TP that represents the correctly predicted cases will lie on the matrix diagonal, while the FN and FP will be on the right, and left sides (see Fig 7.2). As a side effect of the confusion matrix, all the four values (i.e., TP, FP, TN, and FN) are displayed in a way that the relation between them can be easily understandable.

7.1.3 Precision, Recall, and F-Measure

As previously mentioned, under normal operating conditions there is a big differ-
ence between the rate of normal and intrusion data. Thus, the Precision, Recall, and
F-Measure metrics ignore the normal data that has been correctly classified by the
IDS (TN), and focus on both the intrusion data (TP+FN) and FP (also known as
False Alarms) that are generated by the IDS (See Fig 7.3).

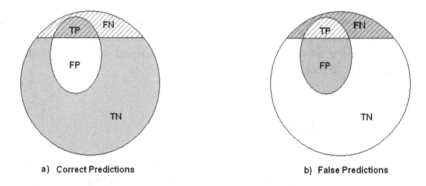

a) Correct Predictions   b) False Predictions

Fig. 7.3 The data space of a two class intrusion detection problem.

Precision: It is a metric defined with respect to the intrusion class. It shows how
many examples, predicted by an IDS as being intrusive, are the actual intrusions
[7, 26, 6]. The aim of an IDS is to obtain a high Precision, meaning that the
number of false alarms is minimized.

$$precision = \frac{TP}{TP+FP} \qquad where \quad precision \in [0,1] \qquad (7.1)$$

The main disadvantage of the metric is the impossibility to express the percent of
predicted intrusions versus all the real intrusions that exist in the data. Figure 7.4
highlights this disadvantage. Both of the depicted classifiers have a HIGH precision, due to the large percent of the correctly predicted intrusions (i.e., TP)
versus the total number of predicted intrusions (i.e., TP+FP). Thus, in both cases
the number of False Alarms is very low. Despite this apparent similarity, it is
obvious that the classifier in Figure 7.4(a) covers less intrusions (i.e. Recall =
LOW) than the one in Figure 7.4(b) (i.e. Recall= MEDIUM).

Recall: This metric measures the missing part from the Precision; namely, the
percentage from the real intrusions covered by the classifier. Consequently, it is
desired for a classifier to have a high recall value [7, 26, 6].

$$recall = \frac{TP}{TP+FN} \qquad where \quad recall \in [0,1] \qquad (7.2)$$

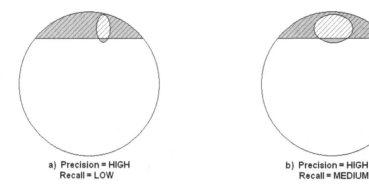

a) Precision = HIGH
Recall = LOW

b) Precision = HIGH
Recall = MEDIUM

Fig. 7.4 The disadvantage of using only precision as a metric: The figure shows two classifiers (IDS) that have almost the same precision (i.e., low False Alarms) but different Recall. While in the first case (a) the Recall is low (i.e., the detected intrusions represent a small part of the real intrusions), in the second case (b) the number of covered intrusions is higher.

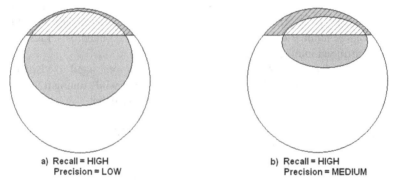

a) Recall = HIGH
Precision = LOW

b) Recall = HIGH
Precision = MEDIUM

Fig. 7.5 The disadvantage of using only recall as a metric: The figure shows two classifiers (IDSs) that have almost the same recall (i.e., very good detection rate) but different precisions. While in the first case (a) the precision is low (because of the high number of false alarms), in the second case (b) even though the recall is a little bit lower, the number of false alarms is improved.

This metric does not take into consideration the number of False Alarms. Thus, a classifier can have at the same time both good Recall and high False Alarm rate. Furthermore, a classifier that blindly predicts all the data as being intrusive will have a 100% Recall (but a very low precision). This case is depicted in Figure 7.5, where the two classifiers have approximately is the rate of false alarms. Even though the first classifier (Figure 7.5(a)) has a higher recall than the second one (Figure 7.5(b)), its false alarm rate is very high.

F-Measure: Due to the fact that the previously discussed two metrics (i.e., Precision, and Recall) do not completely define the accuracy of an IDS, a combination of them would be more appropriate to use.

The F-Measure mixes the properties of the previous two metrics, being defined as the harmonic mean of precision and recall [26].

$$F-Measure = \frac{2}{\frac{1}{precision} + \frac{1}{recall}} \qquad where \quad F-Measure \in [0,1] \qquad (7.3)$$

F-Measure is preferred when only one accuracy metric is desired as an evaluation criteria. Note that when Precision and Recall reaches 100%, the F-Measure is maximum (i.e. 1), meaning that the classifier has 0% false alarms and detects 100% of the attacks. Thus, the F-Measure of a classifier is desired to be as high as possible.

7.1.4 ROC Curves

The Receiver Operating Characteristics (ROC) analysis originates from the signal detection theory. Its applicability is not limited only to intrusion detection, but extends to a large number of practical problems like medical diagnosis, radiology, as well as in artificial intelligence and data mining.

In intrusion detection, ROC curves are used on the one hand to visualize the relation between the TP and FP rate of a certain classifier while tuning it, and on the other hand, to compare the accuracy of two or more classifiers.

The ROC space [16] represents the orthogonal coordinate system used to visualize the classifier's accuracy. The X axis depicts the FP (false alarms rate), while the Y axis accommodates the TP (intrusion detection rate) (see Figure 7.6).

In order to understand the usage of the ROC curves in detecting the accuracy of a classifier, several points on the ROC space must be described [16, 5, 4, 26]:

- The lower-left point (0,0) characterizes an IDS that classifies all the data as normal all the time. Obviously in such situation, the classifier will have a zero false alarm rate, but at the same time will not be able to detect anything.
- The upper-right point (1,1) characterizes an IDS that generates an alarm for each data that is encountered. Consequently, it will have a 100% detection rate and a 100% false alarm rate as well.
- The line defined by connecting the two previous points represents any classifier that uses a randomize decision engine for detecting the intrusions. Any point on this line can be obtained by a linear combination of the two previously mentioned strategies. Thus, the ROC curve of an IDS will always reside above this diagonal.
- The upper-left point (0,1) represents the ideal case when there is a 100% detection rate while having a 0% false alarm rate. Thus the closer a point in the ROC space is to the ideal case, the more efficient the classifier is.

Setting up an IDS to work at its optimal point is a tedious task that the system administrator must accomplish. All IDSs have certain variables (thresholds) that have

Fig. 7.6 The ROC curve for different classifiers

to be tuned in order to produce a good detection result. For example, if the detection threshold is set too high, the classifier will start to miss a lot of intrusions, thus, creating a large number of FN and a small number of TP. Consequently, its corresponding point on the ROC space will migrate towards the origin (0,0). Conversely, if the detection threshold is set too low then, the classifier starts to produce a high volume of both false alarms and TP. As a result, the corresponding point on the ROC space will migrate to the (1,1) point.

The effect of tuning an IDS is materialized in a convex curve that will always pass through the two extreme points (0,0) and (1,1). Consequently, different IDSs will produce different ROC curves. A classifier is said to be more accurate than another one if its ROC curve is closer to the left-top part of the ROC space. Unfortunately, in practice, when comparing two or more IDSs, not all the time one ROC curve completely dominates the other ones. Consequently, a clear-cut of what classifier is the best cannot be made.

Besides IDS analysis, ROC curves are also used in order to combine one or more classifiers into a better hybrid one. For this purpose, Provest and Fawcett [16] propose an algorithm that combines techniques from ROC analysis, decision analysis, and computational geometry.

Axelsson [5, 4] defined a threshold for the ROC curves, that an IDS must meet in order to be relevant for intrusion detection. (see next subsection for the thresholds for TP and FP).

7.1.5 The Base-Rate Fallacy

The *base-rate fallacy* merges from psychology and probability. Scientists noticed the way that people usually ignore or wrongly perceive probabilities when trying to solve daily problems. This is mainly because those problems employ statistics between the population as a whole and a single individual. Consequently, the base-rate fallacy is the belief that probability rates are false [18, 5, 4, 19].

As an example of this phenomenon, let us consider an exercise (i.e., 13.8 from [18]) by Russel and Norvig:

"After your yearly checkup, the doctor has bad news and good news. The bad news is that you tested positive for a serious disease and that the test is 99% accurate (i.e., the probability of testing positive when you do have the disease is 0.99, as is the probability of testing negative when you don't have the disease). The good news is that this is a rare disease, striking only 1 in 10,000 people of your age. Why is it good news that the disease is rare? What are the chances that you actually have the disease?"

At this point, the reader is encouraged to make a quick estimation of the real result. A common answer concerning the probability of that person to have the disease is close to 99% chance. Consequently, without any kind of other reflection on the problem (ignoring the base-rate) the person will certainly be sure that he has that disease, furthermore he might consider the doctor's good news as an insult or a sarcastic remark. The first guess result in this case is too far from the real probability.

This type of perception is called the *base-rate fallacy*. All the problems that fall into this category can be solved by the use of probabilities and Bayesian theory.

Equation (7.4) depicts the Bayes rule (also known as Bayes theorem or Bayes law) [18] for two variables A and B as:

$$P(A|B) = \frac{P(A) \cdot P(B|A)}{P(B)} \tag{7.4}$$

Furthermore, considering that A is a multivalued-variable, the $P(B)$ can be expressed with respect to the total number of mutually exclusive n values of A. (see Equation (7.5))

$$P(B) = \Sigma_{i=1}^{n}(P(A_i) \cdot P(B|A_i)) \tag{7.5}$$

Combining Equation (7.4) with Equation (7.5), the posterior probability of A given B can be computed as:

$$P(A|B) = \frac{P(A) \cdot P(B|A)}{\Sigma_{i=1}^{n}(P(A_i) \cdot P(B|A_i))} \tag{7.6}$$

Let us refer back to the original problem of the patient and define the following variables [5, 4]:

- S denote the *sick*
- $\neg S$ denote the *healthy*

- R denote a *positive test*
- ¬R denote a *negative test*

Furthermore, the statement of the exercise can be probabilistically written as:

- $P(R|S) = 0.99$ denotes the *probability of a positive test given a sick person*
- $P(\neg R|\neg S) = 0.99$ denotes the *probability of a negative test given a healthy person*
- $P(S) = \frac{1}{10,000}$ denotes the *probability of a person to have that disease*
- $P(S|R)$ denotes the *probability of sickness for a person given a positive test*

A direct application of the Bayes theorem (Equation 7.6) to our problem gives:

$$P(S|R) = \frac{P(S) \cdot P(R|S)}{(P(S) \cdot P(R|S)) + (P(\neg S) \cdot P(R|\neg S))} \tag{7.7}$$

Note that
$$P(R|\neg S) = 1 - P(R|S) \quad \Longrightarrow \quad P(R|\neg S) = 0.01,$$
and similarly
$$P(\neg S) = 1 - P(S) \quad \Longrightarrow \quad P(\neg S) = 1 - \tfrac{1}{10,000}$$

Substituting all the previous mentioned values into Equation 7.7 gives:

$$P(S|R) = \frac{\frac{1}{10,000} \cdot 0.99}{\left(\frac{1}{10,000} \cdot 0.99\right) + \left(\left(1 - \frac{1}{10,000}\right) \cdot 0.01\right)} = 0.00980 \quad \approx 1\% \tag{7.8}$$

Consequently, even though the test is positive, and its precision is 99%, due to the small number of persons that have that disease (i.e., one in 10,000) comparing with the number of healthy peoples, ones chance of having the disease is approximately 1%.

This result often surprises people because in contrast with the probability theory, the human judgmental reasoning is more qualitative, and in general do not take the base-rate into account [5, 4, 19].

Axelsson [5, 4], applied this kind of reasoning in intrusion detection. The goal is to find the minimal efficiency point of an IDS in order to be useful with respect to its detection rate and false alarm rate. His analysis is done with respect to a figurative UNIX computer network setup consisting of a few tens of workstations, a few servers, and dozens of users. Such a setup could produce 1,000,000 audit records daily (Note that this statement was made in 2000, see [5, 4]). The "normal" number of intrusions per day was considered to be not more than one or two, and each intrusion will affect 10 audit records. Furthermore, he considers that the network administrator is likely to respond only to a low number of alarms (i.e. 50%), especially when the rate of the false alarms is high.

Consider the following notations:

- *I* denote the *intrusion*

- $\neg I$ denote the *normal* behavior
- A denote an *intrusion alarm*
- $\neg A$ denote the absence of a *alarm*
- $P(A|I)$ denote the probability of an alarm given an intrusion (i.e., TP rate, or Detection Rate)
- $P(A|\neg I)$ denote the probability of an alarm given a normal data (i.e., FP rate, or False Alarm rate)
- $P(\neg A|I) = 1 - P(A|I)$ denote the probability of no alarm given an intrusion (i.e., FN rate, or undetected Intrusions rate)
- $P(\neg A|\neg I) = 1 - P(A|\neg I)$ denote the probability of no alarm given a normal data (i.e., TN rate)

Our ultimate goal is to measure both the probability that an alarm really indicates an intrusion (i.e. $P(I|A)$) as well as the probability that the absence of an alarm indeed indicates a normal data (i.e. $P(\neg I|\neg A)$). Thus, applying the previous notations to Equation 7.6 gives:

$$P(I|A) = \frac{P(I) \cdot P(A|I)}{(P(I) \cdot P(A|I)) + (P(\neg I) \cdot P(A|\neg I))} \tag{7.9}$$

$$P(\neg I|\neg A) = \frac{P(\neg I) \cdot P(\neg A|\neg I)}{(P(\neg I) \cdot P(\neg A|\neg I)) + (P(I) \cdot P(\neg A|I))} \tag{7.10}$$

Furthermore, having 10 audit records per intrusion, 2 intrusions per day, and 1,000,000 audit records per day, the $P(I)$ and $P(\neg I)$ are:

$$P(I) = \frac{1}{\frac{10,000,000}{2 \cdot 10}} \quad \Longrightarrow \quad P(I) = 0.00002 \tag{7.11}$$

$$P(\neg I) = 1 - P(I) \quad \Longrightarrow \quad P(I) = 0.99998 \tag{7.12}$$

Substituting, $P(I)$ and $P(\neg I)$ into Equation 7.9, and Equation 7.10,gives:

$$P(I|A) = \frac{0.00002 \cdot P(A|I)}{(0.00002 \cdot P(A|I)) + (0.99998 \cdot P(A|\neg I))} \tag{7.13}$$

$$P(\neg I|\neg A) = \frac{0.99998 \cdot P(\neg A|\neg I)}{(0.99998 \cdot P(\neg A|\neg I)) + (0.00002 \cdot P(\neg A|I))} \tag{7.14}$$

The base-rate fallacy is clearly shown in Equation 7.13 equation, due to the factor governing the false alarm rate (i.e., 0.99998) that completely dominates the factor of the detection rate (i.e., 0.00002). Furthermore, the equation will have its desired outcome (i.e, 1) when $P(A|I) = 1$ and $P(A|\neg I) = 0$, which complies with the most beneficial outcome regarding the TP and FP.

If the Bayesian detection rate is analyzed versus the false alarm rate, as reported in [5], for an IDS with a 100% detection rate (i.e., $P(A|I) = 1$) a very low false alarm rate is needed (i.e., on the order of 10^{-5}) so that 66% of the alarms to denote a true intrusion. Furthermore, if a more realistic case is considered, an IDS that has a 70% detection rate (i.e., $P(A|I) = 0.7$), for the same false alarm rate (i.e., 10^{-5}), only 58% of the alarms will denote a real intrusion.

At this point, even though that the TP and FP are considered to be close to optimal (i.e. 0.70 and 0.00001, respectively) the system administrator will be faced with almost half false alarms from the total ones. Thus, even though the number of alarms is very low, the human will stop thrusting them, or at least ignore some of them.

Given the previous values for TP and FP, from Equation 7.14, the probability of *no alarm* for a normal data rises no concern (i.e., $P(\neg I|\neg A)$). This is mainly because the 0.99998 value clearly dominates the other factor 0.00002. Thus, $P(\neg I|\neg A)$ is close to 100%.

Conclusively, the author of [5] highlights the base-rate fallacy problem as being one of the real threats that future IDSs must overcome. This becomes highly questionable as computers become faster, and the number of intrusions stays relatively low comparing with the huge amount of normal data generated.

7.2 Performance

The evaluation of an IDS performance is a subject matter. It involves many other issues that go beyond the IDS itself. Such issues include hardware platform, operating system, or even the deployment of the IDS. For a network intrusion detection system (NIDS), the most important evaluation criterion for its performance is the system's ability to process traffic in a high speed link with minimum packet loss while working in real-time.

Schaelicke et al. [20] proposes a methodology to measure the performance of rule-based NIDSs. Rule-based NIDSs inspects every packet on the protected network in an effort to find the particular patterns based on user-defined rules. Given a fixed amount of traffic load, the processing capability of an NIDS depends on the type of the rules and the packet size. Generally, there are two kinds of rules, namely header rules and payload rules. Header rules search the headers for particular combination of features. Since the size of header is generally fixed, the overall processing cost by applying header rules depends on the number of packets to be processed. But for payload rules, which inspect the payload of the packets in an attempt to find specific byte sequences, the overall processing cost is determined by the size of the packets. Real network traffic is comprised of packets of different sizes. Consequently, an effective NIDS must be able to handle packets of any size. Taking all these factors into consideration, the measurement carried out by Schaelicke et al. was performed for four different packet payload sizes: 64 bytes, 512 bytes, 1000 bytes, and 1452 bytes, the NIDS to be measured ran on the 100Mbit link, which was nearly saturated during the evaluation. The number of rules kept increasing until packet loss was reported, the maximum number of supported rules was then the indicator of performance.

Several conclusion were draw by the authors based on their experimental results:

- According to this paper, hardware platform for NIDS is very important in terms of improving performance, thus, general-purpose systems are generally inadequate to be used as hardware platform for NIDS even on moderate-speed networks, since maximum number of rules they support is much smaller than the total number of applicable rules.
- Different system parameters have different degrees of contribution to the improvement of performance. Memory bandwidth and latency are the most significant contributor. While CPU is a not a suitable predictor of NIDS' performance.
- Operating systems also affects the performance of NIDS, the experimental result presented in this paper shows that, Linux significantly outperformed FreeBSD because of its efficient interrupt handling.

In addition to processing speed, the CPU and memory usage can also serve as a measurement of NIDS performance [21]. This is usually used to indirectly measure the time and space complexity of the intrusion detection algorithms.

As we mentioned in previous chapters, special designs such as the one proposed by Kruegel et al. [8] are needed to boost the performance of the intrusion detection systems.

7.3 Completeness

The completeness criterion represents the space of the vulnerabilities and attacks that can be covered by an IDS. This criterion is very hard to assess because having a global knowledge about attacks or abuses of privileges is impossible. However, each IDS can be evaluated against a complete set of known attacks. A comprehensive IDS solution should cover all known vulnerabilities and attacks. Moreover, such a complete solution needs to employ some mechanisms to be able to address the unknown attacks.

7.4 Timely Response

An intrusion detection system that performs its analysis as quickly as possible will enable the security officer or the response engine to promptly react before much damage is done. Thus, preventing the attacker from subverting the audit source or the intrusion detection system itself.

The system response is the most important step when combating an attack. Since the data must be processed in order to discover intrusions, there will always be a delay between the actual moment of the attack and the response of the system (i.e., *Total delay*)

Consider the situation from Figure 7.7. Let on the horizontal time axis, t_{Attack}, $t_{Detection}$, and $t_{Response}$ represent the starting moment of the real attack, the moment when the IDS detects the attack, and the moment when the response mechanism is initiated, respectively.

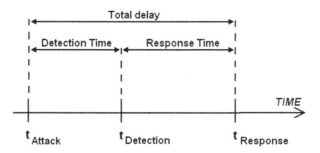

Fig. 7.7 The delta interval

Consequently, the *Total delay* (i.e. difference in time between the t_{Attack}, and $t_{Response}$) consists of two main time intervals the *Detection Time*, and *Response Time*. Thus, the smaller that time is, the better an IDS is with respect to its response.

No matter if an IDS is anomaly based, signature based, or specification based, there will always be a difference between the starting time of the attack and the attack detection. The pioneer IDSs were working off-line, processing the data at the end of the data collection phase (e.g., once a day, once a week). Obviously, the detection time in this case is far too long in order to be useful. There is no point in having a good detection rate if the detection time takes hours or days. Currently, almost all IDSs (commercial and academic) tend to work in real-time, thus, they drastically reduce the *Detection Time*.

Dokas et al. [6] present two metrics for IDS' evaluation with respect to the *Detection Time* [1]. Although both of the metrics (i.e., Brust Detection Rate and Detection Time) are presented with respect to an Anomaly based NIDS, both can be generalized to any kind of IDS.

Figure 7.8 presents a typical scenario of an attack when it is detected by the IDS. Let us define the horizontal axis as being the time, and the vertical axis as the *score value* of the data. The *score value* of each data is the probability that data is believed by the IDS to be an intrusion [2].

The horizontal dotted line represents the detection *threshold*. Even though, the *threshold* variable seems to be suitable only for Anomaly Detection, it can be also defined for specification and signature detection. Thus, whenever that threshold is exceeded, an intrusion is signaled by the IDS.

---

[1] Dokas et al. present the metrics for a simple IDS without a response mechanism [6]. Thus, they refer to the time between the real attack and the actual detection as the *Response Time* of the IDS. We changed the name to *Detection Time* for consistency since it refers to the same thing.

[2] This score can be defined for all three types of major IDS implementations (i.e. anomaly based, signature based, and specification based).

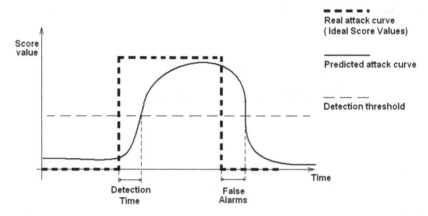

Fig. 7.8 The latency of an IDS detection time (This figure was inspired from [6])

Assume that the *real attack curve* is defined by the dotted discrete line. Due to the computational time (e.g., data capturing, features extraction, and features processing, to name a few), the *predicted attack curve* will have latency in following the *real attack curve*. Thus, the *detection time* can be pictured as the difference between the time when the real attack strikes and the time when the *predicted attack curve* exceeds the *detection threshold*. The *Burst Detection Rate* metric is defined as the rate between the amount of real attack data and the portion of it that the IDS correctly detects [6].

Once the attack is detected, a proper response strategy must be initiated in order to stop it or slow it down. The shorter the *response time* is, the quicker the response is initiated. Thus, a quick response increases the chances to defeat or slow down an attack.

Inline IDSs have a good potential to respond promptly to an already detected suspicious data, mainly because all the communication goes through them, and if an automated response of any kind is triggered, no further delay between the detection and response is needed. In contrast, passive IDSs must communicate with third party inline-devices in order to provide response and this introduces communication delay.

The speed requirements of an Inline IDS are much higher than in the case of a passive IDS. This is mainly because a lazy passive IDS influences only the detection result, while an inline IDS may also influence the data traffick that flows through it. Thus, an inline IDS overwhelmed by the computational power is a bigger threat then a passive IDS in the same situation (i.e., in the first case the IDS might block or delay the whole traffic).

In practice, it is difficult to measure the *total delay* that an IDS has. Consequently, only in a controlled environment (e.g., a standard evaluation data set for intrusion detection), where the starting of the actual attack is known, the *Detection Time* and the *Response Time* can be computed and evaluated.

7.5 Adaptation and Cost-Sensitivity

Besides accuracy, cost-sensitivity also should be considered in the process of developing and evaluating IDSs. Cost-sensitive detection focuses the limited available resources on the most serious and damaging attacks. A cost-benefit justification is required for detecting an attack and detection of an attack is pointless if the operational cost of detecting is larger than its damage cost. Similarly, because of limited labor and computational resources, analyzing and responding to every alarm raised by an IDS is not feasible. A cost-sensitive (i.e., adaptive) intrusion detection system balances the trade-offs of its performance objective to minimize its costs and maximize its benefits according to the current operational condition [10]. For example, if an IDS was forced to miss some intrusions because of stress or overload attacks and if we consider buffer-overflow as more damaging than port-scan, then missing a port-scan would be better than missing a buffer overflow [10]. Systems with adaptive intrusion response capabilities may adapt to the changing operational conditions by selecting responses that are tailored for the current condition.

Lee et al. [9] describe the principles of cost analysis and modeling for intrusion detection and response. They also propose cost factors and cost models relevant to IDSs. The major cost factors associated with an attack are identified by the authors as *Damage Cost* or *DC* (i.e., the amount of damage to the targeted resource), *Response Cost* or *RC* (i.e., the cost of responding to an attack), and *Operational Cost* (i.e., the cost of analyzing events using an IDS). For example, in a cost-sensitive IDS, an intrusion with a higher response cost than damage cost would not be responded to. They argue that the use of attack taxonomy as well as site-specific policies and priorities are necessary in determining the cost factors of detection and response.

According to the authors, a cost model is the total expected cost of intrusion detection and shows the trade-off among all relevant cost factors. To build a cost model, the authors define the *Consequential Cost (CC)* as the cost associated with the prediction of an IDS. For example, the false negative detection cost of the event *e* is equal to damage cost associated with event *e* because it happens when an IDS falsely decides that an event is not an attack and lets the attack succeed by not responding to it. The total cost of intrusion detection is defined as the sum of consequential and operational costs.

Lee et al. also represent cost-sensitive models for intrusion detection and response by proposing methods to reduce operational and consequential costs. The authors are well-respected in the intrusion detection research community. Although Lee et al. have been unable both to propose a systematic way of measuring cost factors and to solve the important problems such as comparing different types of costs in different measurement units, their work is one of the most useful and important sources of the research on cost-sensitive intrusion detection and response.

Some of the cost factors of intrusion detection and response systems are listed in the following:

Damage Cost (DC) or severity   is associated with the ongoing attack and shows the amount of damage caused by an attack when IDS does not operate.

Operational Cost (OC)   is the cost of running the IDS in detecting an attack in terms of labor and computational resources.

Confidence metric   is confidence degree of a cost-sensitive IDS that an alarm is a real intrusion.

Response Cost (RC)   is the cost of response in terms of the resources that are required and the potential negative impacts of the response on legitimate network operations.

Consequential Cost   is associated with the outcome of detection i.e., False Positive (FP), False Negative (FN), True Psitive (TP), True Negative (TN), Missclassified hit.

Detection of an attack is not beneficial if the operational cost of the detection exceeds the damage cost that may be inflicted by the attack. A cost-sensitive IDS needs to compute a confidence metric for each of its alerts. A low confidence metric prohibits a cost-sensitive IDS from responding to the attack. Furthermore, having a high confidence about occurrence of an attack is not sufficient for launching a response. Thus, the response cost needs to be evaluated and if it is more than the damage cost taking an action will not have any beneficial effect. The cost of missing an intrusion (FN), is equal to damage cost of occurring intrusion e. The cost of true normal classification (TN) of an event is always zero.

When an IDS falsely classifies a normal event e as an intrusion e' (FP), it may launch a response to defend against intrusion e'. In this case, the consequential cost of intrusion detection is equal to the cost of launching response for event e', i.e. $RC(e')$. Moreover, since an unnecessary response may negatively impact normal activities (e.g. resetting a legitimate connection), a *penalty cost* is considered for labeling legitimate activities as malicious. Obviously, if the IDS does not take any action due to the higher cost of response than the falsely detected event, the consequential cost of FP is zero.

When an IDS correctly classifies an event as an intrusion, the consequential cost includes the cost of detecting the attack and possibly the cost of responding to attack. If the damages inflicted by the attack were less than the response cost, then the cost-sensitive IDS would not take any action and, consequently, the CC resultant from the attack event e, would be $DC(e)$, the damage caused by the attack. If the IDS took an action, the CC of detecting the attack e would be equal to the cost of response, $RC(e)$. However, because of the possible delay in the detection process, partial damage may have incurred by the time the attack is detected and response is launched.

In case of an incorrect detection (misclassification), if the IDS does not launch a response the CC of the attack is equal to the damage inflicted by the real attack$e$, $DC(e)$. If IDS launch a response, due to higher damage cost of the incorrectly detected attack, the CC will include the response cost to the attack e'. The response to event e' may limit the damage cost of the real attack e.

7.6 Intrusion Tolerance and Attack Resistance

The first generation of IDSs were implemented inside the host systems (mostly mainframe computers) that they were monitoring. This was a major problem because any attacker that could successfully compromise the target system could also disable the IDS. There are still many host-based IDSs that run on the target system to monitor and analyze the operating system and host activities and to detect malicious activities. All such implementations are vulnerable to compromise by an attacker that is able to gain system-level access.

In the next generation of IDSs, the intrusion monitoring and analysis moved from the target system to a separate system. This improved the security and survivability of the IDS because it became easier for IDSs to hide from attackers. However, because of the important role of IDSs in a system defense, sophisticated attackers might attempt to disable an IDS or take over its capabilities [28].

In a generic IDS, each individual component is centralized and is vulnerable to be a single point of failure. Failure of an IDS's components may also happen as the result of DoS attacks. An IDS's components may also be compromised by the attackers to send misleading reports. The communication link failure may happen as the result of a fault or a DoS attack. Finally, data collected by a network-based IDS are vulnerable to insertion and evasion attacks [17].

Intrusion detection systems should be able to continue operating regardless of the ongoing attacks. They need to provide continued network and application services with the goal of minimum degradation of service to critical users while they are under attack. To achieve this objective, IDSs employ several techniques which are discussed in this subsection.

7.6.1 Redundant and Fault Tolerance Design

AAFID architecture uses agents to avoid having a single point of failure in the system [22]. Each AFFID agent is designed both to collect and to analyze the information from a single host. Therefore, the architecture is not reliant on a single component and eliminates the vulnerability of a single failure point.

AAFID agents are also organized into layers. This layered architecture may enable the IDS to tolerate the DoS attacks more successfully. However, the fact that all of AAFID agents utilize the same code makes them vulnerable to attacks that target the agents' code. Here, the assumption that agents will only fail independently is not valid, and a successful compromise may impact all of the agents.

Yu and Frincke [28] propose a fault tolerant based IDS called Survivable IDS (SIDS). They also propose a systematic way to transform a generic IDS architecture into a survivable architecture. The survivable architecture includes a Dual-Functionality Forward-Ahead (DFFA) structure, backup communication paths, component recycling, system reconfiguration, and an anomaly detector.

A generic IDS is considered as a set of components $(C_1, C_2, ..., C_N)$ in which, each component has only one function. If in an IDS one component is responsible for more than one function, it can be transformed into SIDS by first separating it into components that each performs only one function. For example, if we want to transform an agent based system that relies on individual agents to perform data gathering and analysis, each agent would be comprised of at least two components. A component's functionalities are labeled as $F_1, F_2, ..., F_N$, respectively. Figure 7.9 adapted from [28] shows the generic IDS architecture, which consists of four components and its transformation using DFFA structure. As seen in Figure 7.9, each component, C_n, of the original IDS is associated with a single functionality, F_n, whereas in the DFFA each component has two functionalities, and each functionality is implemented in consecutive components. To provide redundancy and diversity, the two implementation of each functionality is different. Therefore, attacks against one function will not necessarily succeed in compromising both components.

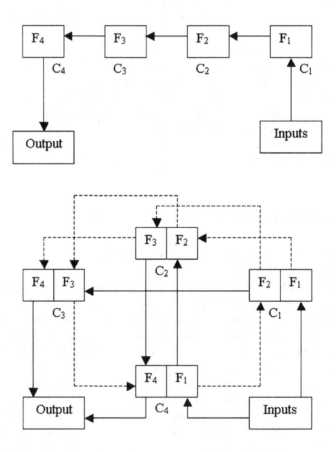

Fig. 7.9 DFFA structure to transform a four component IDS into SIDS [28]

In DFFA structure, components are ordered counter clock-wise into a circle. Within each component, the output of first functionality is passed directly to the second one (e.g., F_1 to F_2) (F_N is an exception). In contrast, the output of each component is forwarded one component ahead. For example, under normal condition, F_3 in C_2 sends its output to F_4 in C_4.

The dotted lines in DFFA structure of Figure 7.9 represent the backup connections between components. These backup connections provide functionalities located in different components with backup communication path and are not used under normal conditions. In case of a connection failure, a backup connection is used to increase the survivability of the system.

Component recycling is defined as a process that restarts disabled components and bring them back to normal operation. Instead of replacing components with new components, the component recycling would change the executable loaded into memory by reconfiguration. In DFFA, reconfiguration is triggered when a connection or a component failure is detected. The efficiency of the detection subsystem is vital to the success of SIDS. An aggressive detection would result in many false positives and reconfigurations. On the other hand, a conservative detection may not react to failure on time. In addition, Yu and Frincke propose a light anomaly detector for their architecture. Yu and Frincke envision the use of an embedded detector strategy similar to the one proposed by [29]. If the failure also affected the internal detector, it would be up to the detectors inside the other components to detect the failure. This is done by observing inconsistencies in output, or delayed response to a query, or by some other means.

We reviewed the SIDS proposal by Yu and Frincke as a classic research in applying fault tolerance and survivability to IDSs. The proposed SIDS could theoretically avoid having single point of failure and could restore IDS back to a safe state. However, it requires further research and implementation to validate the approach.

7.6.2 Obstructing Methods

Obstructing methods are intended to hide the IDS from the potential attackers. Obscurity can be achieved by hiding many aspects of an IDS (e.g., avoiding noisy broadcasting of alerts in the network) or by creating a false impression about the presence of an IDS in the network to prevent an attacker from discovering the actual IDS [28].

One obstructing method is the use of encrypted tunnels or other cryptographic measures to hide and authenticate IDS communication. The AALCP protocol is proposed for agent communication by Xue et al. [27]. They propose a multi-agent system for distributed intrusion detection. The architecture consists of many different types of agents that communicate with each other. A public-key encryption algorithm is used to encrypt all the communication and passwords in the system.

Takada and Koike [24] propose NIGELOG (NIGE in Japanese means run away), a method to protect the log files. The idea is that making multiple backups is not sufficent for protecting a log file because if the intruder already knows their names and their locations, he or she can easily compromise those backups. NIGELOG makes multiple backups of the log information, hide them in arbitrary locations, and periodically moves them to other locations. This method increases the difficulty of corrupting the log files by the attackers. If for any reason the original log file is altered or deleted, NIGELOG will restore the log information from the backup files. Takada and Koike reported in [24] that they have implemented the NIGELOG as a C++ program.

7.7 Test, Evaluation and Data Sets

Testing and evaluating IDSs are controversial topics. Although there is not any standard test framework capable of comprehensive evaluation of proposed prototypes, there are several data sets that have been used throughout the recent years.

DARPA 98:   The first intrusion detection evaluation effort sponsored by DARPA was carried out in 1998 [11, 1]. The evaluation contained two parts: an off-line evaluation and a realtime evaluation that were conducted by MIT Lincoln Laboratory and Air Force Rome Laboratory (AFRL/SNH-1), respectively. Both of the evaluations involves setting up simulated networks to generate network traffic. The simulated network includes inside and outside segments separated by a router. Besides the real network traffic, some background traffic and attack traffic is artificially generated by software tools. The primary services used in the simulated network includes *HTTP, FTP, SMTP, POP, DNS, X, IRC, SWL/Telnet, SNMP, Time* and *Finger*, which covers most of the frequently used services in real network. The traffic contains 38 types of attacks that falls into following four categories:

- Denial of service (DOS).
- Remote to user (R2L).
- User to root (U2R).
- Survellance/Probing.

Seven weeks of network based attacks in the midst of normal background data is collected for training. The two weeks of testing data contains some attacks that do not exist in the training data. In the experiments two types of data have been collected: 1) tcpdump data captured from the network link and; 2) system audit data including Sun Basic Security Module (BSM) audit data from one UNIX Solaris host and file system dump.

DARPA 99:   The primary goal of DARPA 99 evaluation was to measure ability of intrusion detection system to detect novel attacks since this was a major problem discovered in 98 evaluation. As a result, Windows NT workstation were added to the simulated network, and 17 new attacks targeting NT systems were inserted to the traffic. The other major change is the addition of inside attacks. The inside sniffering data, which was not used in 98 evaluation, is provided as the training and testing data in order to detect these inside attacks. Moreover, the evaluation of IDSs is more comprehensive since both attack detection and attack identification are evaluated.

KDD CUP 99: Since 1999, KDD CUP 99 [2] has been the most wildly used data set for the evaluation of network-based anomaly detection methods. This data set is prepared by Stolfo et al. [23] and is built based on the data captured in DARPA'98 IDS evaluation program. The KDD training data set consists of approximately 4,900,000 single connection vectors each of which contains 41 features and is labeled as either normal or an attack with exactly a specific attack type, while the test set contains about 300,000 samples with a total number of 24 training attack types, plus additional 14 types in the test set only. The name and detail description of the attack types are listed in [1].

NSL-KDD: The analysis of the KDD data set shows that there are two important issues in the data set which highly affects the performance of evaluated systems, and results in a very poor evaluation of anomaly detection approaches [25]. To solve these issues, a new data set is proposed called NSL-KDD [3], which consists of selected records of the complete KDD data set. This data set is publicly available for researchers and has the following advantages over the original KDD data set:

- It does not include redundant records in the train set, so the classifiers will not be biased towards more frequent records.
- There is no duplicate records in the proposed test sets; therefore, the performance of the learners are not biased by the methods which have better detection rates on the frequent records.
- The number of selected records from each difficulty-level group is inversely proportional to the percentage of records in the original KDD data set. As a result, the classification rates of distinct machine learning methods vary in a wider range, which makes it more efficient to have an accurate evaluation of different learning techniques.
- The number of records in the train and test sets are reasonable, which makes it affordable to run the experiments on the complete set without the need to randomly select a small portion. Consequently, evaluation results of different research works will be consistent and comparable.

DARPA 2000: DARPA 2000 evaluation targeted the detection of complex attacks that contain multiple steps. Two attack scenarios are simulated in the 2000 evaluation, namely LLDOS (Lincoln Laboratory Scenario (DDoS)) 1.0 and LLDOS 2.0. Both attack scenarios are carried out over multiple network and audit sessions. These sessions are grouped into four attack phases: 1) probing; 2) breaking in to the system by exploiting vulnerability; 3) installing DDOS software on the compromised system; and 4) launching DDOS attack against another target. LLDOS 2.0 is different from LLDOS 1.0 in a sense that attacks are more stealthy and thus harder to detect. Since this data set contains multistage attack scenario, it is also commonly used for evaluation of alert correlation methods.

DEFCON 9: The DEFCON 9 data set is another commonly used data set for evaluation of IDSs. The data contains network traffic that are captured during the hacker competition called Capture The Flag (CTF), in which the competing teams were divided into two groups: attackers and defenders. The traffic produced during the CTF is very different from the real world network traffic since it only contains intrusive traffic without any normal background traffic. Due to this shortcoming, this data set is usually used for evaluation of alert correlation techniques.

These data sets are valuable assets for the intrusion detection community. However, they all suffer from the fact that they are not good representatives of the real world traffic. The DARPA data set, for example, has been questioned about the realism of the background traffic [13, 12] because it is synthetically generated. In addition to the difficulty of simulating real world network traffic, there are some other challenges in IDS evaluation [14], these include difficulties in collecting attack scripts and victim software, differing requirements for testing signature based vs. anomaly based IDSs, network based vs. host based IDSs, etc.

References

1. MIT Lincoln Labs, 1998 DARPA Intrusion Detection Evaluation. Available on: http://www.ll.mit.edu/mission/communications/ist/corpora/ideval/ index.html, February 2008.
2. KDD Cup 1999. Available on: http://kdd.ics.uci.edu/databases/kddcup 99/kddcup99.html, Ocotber 2007.
3. *Nsl-kdd data set for network-based intrusion detection systems*, Available on: http://iscx.cs.unb.ca/NSL-KDD/, March 2009.
4. Stefan Axelsson, *The base-rate fallacy and its implications for the difficulty of intrusion detection*, Proceedings of the 6th ACM conference on Computer and communication security (Kent Ridge Digital Labs, Singapore), ACM Press, November 1999, pp. 1–7.
5. _____ , *The base-rate fallacy and the difficulty of intrusion detection*, ACM Transactions on Information and System Security (TISSEC) **3** (2000), no. 3, 186–205.
6. P. Dokas, L. Ertoz, V. Kumar, A. Lazarevic, J. Srivastava, and P. Tan, *Data mining for network intrusion detection*, Proceedings of NSF Workshop on Next Generation Data Mining (Baltimore, MD), November 2002.
7. Mahesh V. Joshi, Ramesh C. Agarwal, and Vipin Kumar, *Predicting rare classes: Can boosting make any weak lerner strong?*, Proceedings of the SIG KDD (Edmonton, Alberta, Canada), 2002.
8. C. Kruegel, F. Valeur, G. Vigna, and R.A. Kemmerer, *Stateful intrusion detection for high-speed networks*, Proceedings of the IEEE Symposium on Security and Privacy (Oakland, CA), IEEE Press, May 2002, pp. 285–293.
9. W. Lee, W. Fan, M. Miller, s. Stolfo, and E. Zadok, *Toward cost sensitive modeling for intrusion detection and response*, Journal of Computer Security **10** (2002), no. 1,2, 5–22.
10. Wenke Lee, Joo B.D. Cabrera, Ashley Thomas, Niranjan Balwalli, Sunmeet Saluja, and Yi Zhang, *Performance adaptation in real-time intrusion detection systems*, Proceedings of Recent Advances in Intrusion Detection, 5th International Symposium, (RAID 2002) (Zurich, Switzerland) (A. Wespi, G. Vigna, and L. Deri, eds.), Lecture Notes in Computer Science, Springer-Verlag Heidelberg, October 2002, pp. 252–273.

11. R. Lippmann, D. Fried, I. Graf, J. Haines, K. Kendall, D. McClung, D. Weber, S. Webster, D. Wyschogrod, R. Cunningham, and M. Zissman, *Evaluating intrusion detection systems: The 1998 darpa off-line intrusion detection evaluation*, Proceedings of the 2000 DARPA Information Survivability Conference and Exposition (DISCEX-00), 2000, pp. 12–26.
12. M.V. Mahoney and P.K. Chan, *An Analysis of the 1999 DARPA/Lincoln Laboratory Evaluation Data for Network Anomaly Detection*, LECTURE NOTES IN COMPUTER SCIENCE (2003), 220–238.
13. John McHugh, *Testing intrusion detection systems: a critique of the 1998 and 1999 darpa intrusion detection system evaluations as performed by lincoln laboratory*, ACM Transactions on Information and System Security (TISSEC) **3** (2000), no. 4, 262–294.
14. NIST, Technology ITL, MITLL, Peter Mell, Vincent Hu, Richard Lippmann, Josh Haines, and Marc Zissman, *An overview of issues in testing intrusion detection*, July 2003.
15. Bryan Pfaffenberger, *Webster's new world dictionary*, ninth edition ed., ch. AC-3, p. 9, Hungry Minds, 2001.
16. Foster Provost and Tom Fawcett, *Robust classification for imprecise environments*, Machine Learning **42** (2001), no. 3, 203–231.
17. T. Ptacek and T.Newsham, *Insertion, evasion, and denial of service: Eluding network intrusion detection*, 1998.
18. Stuart Russell and Peter Norving, *Artificial intelligence a modern approach*, second edition ed., ch. Uncertainty, pp. 462–491, Prentice Hall, 2003.
19. ———, *Artificial intelligence a modern approach*, second edition ed., ch. Probabilistic Reasoning, pp. 492–536, Prentice Hall, 2003.
20. Lambert Schaelicke, Thomas Slabach, Branden Moore, and Curt Freeland, *Characterizing the performance of network intrusion detection sensors*, Proceedings of Recent Advances in Intrusion Detection, 6th International Symposium, (RAID 2003) (Pittsburgh, PA, USA) (G. Vigna, E. Jonsson, and C. Kruegel, eds.), Lecture Notes in Computer Science, Springer-Verlag Heidelberg, September 2003, pp. 155–172.
21. R. Sekar, Y. Guang, S. Verma, and T. Shanbhag, *A high-performance network intrusion detection system*, CCS '99: Proceedings of the 6th ACM conference on Computer and communications security, ACM Press, 1999, pp. 8–17.
22. Eugene H. Spafford and Diego Zamboni, *Intrusion detection using autonomous agents*, Computer Networks **34** (2000), no. 4, 547–570, http://www.sciencedirect.com/science/article/B6VRG-411FRK9-2/2/f818f61028e80aa2cd740fdc4a3cd696.
23. SJ Stolfo, W. Fan, W. Lee, A. Prodromidis, and PK Chan, *Cost-based modeling for fraud and intrusion detection: results fromthe JAM project*, Proceedings of the DARPA Information Survivability Conference and Exposition (DISCEX), vol. 2, 2000.
24. T. Takada and H.Koike, *Nigelog: Protecting logging information by hiding multiple backups in directories*, Proceedings of the International Conference on Electronic Commerece and Security, IEEE, IEEE, 1999, pp. 874–878.
25. M. Tavallaee, E. Bagheri, W. Lu, and A.A. Ghorbani, *A Detailed Analysis of the KDD CUP 99 Data Set*, Proceedings of the IEEE Symposium on Computational Intelligence for Security and Defense Applications (CISDA), 2009.
26. Sholom M. Weiss and Tong Zhang, *The handbook of data mining*, ch. Performance Alanysis and Evaluation, pp. 426–439, Lawrence Erlbaum Assoc Inc, 2003.
27. Q. Xue, J. Sun, and Z. Wei, *Tjids: an intrusion detection architecture for distributed network*, Proceedings of the Canadian Conference on Electrical and Computer Engineering, IEEE CCECE 2003, May 2003, pp. 709–712.
28. Dong Yu and D. Frincke, *Towards survivable intrusion detection system*, Proceedings of the 37th Annual Hawaii International Conference on System Sciences, January 2004, pp. 299–308.
29. D. Zamboni, *Using internal sensors for computer intrusion detection*, Ph.D. thesis, Purdue University, Center for Education and Research in Information Assurance and Security, August 2001.

Chapter 8
Intrusion Response

The function of intrusion detection systems without a timely response against intrusions and threats will be largely limited even they can detect attacks and generate alarms. A comprehensive security solution usually has a timely countermeasure against intrusions. IDSs aim to cover vulnerabilities by detecting different attack types, some of which can be responded by hand. The manual response, however, can not protect the system against fast attacks such as highly distributed DDoS attacks. Since it is impossible to provide a highly efficient way of responding to high-speed threats manually, automated response is proposed. In this chapter, we discuss in details different response approaches.

8.1 Response Type

An alternative way to classify IDSs is according to their response mechanism. Passive IDSs usually work off-line to analyze system log files and network traffic traces. In some cases, they also operate online to monitor host audit data and network traffic passively. Passive IDSs report intrusion alarms to system/network administrator after detecting possible attacks. On the other hand, active IDSs work on the fly and can launch immediate reactive or proactive responses to the attackers, automatically.

8.1.1 Passive Alerting and Manual Response

Passive IDSs notify or detect attacks instead of stopping them entirely. They monitor host audit data and network traffic data passively and then report to system/network administrator after detecting possible intrusions or suspicious behaviors. Although manual response can help to stop intrusions and network level attacks as an after event mechanism, it creates a considerable gap between detecting intrusion and

A.A. Ghorbani et al., *Network Intrusion Detection and Prevention: Concepts and Techniques*,   185
Advances in Information Security 47, DOI 10.1007/978-0-387-88771-5_8,
© Springer Science + Business Media, LLC 2010

launching a response against the intrusion [4]. The duration of this time gap may range from minutes to hours, leading a successful attack.

8.1.2 Active Response

Active IDSs analyze and monitor host audit data or network traffic data on the fly. Once an intrusion is found they will first report it to the system/network administrator and then launch immediate reactive or proactive responses to the attacks. During an attack, the approximate responses will be activated without any human intervention. Most current automatic response systems apply a simple decision table to associate specific responses with particular attacks [4]. A major limitation is that they do not take into account the collateral damage to legitimate users. Moreover, such a predictable response can be easily compromised by an adversary [11], in particular, the network level response to denial of service attacks will be triggered and applied by the attack to damage the network itself by using large number of spoofing IP addresses. Traditionally, the active response can be divided into two categories, reactive response and proactive response. Reactive responses are activated and executed after intrusions have detected. Proactive responses refer to a set of preemptive actions to prevent an intended attack. The effectiveness of proactive responses is highly dependent on the ability of the system to predict the attacks or the violations [16].

8.2 Response Approach

8.2.1 Decision Analysis

The main goal of decision analysis is to apply automated reasoning and decision making theory into the human-mediated or automatic response. One of the most important criteria for effective response is based on the cost benefit for conducting the response. Two typical intrusion response systems based on decision analysis include Emerald [14] and Cooperating Security Managers (CSM) [19], in which they use severity and confidence metrics to minimize the interferences of the inappropriate responses with legitimate activities. The confidence metric measures the degree of confidence for an alarm being a real intrusion. The severity metric estimates the potential negative effects of each response on legitimate network operations.

In [14], the generic EMERALD monitor proposed by Porras et al. is composed of a profiler engine, a signature engine, and a resolver. The signature analysis engine is combined with the statistical profiling technique to carry out different forms of analysis regarding the operation of network services and infrastructure. In particular, the profiler engine implements the statistical analysis using historical profiles, and the signature engine set up a rule-coding scheme to provide a distributed signature analysis model. The combination of profiler and signature generates intrusion or suspicion alerts, and then sends them to the corresponding resolver.

The main functions of resolver in the EMERALD include alert correlation and intrusion response. Once the resolver receives the intrusion and suspicion reports, it will conduct the further correlation, response and dissemination to the other EMERALD monitors. All the intra-monitor communications are carried out by the resolver. Resolvers can request and receive intrusion reports from other resolvers at lower layers in the analysis hierarchy. Moreover, they can launch real-time countermeasures in response to malicious or anomalous activity alerts sent by the analysis engines. There are two types of responses in the EMERALD, one is aggressive response and the other is passive response. Aggressive responses make direct countermeasures against the attacks, such as closing connections or terminating processes. Passive responses mainly dispatch integrity checkers to verify the state of the analysis target. Each valid EMERALD response is evaluated by two performance metrics for determining which response activities should be launched, namely threshold metric and severity metric.

In [2], Balepin et al. propose the Automated Response Broker (ARB) for intrusion response, in which a map-based action cost model is designed to select optimal response strategy for a host computer. The proposed response system is integrated with a specification based, host-based intrusion detection system called SHIM [9]. The response mechanism is based on a resource type hierarchy and a system map. Resource type hierarchy stores general response actions that might apply to a resource, not including any information about specific instances of resources on a system. The system map applied by ARB is a directed graph. The vertices of the graph stand for the resources in the system and the edges of the map represent dependencies between the resources. Nodes with non-zero cost are important nodes and they are included in the system map. The underlying basic resources that the important nodes need for proper operation are also included in the map.

In the system, every node has a list of basic actions with corresponding functionalities and it is constructed from response actions that are listed for this type of node and its parent types in the type hierarchy. The damage assessment procedure and response selection are other two components in the system that are mainly focused on handling uncertainty and producing the optimal response strategy.

The cost model is based on the numerical cost values that are related to every map node. Only a few priority nodes have actual cost value in the model, e.g. a Web server, and generally the response action that affects zero-cost nodes is not harmful for the system. According to Balepin et al. [2], the cost of an intrusion is defined as the sum of costs of map nodes that stay in a safe state previously, but get negatively affected by an action. The benefit of a response action is defined as the sum of costs of nodes that were previously in the set of affected nodes but are restored to a working state caused by this response action. The cost of a response action is defined in terms of costs of the nodes that get negatively affected by the response action.

The main goal of the response system is to carry out the response sequence that produces the maximum benefit with the minimum cost. The final decision is made by the Minmax, Maxmin or Hurwicz approach from the decision theory. Balepin et al. believe that the selection of these approaches is subjective and they suggest that it would be useful if the situation can be analyzed using various approaches [2]. Experimental reports from Balepin et al. show that the proposed ARB system successfully responds to several host attacks.

Another typical example on intrusion response is conducted by Wu et al. [20], in which they design and implement an Adaptive Intrusion Tolerant System (ADEPTS). The main function of the system is to respond to intrusions automatically in a distributed e-commerce site. The system does not have any intrusion detection module. Intrusion alerts are provided by the existing IDSs. A directed acyclic graph, called Intrusion-DAG (I-DAG), is used to represent intrusion goals. Nodes in an I-DAG are sub-goals of an attack. To achieve a specific attack goal, the first step is to complete the goal corresponding to its child nodes.

The ADEPTS receives alerts from IDSs and then calculates three index for each model, namely Compromised Confidence Index (CCI), Response Index (RI) and Effectiveness Index (EI). CCI measures the confidence that the goal of the node has been achieved and classifies the node into 4 categories ranging from strong candidate to non-candidate. RI represents the confidence that a candidate response action is suitable for the specific attack. EI is adjusted by the feedback mechanism of ADEPTS according to whether the response has been successful in containing the attack or not. Wu et al. implemented the ADEPTS on a lightweight e-commerce system as the testbed including a web server, a database server, and a directory server and then evaluated the response system by simulating a lot of alerts from different attack types. The evaluation results showed the proposed system is very effective compared to statically mapped intrusion response systems.

Another system using confidence metric in the response process is the Adaptive Agent-based Intrusion Response System (AAIRS) [3, 15] and in [15], Ragsdale et al. present several adaptation techniques that can be used in AAIRS. The agents defined in AAIRS consist of Interface agents, Master Analysis agent, Analysis agents, Response Taxonomy agent, Policy Specification agent, and Tactics agent. The interface agents build a model for each IDS based on the number of false alarms they have already generated and they are adapted by modifying the confidence metric. Particularly, Ragsdale et al. propose the response to be proportionate to the degree to which system believes that an event is a real attack and not a false alarm. The system administrator updates the value of confidence metric after each attack is analyzed and determined regarding its trueness or falseness. The master analysis agent classifies an event according to the intrusion report and confidence metric obtained from the interface agent. Other analysis agents are controlled and assigned by the master analysis agent to handle an event. They analyze an event until an abstract response is decided. Analysis agents are adapted by reclassifying the type of the attack when they receive additional incident reports. Response taxonomy agents are called by an analysis agent to classify the attack. Policy specification agents are invoked by an analysis agent to determine a response goal and to limit the response based on the different predefined constraint such as legal and ethical. Finally, tactics agents translate an abstract response into specific actions and apply several techniques for implementing a plan step.

8.2.2 Control Theory

The feedback control theory is applied by Kreidl and Frazier in [10] to improve survivability for a single host computer. Authors in [10] design and develop a realtime, host-based software prototype called Automatic Defense System (ADS) . The general ADS architecture includes: (1) the host to be protected, (2) a set of sensors that report on intrusive activities, (3) a set of actuators that implement responses, and (4) a controller that coordinates all available sensors and actuators for maximizing host survivability.

The controller includes two main components: one is a recursive estimator and the other one is a response selector. The recursive estimator processes a stream of sensor observations to update its state estimation and drive the response selector consequently. Response selector is dynamically selected from the available defensive actuators. According to Kreidl et al., feedback control is involved with three major processes, namely receiving new observations, estimating the implication according to past observations and responses, and using the estimation to select new responses.

Although the attack attribute, the implication of a sensor, and the effect of an actuator response are not 100% predictable, it is necessary that they can be estimated by some statistical models before each control decision is made. The objective function of survivability is formulated as the minimization of a certain mathematical cost formula that quantifies a tradeoff between the operational cost of response versus an overall failure cost associated with attack completion. In practical implementation, Kreidl et al. developed the prototype of ADS based on a feedback control technique called Partially Observable Markov Decision Process (PO-MDP). The experimental results with their prototype show that the ADS can successfully protect a web server against an automated Internet worm attack.

8.2.3 Game theory

Game theory has been applied for intrusion response and cyber warfare in recent years. Typical examples include literatures [1, 6]. Although game-theoretic techniques can be potentially utilized for intrusion detection and response, the complexity of a simple scenario has to be investigated and it is not an easy task to incorporate these techniques to a working system. Next we briefly introduce those two examples.

In [1], Alpcan at al. investigate the possible application of game theory to the network security and consider a generic model of an intrusion detection system with several distributed sensors. The game theory is studied in two example scenarios: a security warning system and a security attack game. The security attack game models and analyzes the behaviors of attackers and IDSs within a two-person, non-zero sum, non-cooperative game. Two patoff matrixes are used in the game to represent the attacker and the IDS. Each entry in the IDS payoff matrix represents a cost value, such as the gain of the IDS to detect an attack, its cost for false alarms, and its cost for missing alarms. Each entry in the attacker payoff matrix represents the cost value including the detection penalty for the attacker and gain of the attacker from the undetected attack. The action (or strategy space) available to attackers is attack a single subsystem, set an alarm for one target in the information set or do nothing. The game does not have any dominant strategy and Nash Equilibrium (NE) in pure strategies. In [1], the authors extend the analysis by considering mixed strategies of players defined as probability distributions on the space of their pure strategies and they also report the existence of NEs for some specific subgames.

In [6], Hamilton et al. attempt to apply game theory in the information warfare. They identify three areas that are particularly associated with the information warfare. The first area is called pruning, which is defined due to a belief that the difference between defender's evaluation function and opponent's evaluation function in an information warfare demands particular types of techniques for search in the strategy space and traditional techniques, however, are not appropriate. As a result, pruning is then used to limit the explosion of the search space in such a complex game. The second important area of game theory is modeling the opponent, in order to predict the opponent's behavior. The third area is to tune local site's (or defender side's) evaluation functions. As claimed by the authors in [6], the main contribution of the paper is to collect preliminary thoughts and identify the research areas for the future work.

8.2.4 Fuzzy theory

Fuzzy theory developed by Zadeh can be used for approximate reasoning with vague and incomplete information. Fuzzy logic can be utilized for effective intrusion response because the crisp detection does not provide the response module with enough granular analysis about an attack event. Moreover, an intrusion response system should be able to make reasonable decisions in spite of uncertainties and fuzzy decision theories are designed for this purpose. Although there is only few papers that directly address the application of fuzzy logic in intrusion response, several applications of fuzzy theory in intrusion detection that could accommodate for successful response more effective than conventional detection are also described in this section. For more information about applying fuzzy theory to detect network intrusions can see Section 5.2 in Chapter 5.

Dickerson et al. [7] present one of the first fuzzy logic-based intrusion detection systems. The Fuzzy Intrusion Recognition Engine (FIRE) is a network intrusion detection system that uses fuzzy systems to assess malicious activity against computer networks. The FIRE intrusion detection system utilizes the Autonomous Agents for Intrusion Detection (AAFID) architecture developed at Purdue University. FIRE uses the Fuzzy C-Means Algorithm to determine membership functions for each observed feature. The traffic data collected during a two-week sliding window is used for this purpose. There are five membership functions in each fuzzy input: LOW, MED-LOW, MEDIUM, MED-HIGH, and HIGH. Fuzzy rules define individual attack signatures by using membership functions. Individual agents perform their own fuzzification of the input data sources. All agents communicate with a fuzzy evaluation engine that combines the results of individual agents using fuzzy rules to produce alerts that are true to a degree. The authors have reported that the proposed system can detect several attacks such as host- and port-scan and pingflood. Although Dickerson et al. provide no comprehensive report on the results and the evaluation of the system based on the real data, their granular detection method could be a valuable asset to determine the time and the necessity of a response.

Jian et al. [8], researchers at the Southeast University in China, propose a Fuzzy Default Logic-based Intrusion Detection System (FDL-IDS). Fuzzy default logic incorporates both fuzzy logic and default logic. Default theory was developed by Ray Reiter. The idea is to reason in first order logic but to have available a set of default rules which are used only if an inference cannot be obtained within the first order formulation.

In this paper, fuzzy logic is used for fuzzy reasoning, and the default logic is used in plan recognition and response rollback. The proposed system is composed of a fuzzy default logic knowledge-base (FDL-KB), the corresponding reasoning engine (FDL-IRE), and a response engine (REE), which responds to intrusions based on a cost-sensitive model and is capable of rollback of the false responses. Jian et al. report an experiment that transforms the rule-base of Snort into FDL-KB and the packet-matching module of Snort to FDL-IRE. The performance of the resulting FDL-IDS is compared with Snort. The reported result shows significant improvement in speed and sensitivity. The major problem with the paper is the lack of examples of typical fuzzy-default rule-bases, proposed responses, rollbacks, and reasonings. It also relies heavily on the experts' knowledge of parameters such as the threshold of the confidence of each rule and the different costs associated with intrusion detection and response.

Botha and Solms [12] use fuzzy logic to compare the generic intrusion phases to the actions of a user or intruder. The intrusion phases are identified in the paper as:

- probing phase
- initial access phase
- super-user access phase
- covering phase
- backdoor phase

Each phase is represented by 2 graphs. The first graph is called the template, which represents an intrusion phase, and the second graph is called the action graph, which represents actual actions of the user/intruder.

Input variables are defined for each intrusion phase. For example, *invalid password attempt*, *user terminal*, and *user working hours* are the input variables for phase 2, *gaining initial access*. The information obtained from the input variables represents real-world values and must be converted to truth values in order to accurately map the intruder's action onto the user action graph. The truth-value represents the possibility that an input value is true. Input values are converted to truth-values using membership functions. Simple membership functions are defined for each input variable. For example, a membership function is defined for the Illegal firewall access as:

if *numberofattempts* < 3, then the value of *Illegalfirewallaccess*$(x) = 0$;
if *numberofattempts* $= 3$, then the value of *Illegalfirewallaccess*$(x) = 0.33$;
if *numberofattempts* $= 4$, then the value of *Illegalfirewallaccess*$(x) = 0.66$;
if *numberofattempts* > 4, then the value of *Illegalfirewallaccess*$(x) = 1$;

This simple membership expression is also represented as a graph that translate real-world values to truth-values (*fuzzification* step).

In the next step of the fuzzy process (called *inference* step in this paper), each input value is assigned to one of the fuzzy output values such as *low, medium*, or *high*. This step is carried out using fuzzy rules. An example of a fuzzy rule mentioned in the paper has the following form: *If the user types his/her password incorrectly four times, then the contribution of this input should be high.*

In the third step of the fuzzy process that is called the *composition* step, all 11 output membership functions are combined. It includes cutting the output triangles according to truth-values of input and superimposing the resulting trapezoids over each other to create a new geometrical shaped graph.

The last step of the fuzzy process or *defuzzification* is carried out by mapping the geometrical graphs (one for each variable) resulting from the composition step to a single output that shows the degree of certainty that an intruder has moved through all six phases of intrusion. The proposed system first constructs the template graph by maximizing the various output membership functions and then combining them. Then, a user action graph is constructed. This graph is built by applying the information gained from the user profile and the audit logs to the first three steps of the fuzzy process.

Finally, two graphs are compared to determine that a user or intruder is involved in an illegal activity. The Center of Gravity (CoG) defuzzification method is used here. The CoG for the template graph shows the center of the graph and since the template graph covers the range from 0 to 100, its value is 50. The CoG of the user action graph in comparison to the CoG of the template graph shows the possibility of illegal activity. For example, the value of 50 for the user action graph shows that the system is confident that a user or an intruder has completed all 6 intrusion phases.

The implementation of a prototype called Hybrid Intrusion Detection System (HIDS) and the results of several tests are also reported by Botha and Solms. Although this work oversimplifies the problem and does not seem to be applicable to a real-world situation, a more sophisticated fuzzy system that highlights different stages of an attack would be an indispensable asset for response planning.

Siraj et al. [18] describe a decision engine based on Fuzzy Cognitive Maps (FCMs) for the proposed Intelligent Intrusion Detection (IIDS) System. Using FCMs, this engine fuses information from different intrusion detection sensors.

The Decision Engine of the IIDS architecture has the following major components: 1) *Misuse Alert Interface*, 2) *Network Anomaly Alert Interface*, 3) *Interface Integration Module*, and 4) *Alert Report Generation Module*. According to the authors, the decision agent provides the security administrator with a big picture of the overall security status, which is determined by the following factors: 1) Misuse alert level of all hosts and users in the network and 2) Anomaly alert of traffic.

For misuse detection, IIDS uses multi-sensor data fusion Fuzzy Cognitive Maps (FCMs). The system is host-based and uses a rule-based detection mechanism for misuse detection. The output of a misuse detection module could be fuzzy (e.g., number of failed logins) or crisp (e.g., SYNflooding attack).

As an example the following scenario is presented: *an intruder is trying to access the network by breaking into a particular host. The intruder tries to login with several users/ passwords and fails.* An FCM represents the scenario in which the nodes that positively impact the suspicious event are *number of login failures*, *the different users*, and *same host*. Each of them is represented by a node in the FCM and is connected to the central node (i.e. *Suspicious Login Failure* Event) by a positive labeled edge. On the other hand, the concept *Interval between failures* negatively impacts the suspicion about the event and is connected to the event node by a negatively labeled edge.

The concept *Login-Failure Suspicious Event* is implemented as fuzzy variable and fuzzy sets such as Low, Medium, and High are used to describe the concept. The activation of the output concept Suspicious-Event-Login-Failure by the input concepts is carried out using simple fuzzy rules such as: *If number of login failures is high and interval is short and this happened for same host and different users, then Suspicious-Event-Login-Failure is activated highly.*

The next step of misuse inference in IIDS is dedicated to computing the level of alert for each host by combining the individual suspicious alerts. A FCM (designed based on expert knowledge) is used to combine evidence of malicious activities to generate user and host alerts.

Design and implementation of the decision engine and some examples of the results are also reported in the paper. As mentioned before the concepts such as suspicion to an event can be best represented by a fuzzy variable. Combining different evidences to represent the degree of suspicion of different events also can be implemented by using fuzzy systems. The fuzzy output variables such as the one proposed in [18] could enable the response module to have more granular information and to provide more accurate response to attacks.

8.3 Survivability and Intrusion Tolerance

Survivability is an emerging subject for aiding a system to maintain its essential services and properties (e.g. integrity, confidentiality, and performance) during the period of intrusions [5]. Any survivable system's architecture should have a survivability component with the function of response and adaptation. In [13], the concept of survival by defense is proposed to protect an application rather than the network. In case of the protection fails and the attacker gains some privileges, the survival by defense can frustrate an attacker. According to Sanders, both the protection and the defense mechanisms aim to keep a system functioning (i.e., survival), while the protection tends to be all-or-nothing (i.e. it works or it does not) and the defense is more flexible since it can be chosen from a range of responses, some more appropriate and cost-effective than others under different circumstances. The paper is focused on malicious attacks that exploit flaws in an application's environment. The main goal of survival by defense is to delay or prevent this kind of corruption. The other two substantial goals of defense are slowing down the acquisition of privileges and controlling of resources.

Slowing down the acquisition of privileges is very important because if an attacker could obtain the privileges that he needed, he could instantly stop all processes and deny all services. To prevent the quick acquisition of privileges by the attacker, the entire system is divided into several security domains, each with its own set of privileges so that it can delay the attacker in collecting the privileges required to corrupt the application. In addition to typical privileges (i.e. anonymous user privilege, domain user privilege, and domain administrator privilege), a new kind of privilege, called Application-level privilege, is created to defend an application by using cryptographic techniques.

Controlling of resources is another important objective for the defense. During an intrusion, the attacker and the applications compete for the system resources. In the paper Pal et al. propose three mechanisms allowing the domain administrator to dispute the attacker's control of domains. These mechanisms include the use of redundancy, monitoring, and adaptation, in which the most important one is adaptation. This is because if the application could not adapt to the changing environment, the application would not survive. According to Pal et al., the defensive adaption can be divided into three classes, namely the application level, the QoS management level and the infrastructure level. The adaptation on the application level degrades service expectations in the face of an attack, the defensive adaptation in QoS level applies QoS management facilities such as reserving CPU or bandwidth to obtain the QoS that it needs, and the adaptation in the infrastructure level involves services from the operating system and networks, such as blocking IP sources to improve the quality of service.

In [5], Ellison et al. consider the survivability as a subject that can help a system to maintain its essential services and properties (e.g., integrity, confidentiality, and performance) during an intrusion. Mission is defined as the high-level organizational goals and it can be judged in the context of external conditions. For example, we say a financial system fulfilling its mission if in case a power outage caused by a hurricane shuts down the system for 12 hours, the financial system still preserves its integrity and confidentiality during that period and can resume essential services after the period of downtime. The other potential damaging events are explained in terms of attack, failure and accident.

The Survivable Network Analysis (SNA) is a practical engineering process for the systematic assessment of the survivability features of systems, which includes four steps: (1) System Definition, (2) Essential Capability Definition, (3) Compromisable Capability Definition, and (4) Survivability Analysis. During the system definition the mission objectives and requirements and the properties of the system architecture are investigated. The essential capability definition identifies essential services and assets based on mission objectives and the consequences of the failure. The compromisable capability tests the system architecture against intrusion scenarios in order to identify compromisable components (i.e., vulnerabilities). Finally in survivability analysis the essential compromisable components are analyzed for the key survivability properties of resistance, recognition, and recovery. A systematic way for using a survivability map is proposed to improve the key survivability properties, in which for every intrusion scenario and its corresponding soft spots, the current and recommended architecture strategies for resistance, recognition and recovery are recorded. Moreover, an iterative model is presented to define survivable system requirements and based on this model, survivability properties can be integrated into the requirement definition phase of new and evolving systems.

The other important work aiming at the survivability of intrusion detection systems is proposed by Shajari and Ghorbani, called Fuzzy Adaptive Survivability Tool (FAST) [17]. The FAST system is an intelligent multi-agent based intrusion detection system that enables the network to survive in the face of large-scale intrusion problems. The proposed system is based on an automated detection and response approach for survivability. Survivability is the ultimate goal of FAST. The tool is designed to maintain essential network services and unlike current commercial systems cannot be triggered by an attacker to block important network services. Blocked unessential network services are automatically resumed after an attack. The general architecture of FAST for detecting and responding to network-level attacks is illustrated in the Figure 8.1 [17]. Monitor agents identify anomalous network activities (represented by different variables) and use them to detect known attacks and events of interest. Using the information provided by Monitor agents, Detection agents can detect known multiple-packet type attacks by using their specific signatures. FAST divides the traffic into 3 categories:

1. Normal traffic is allowed to pass.
2. Attack traffic is blocked.
3. Suspicious traffic is logged into the Suspicious Flow Table (SFT).

When there is no indication of suspicious activity in the network, all flow data are forwarded to their destinations without being logged into the SFT. Detection agents inspect each flow as they appear on the network. When one of the detection agents detects the intention or suspicion of an attack, the flow information is recorded into the SFT of that agent. SFT maintains records of all suspicious active flows in the network. In case of false intention or false suspicion alarm, the flow data in the SFT will be forwarded to their destinations after a time-out. But, if the state of the detection changes from suspicious to attack, the trace of the attack traffic will be available in the SFT.

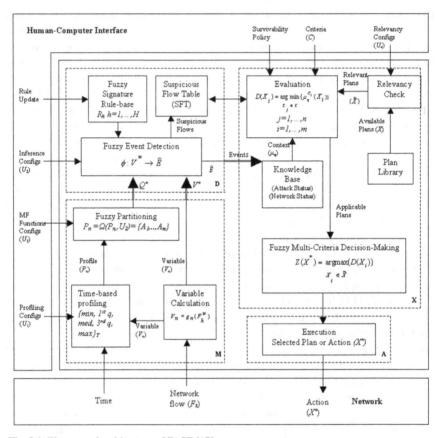

Fig. 8.1 The general architecture of FAST [17]

A Decision agent analyzes the attack flows and decides on proper countermeasure. When a Decision agent receives an attack event, the agent initiates a task to handle it. This task involves selecting and executing a desirable plan that is both relevant and applicable to the event. To decide which plan is desirable, the following steps are carried out:

1. Identifying the plans, which can handle the attack type.
2. Finding relevant plans for this particular attack instance based on the severity associated with the attack.
3. Identifying applicable plans in the current context - i.e. instances of relevant plans that are consistent with the current context.

4. Deciding on a desirable plan based on the evaluation of the relevant decision criteria.

Severity is defined for each attack and is evaluated by the Detection agent that is responsible for the attack. Severity is representative of the size of the damage that is possible by ongoing attack. This factor is a go/no go criterion in the decision for automated response. Low severity may prevent FAST from taking any countermeasures even when there are suitable alternatives. Severity of an attack is calculated from the other relevant attributes. For example, in calculating the severity of a probing attack, attributes such as status, speed of escalation, intensity and type are considered. FAST responds to highly severe attacks automatically. Meanwhile, severity of an attack increases with its intensity. Intensity is an attack attribute that is related to the number of suspicious flows in the SFT at any instant of time. During large-scale attacks such as a worm attack that consists of several attack elements from different sources, intensity increases steadily. High intensity is translated to high severity and causes the Decision agent to respond to the attack proactively. High severity forces the decision agent to respond even when the status of the attack is still suspicious.

References

1. T. Alpcan and T. Basar, *A game theoretic approach to decision and analysis in network intrusion detection*, Proceedings of the 42nd IEEE Conference on Decision and Control, vol. 3, December 2003, pp. 2595–2600.
2. Ivan Balepin, Sergei Maltsev, Jeff Rowe, and Karl Levitt, *Using specification-based intrusion detection for automated response*, Proceedings of Recent Advances in Intrusion Detection, 6th International Symposium, (RAID 2003) (Pittsburgh, PA, USA) (G. Vigna, E. Jonsson, and C. Kruegel, eds.), Lecture Notes in Computer Science, Springer-Verlag Heidelberg, 2003, pp. 136–154.
3. C. A. Carver, J. M. D. Hill, and U. W. Pooh, *Limiting uncertainty in intrusion response*, Proceedings of the 2001 IEEE Workshop on Information Assurance and Security (United States Military Academy, West Point), June 2001, pp. 142–147.
4. A. Curtis and Jr. Carver, *Intrusion response systems: A survey*, Tech. report, Texas A&M University, Department of Computer Sciences, 2000.
5. Robert J. Ellison, Nancy R. Mead, Thomas A. Longstaff, and Richard C. Linger, *The survivability imperative: Protecting critical systems*, CrossTalk: The Journal of Defense Software Engineering **13** (2000), no. 10, 12–15.
6. S. N. Hamilton, W. L. Miller, A. Ott, and O. S. Saydjari, *The role of game theory in information warfare*, Proceedings of the 4th Information Survivability Workshop (ISW-2001/2002) (Vancouver, BC, Canada), March 2002.
7. O. Koukousoula J. Dickerson, J. Juslin and J. Dickerson, *Fuzzy intrusion detection*, Proceedings of IFSA World Congress and 20th North American Fuzzy Information Processing Society (NAFIPS) International Conference, July, 2001, pp. 1506–1510.
8. Zhang Jian, Ding Yong, and Gong Jian, *Intrusion detection system based on fuzzy default logic*, Proceedings of The 12th IEEE International Conference on Fuzzy Systems, FUZZ'03, vol. 2, May 2003, pp. 1350 – 1356.
9. C. Ko, *System health and intrusion monitoring (shim): project summary*, Proceedings of The DARPA Information Survivability Conference and Exposition II (DISCEX), vol. 2, April 2003, pp. 202–207.

10. O. P. Kreidl and T. M. Frazier, *Feedback control applied to survivability: A host-based autonomic defense system*, IEEE Transactions on Reliability **53** (2004), no. 1, 148–166.

11. S. Lewandowski, D. J. Van Hook, G. C. OLeary, J. W. Haines, and L. M. Rose, *Sara: Survivable autonomic response architecture*, Proceedings of DARPA Information Survivability Conference and Exposition II (DISCEX II01) (Anaheim, CA, USA), June 2001, pp. 77–88.

12. Botha M. and R. Solms, *Utilising fuzzy logic and trend analysis for effective intrusion detection*, Computers & Security **22** (2003), no. 5, 423–434.

13. P. Pal, F. Webber, and R. Schantz, *Survival by defense-enabling*, Proceedings of the 2001 workshop on New security paradigms, ACM New York, NY, USA, 2001, pp. 71–78.

14. A. Ph. Porras and P. G. Neumann, *Emerald: Event monitoring enabling responses to anomalous live disturbances*, Proceedings of the National Information Systems Security Conference, 1997, pp. 353–365.

15. D.J. Ragsdale, C.A. Jr. Carver, J.W. Humphries, and U.W. Pooch, *Adaptation techniques for intrusion detection and intrusion response systems*, Proceedings of the 2000 IEEE International Conference on Systems, Man, and Cybernetics (Nashville, TN USA), vol. 4, 2000, pp. 2344–2349.

16. R. Sandhu and P. Samarati, *Authentication, access control and intrusion detection*, The Computer Science and Engineering Handbook (Boca Raton, FL) (A. Tucker, ed.), CRC Press, 1997.

17. M. Shajari, *Enhancing network survivability using intelligent agents*, Ph.D. thesis, Faculty of Computer Science, University of New Brunswick, Fredericton, NB, Canada, 2005.

18. Vaughn R.B. Siraj A. and S.M. Bridges, *Intrusion sensor data fusion in an intelligent intrusion detection system architecture*, Proceedings of the 37th Annual Hawaii International Conference on System Sciences, January, 2004, pp. 279–288.

19. G. B. White, E. A. Fisch, and U. W. Pooh, *Cooperating security managers: A peer-based intrusion detection system*, IEEE Network **10** (1996), no. 1,2, 20–23.

20. Yu-Sung Wu, Bingrui Foo, Blake Matheny, Tyler Olsen, and Saurabh Bagchi, *Adepts: Adaptive intrusion containment and response using attack graphs in an e-commerce environment*, Tech. Report 2003-33, CERIAS, 2003, http://www.ece.purdue.edu/ sbagchi/Research/Papers/adepts_ceriastr03.pdf.

Appendix A
Examples of Commercial and Open Source IDSs

We introduce in this appendix some examples of existing available commercial and open source IDSs. In particular, we briefly describe some typical examples of IDSs, namely Bro, Snort, Ethereal, Prelude, Multi Router Traffic Grapher and Tamandua network based IDS, and then give a collection of existing available commercial IDSs products. We briefly summarize these products in terms of type of attacks they can cover, their detection approach and response type, and their strong features.

A.1 Bro Intrusion Detection System

Bro was developed by Vern Paxson of Lawrence Berkeley National Labs and the International Computer Science Institute. It is a Unix-based Network Intrusion Detection System (NIDS). Being similar to Snort, another well-known public domain NIDS, Bro also detects intrusion attempts by searching particular patterns in network traffic. So they both fall into the category of signature-based NIDS. But, Bro distinguishes itself by offering high speed network capability. In order to achieve real time, high-volume intrusion detection, Bro uses two network interfaces (one for each direction) to capture the network traffic. In addition, Bro provides a patched kernel for FreeBSD to reduce CPU load. With proper hardware and OS tuning, Bro is claimed to be able to keep up with Gbps network speed and perform real-time detection. More information about Bro intrusion detection system can see http://www.bro-ids.org/.

A.2 Prelude Intrusion Detection System

Prelude is a Hybrid Intrusion Detection System distributed under GNU General Public License, primarily developed under Linux. It also supports BSD and POSIX platforms. Prelude works at both host and network levels providing a more complete solution. It also has dedicated plugins in order to enable communication with several other well known IDSs. The sensors send messages to a central unit (i.e. Manager) which processes them and is responsible for event logging. Besides the Manager, Prelude also includes a module responsible for graphical feedback to the user. It relies on signature based detection. Since Prelude analyzes user, system, and network activities, it targets both the host and network based intrusions. More information about Prelude intrusion detection system can see http://www.prelude-ids.com/.

A.3 Snort Intrusion Detection System

Snort is an open source intrusion detection system, which is capable of packet logging, traffic analysis, and signature-based intrusion detection. In addition to protocol analysis, Snort carries out various content matching on network packets looking for patterns of known attacks and probes. Snort uses a flexible language for rules, enables users to describe traffic that should be collected or passed, and has a detection engine that utilizes a modular plug-in architecture. The real-time alerting system provided by Snort incorporates alerting mechanisms for syslog, user specified files, UNIX sockets, or WinPopup messages to Windows clients using Samba's SMB client. Snort runs on a variety of platforms: Linux (i386, Sparc, M68k/PPC, Alpha), OpenBSD (i386, Sparc, M68k/PPC), FreeBSD (i386), NetBSD (i386, M68k/PPC), Solaris (i386, Sparc), SunOS 4.1.X (Sparc), MacOS X Server (PPC), and Win32 (i386), to name a few. More information about Snort intrusion detection system can see http://www.snort.org/.

A.4 Ethereal Application - Network Protocol Analyzer

This application is a data capture and network-monitoring tool for the network. This software includes different protocols such as TCP, UDP, ICMP, ARP, etc. The ETHEREAL program is capable of near real time operation. It can refresh its browser or resample automatically. Some of its abilities include:

1. It provides a summary on the captured data.
2. Provides a list of connections made using either of the selected protocols. This list provides information regarding the source and destination of the connections as well as the direction of the data transfer and the volume of the packets/bytes transferred (conversation option).
3. It provides a list of End points for the different overall packets/bytes as well as the number of the received/transmitted packets/bytes.

User can enable/disable monitored protocols. It is also possible to filter desired protocols that have to be captured or displayed. Ethereal program is capable of providing statistical information regarding the packet counts for the HTTP, GSM, etc.

For example, it can provide the number of transferred packets for the different types of DHCP packets e.g. Inform, ACK, Request and Offer.

The main browser that is capable of a near real time operation has the following fields: Item (transaction) number, Time, Source address (IP), Destination address (IP), Protocol and Info. The Info field is an interesting item in this browser. This field uses a descriptive natural language to explain the purpose of the transaction. There is an additional window just below the browser where once a record on the browser is selected, information regarding the frame/protocol and the address resolution protocol for that record will be displayed. There is another window below these two windows, where the binary contents (in bytes) of the selected items on either of the above windows is displayed.

One of the issues concerned with this application is the way it saves the captured data. It can both filter the data with regard to the protocols and use different file formats to save the information on the file. Using the different file format will ease connecting this application to other applications that can be used for processing this type of data. At the same time, as for a drawback for this application, there is no text format option provided for saving the data. Therefore, using this information for programmers in their programs can be difficult.

This program can also plot a graph of the network traffic for the selected protocols. Using the filtering feature in this application, different protocols can be selected for the plotting. More information about Ethereal can see http://www.ethereal.com/.

A.5 Multi Router Traffic Grapher (MRTG)

The Multi Router Traffic Grapher (MRTG) is available as a public-domain tool for monitoring the network traffic variables. It generates HTML pages containing graphical images in PNG format. Although it can be used for monitoring any continuous data, its main application is to provide a live visual representation of traffic on network links. MRTG creates the visual representations of traffic seen during

- The last 24 hours
- The last seven days
- The last five weeks
- The last twelve months

To generate the above-mentioned graphs, MRTG keeps a log of the data it collects. However, to prevent this log from growing over time, it automatically consolidates the log while keeps all the relevant data for all the traffic that have been monitored over the last two years. The MRTG site claims this operation is so efficient that 200 or more network links (or other network and computer variables) can be monitored using a regular UNIX computer. By using MRTG, monitoring any SNMP variable is possible. However, MRTG functionality is not limited to only monitoring network traffic. An external program can be used to gather the particular type of data that should be monitored via MRTG. MRTG have been used for monitoring variables such as System Load, Login Sessions, Modem availability and more. MRTG even allows accumulating two or more data sources into a single graph. More information about MRTG can see http://oss.oetiker.ch/mrtg/.

A.6 Tamandua Network Intrusion Detection System

Tamandua is an open source, light-weight, signature-based, distributed network intrusion detection system created by Tamandua Laboratories, Brazil. The design consist of a central console and distributed sensors. It has a long list of features that make it attractive:

- It has support for defragmentation/reassembly of packets to analyze fragmentation attacks carried out using tools like fragroute.
- It has a Multi-Layer Boolean mechanism which allows rules to be arranged in an order in which they should be examined.
- It has a rich instruction set to write signatures that consists of a language of opcodes which have the facilities of specifying header fields as well as some powerful data inspection options. It also has support for logging portions of payload for handling legal issues.
- There is an experimental response system which for now has two options: Either an ip-address can be placed under firewall quarantine for a given amount of time or the network connection can be reset.
- It allows for creation of separate sets of signatures, each set being called a sensor-profile to match the varying requirements of different sensors.
- There is a snrt2tamandua command which can be used to convert snort's **.rule** file into a set Tamandua's **.trs** files containing one signature each.
- It can function well for networks with small MTU as well.

Despite all of these features, it is not very popular (considering that its first release came in 1997) which is probably because it does not have comprehensive documentation. There are no man-pages and there is only a brief user-manual describing installation and use in a non-comprehensive manner. Another reason is that there are no binary RPM packages available for installation so it forces a source compilation which is not as user friendly. Strangely, the user-manual has a section devoted to installing Tamandua using RPMs but the RPMs themselves were not available at the time of this report.

A.7 Other Commercial IDSs

Product Name	Company Name	Type	Appliance or Software	OSI Layers	Covered Attack Types	Detection Approach	Record Type	Strong Features
FG-A 1000	net/Zentry	passive	appliance	network, transport	DoS/DDoS, worm propagation	anomaly detection	manual through UI	IP traffic graphs and packet traces, dynamic filter refinement and retirement, detailed logging and reporting
FG-Z 1000	net/Zentry	passive	appliance	network, transport	DoS/DDoS, worm propagation	anomaly detection	automatic, user assisted, user combined mitigation	IP traffic graphs and packet traces, dynamic filter refinement and retirement, detailed logging and reporting
Sleuth9	DeepNines Technologies	inline	appliance	network, transport	DoS/DDoS, port scans, worm propagation, Trojan horses, malicious insider	signature based detection, protocol specification based detection, traffic anomaly detection	active filtering, adaptive rate control	zero footprint technology, holistic management console, IPv6 support, self-monitoring intelligence, forensic database
Peakflow SP	Arbor Networks	passive	appliance	network, transport	DoS/DDoS, worm propagation	anomaly detection	dynamic filtering, recommended filters, rate limiting	transit/peering management, customer accounting, backbone management, reporting and analysis (XML, CVS, XLS, HTML)
Mazu Profiler	Mazu Networks	passive	appliance	network, transport	DoS/DDoS, worm propagation, host scans, port scans, unauthorized access, malicious insider activities	host detection	visual analysis and manual response	Mcube technology for intelligent profiling, dynamic baselining, host grouping, real-time analysis module, real-time event detection module

Product Name	Company Name	Type	Appliance or Software	OSI Layers	Covered Attack Types	Detection Approach	Record Type	Strong Features
Mazu Enforcer	Mazu Networks	inline, passive, mixed	appliance	network, transport	DoS/DDoS, worm propagation, fragmentation attacks	anomaly detection	active filtering (on filters itself or routers)	enforcer filters (packet attribute filters, intelligent SYN flood filters, TCP payload filters, Cisco router ACL filters)
netDetail	Esphion Ltd.	passive monitoring	software	network, transport	DoS/DDoS, worm propagation, unauthorized activities, network failures	anomaly detection	manual	nTAIS architecture for direct traffic observation
netDeFlect	Esphion Ltd.	passive alerting	software	network, transport	DoS/DDoS, worm propagation, unauthorized activities, network failures	anomaly detection	manual	nTAIS architecture for direct traffic observation
NetScreen	NetScreen	inline	appliance	network, transport	protocol vulnerability attacks	signature based detection	active filtering, TCP reset	
StealthWatch	Lancope	passive	appliance	network, transport	DoS/DDoS, worm propagation, unauthorized activities, malicious insider	anomaly detection	manual	flow based, concern index, virtual security zones, traffic analysis, forensic flow analysis
StealthWatch+Therminator (SW+T)	Lancope	passive	appliance	network, transport	DoS/DDoS, worm propagation, unauthorized activities, malicious insider	anomaly detection	manual	flow based, concern index, virtual security zones, traffic analysis, forensic flow analysis
QRadar	Q1Labs	passive	software	network, transport, application	DoS/DDoS, worm propagation, unauthorized activities, malicious insider	anomaly detection	manual	flow based, various behavior views, intelligent alerting, selective application content capture
V-Secure IPS	V-Secure	passive, inline	appliance	network, transport	DoS/DDoS, worm propagation, probes, unauthorized activities	anomaly detection	manual and active blocking	network traffic monitoring, spectrum analysis module, adaptive smart dynamic filters, closed feedback module

Product Name	Company Name	Type	Appliance or Software	OSI Layers	Covered Attack Types	Detection Approach	Record Type	Strong Features
FloodGuard	Reactive Network Solutions	passive	appliance	network, transport	DoS/DDoS/DRDoS fixed and randomly spoofed sources	anomaly detection	active blocking	historical analysis of IP address patterns, measurement and enforcement of appropriate flow-control behavior (TCP back-off)
RS 6300	NetScaler	inline	appliance	network, transport, application	traffic surges, DoS	policy based content-intelligent traffic control	active packet filtering, request rate control, request limit, connection rate control, connection limit	load balancing, content aware security
IPS 400	Captus Networks	inline	appliance	network, transport	DoS/DDoS, worm propagation, prot scan, spam detector, unauthorized activities, malicious insider	anomaly detection, policy based	active filtering, traffic throttling	policy statements
StormWatch	OKENA	host-based	software	application	application-specific vulnerability malicious code attacks	anomaly detection, policy driven	applying policies created in the management console to stop unauthorized processes	protecting the application by residing on the workstation or server

Product Name	Company Name	Type	Appliance or Software	OSI Layers	Covered Attack Types	Detection Approach	Record Type	Strong Features
StormFront	OKENA	host-based	software	application	application-specific vulnerability attacks, malicious code attacks	anomaly detection, policy generator		learning and profiling the behavior of applications
StormTrack	OKENA	host-based	software	application	application-specific vulnerability attacks, malicious code attacks	anomaly detection, policy driven	proactive behavior enforcement	management console, highly integrated user interface, INCORE architecture
AppShield	Sanctum	web application firewall	appliance	application	web application attacks (cross site scripting, parameter tampering, forceful browsing, application buffer overflow, etc.)	policy based	IP blocking (OPSEC compatible for firewall based network blocking)	positive security model built around dynamic policy recognition engine, preventing repeated attacks by using an open platform for OPSEC standard to block the IP addresses on firewalls
InterDo	KaVaDo	web application firewall	appliance	application	web application attacks (cross site scripting, parameter tampering, forceful browsing, application buffer overflow, etc.)	policy based	IP blocking (OPSEC compatible for firewall based network blocking)	positive security model, flexible policy configuration
SecureIIS	eEye Digital Security	web application firewall	appliance	application	web application attacks (cross site scripting, parameter tampering, forceful browsing, application buffer overflow, etc.)	signature based	request blocking	negative model application firewall, friendly user interface, ease of deployment

Product Name	Company Name	Type	Appliance or Software	OSI Layers	Covered Attack Types	Detection Approach	Record Type	Strong Features
NC-1000	NetContinuum	web application firewall	appliance	application	web application attacks (cross site scripting, parameter tampering, forceful browsing, application buffer overflow, etc.)	specification based	request blocking, TCP termination, dropping unwanted traffic, ICMP rate limiting	positive model application firewall, attack blocking at all network layers
AppScan Audit	WatchFire	web application security testing	software	application	DoS/DDoS, web application attacks (cross site scripting, parameter tampering, forceful browsing, application buffer overflow, etc.)	signature based testing and validation	testing and validation	automated application vulnerability assessment, software for auditors and compliance officers
AppScan DE	WatchFire	web application security testing	software	application	web application attacks (cross site scripting, parameter tampering, forceful browsing, application buffer overflow, etc.)	signature based testing and validation	testing and validation	real time security testing and secure coding solution for rapid development of secure web applications
AppScan QA	WatchFire	web application security testing	software	application	web application attacks (cross site scripting, parameter tampering, forceful browsing, application buffer overflow, etc.)	signature based testing and validation	testing and validation	automated progressive web application testing software that provides QA personnel with comprehensive security defect analysis

Product Name	Company Name	Type	Appliance or Software	OSI Layers	Covered Attack Types	Detection Approach	Record Type	Strong Features
IntruShield	McAfee	passive, in-line	appliance	network, transport, application	known attacks, malicious codes, DoS/DDoS	signature based detection, anomaly detection	dropping attack packets, session terminating, modifying firewall policies, real-time alerting, packet logging	stateful analysis, IP defragmentation and TCP stream reassembly, protocol analysis

Index